VISUAL QUICKSTART GUIDE

PAGEMAKER 7

FOR WINDOWS AND MACINTOSH

Ted Alspach

 Peachpit Press

Visual QuickStart Guide
PageMaker 7 for Windows and Macintosh
Ted Alspach

Peachpit Press
1249 Eighth Street
Berkeley, CA 94710
510/524-2178
800/283-9444
510/524-2221 (fax)

Find us on the World Wide Web at http://www.peachpit.com
To report errors, please send a note to errata@peachpit.com

Peachpit Press is a division of Pearson Education

Editor: Becky Morgan
Production Coordinator: Kate Reber
Updated by: Susan Prosser
Copyeditor: Doug Clark
Cover design: The Visual Group
Indexer: Karin Arrigoni

ISBN 0-201-77584-0
9 8 7 6 5 4 3 2
Printed and bound in the United States of America

Acknowledgements

Many individuals contributed to this book in one way or another.

Special Triple thanks go to Susan Prosser, for the incredible job that was done in updating this book for PageMaker 7.

Thanks to Becky Morgan, my wonderful editor at Peachpit.

Thanks to Kate Reber, who kept the book rolling and made sure it looked great.

Thanks to Jen Alspach, my favorite accomplished author.

Thanks to everyone at Peachpit Press who helped move this book along until it hit paper.

TABLE OF CONTENTS

INTRODUCTION

It's easy to be intimidated by Adobe PageMaker's vast array of palettes, menus, and dialog boxes. Even if you have some idea of what you're supposed to be doing, just *finding* the correct command or dialog box can feel like an exercise in futility.

That's where this book comes in handy. It covers each of the most common tasks that you'll want to take on in PageMaker, along with some useful techniques that you might not even have imagined. Each task is presented in the most basic format possible, so newbies to PageMaker can read each step and refer to the accompanying figure, while experts can skim the text looking for just the information they need. Teachers can use this book as their students follow along, step by step, with each technique.

How to Use This Book

If you've never used a Visual QuickStart Guide from Peachpit Press (of which there are many, covering every major software package), then you'll be pleasantly surprised. This book takes you on a whirlwind tour of PageMaker 7 in a format that is both easy to understand and fun to read. Tasks are presented so you can follow along on your computer, comparing what you see on screen to the pictures on each page. All of the typical tasks for which you would use PageMaker are included, as well as other, not-so-common ones that you'll find useful when you move beyond the basics.

While you can read the book from front to back if you want to, the book's design allows you to easily find the task you need to know about. When you've found the appropriate task, just read through the task, which is presented in a simple, step-by-step style.

You may find it useful to read a few pages in the chapter where you find the main task. You'll often find related features that will make your work flow more efficiently.

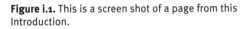

Figure i.1. This is a screen shot of a page from this Introduction.

Working Through a Task

The directions below tell you how to use the step-by-step instructions in this book.

To work through a task:

1. Find the appropriate topic in the table of contents, the index, or by flipping through the pages looking at the thumbtabs.

   The numbered step (above) tells you what to do. The paragraph below it (what you're reading right now) tells you what happens when you do it, or it contains supplementary information you may find useful.

2. Go to the page where the task you need appears.

3. Read that task's steps.

4. At your computer, go through the steps one by one, following the directions.

   Most of the pages contain just one task with appropriate illustrations and screen shots. The pages before and after each task contain related topics that may be pertinent to the task you're learning about.

Why PageMaker?

Page layout can be a daunting task, especially if you are learning how to design at the same time that you're learning a new software program. One of PageMaker's strengths is its relative simplicity, compared to some other layout packages. You can use the program for a one-page, one-color advertisement or stretch your wings and publish a book, taking advantage of PageMaker's Table of Contents, Book compilation and Indexing features. In other words, the program is as versatile as it is elegant.

And because it looks like other Adobe products, you may find that PageMaker looks familiar from the first time you launch it.

One of the real treats about writing this book was that I was able do almost all the work right in PageMaker. In fact, this entire book was designed, created, and laid out in PageMaker, allowing me to use real-world tasks for each of the techniques you'll see presented.

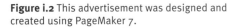

Figure i.2 This advertisement was designed and created using PageMaker 7.

Figure i.3 You'll see this redesigned title screen each time you launch PageMaker 7.0.

What's New in PageMaker 7.0?

PageMaker 7.0 includes several new features that will be useful in your regular use of the program.

◆ You've always been able to merge databases and spreadsheets with PageMaker documents, if you were willing to jump through some hoops. Adobe has automated the process with version 7 to make the production of form letters, mailing labels, envelopes, catalogs, or other merged publications quicker and easier.

◆ Adobe has beefed up PageMaker's PDF creation power. You now have more control of the creation of Adobe Portable Document Format (PDF) files because an updated version of Adobe Distiller is included with every copy of PageMaker.

◆ There are new import filters. Now you can place PDF files created with Photoshop 5.0–6.0 or Illustrator 9.0 directly into PageMaker publications.

◆ There is no need to save multiple copies of your graphics in a work and placement formats. You can save time and hard disk space by importing native Photoshop and Illustrator files. Drag and drop the native file on a PageMaker document or use the Place dialog box to import these files.

◆ An improved converter utility opens QuarkXPress 3.3–4.1 publications directly in PageMaker. The converter now converts Microsoft Publisher 95–2000 documents (Windows only).

Software Updates

At the time of this writing, Adobe had posted three bug fixes to its Web site. An update to the ColorSync files fixes a conflict that occurs on some versions of the Mac OS 9. Another update fixes a problem with deletion of files when using the Publication Converter plug-in on Windows. The third is a utility that allows Windows users to run PageMaker versions 6.0 and 7.0 simultaneously. Check the Adobe Web site at www.adobe.com/support/downloads for more information about this and other late-breaking updates.

PageMaker Basics

The first step toward harnessing Adobe PageMaker's power is understanding what it does best. Although PageMaker has many powerful word processing and graphics features, its strength lies in the assembly of text and art, not in their creation.

To get the most out of PageMaker, you'll need to have the elements of your document already created in other programs. You'll organize them on your hard drive so that they're easy to find. Once the parts have been created and gathered together, you'll finally launch your page layout program. Only then will you call on PageMaker's formidable importing and formatting features to do the most rewarding part of creating a publication—the design.

What is Page Layout?

PageMaker is a page layout program. The concept behind page layout is that the tedious work of research, gathering graphics, writing text, and so on, has already been done. You only launch your page layout software when you're ready to assemble all this stuff on the page. Or pages. Or a book. Or a magazine. Or a print ad. Or a Portable Document Format (PDF) file for transparent exchange between computers, platforms and even over the Web.

PageMaker is the final stop on your journey for print publications, and your second-to-last stop for online documents. Here is where you place text and graphics side by side, a page at a time, until your publication is complete (**Figure 1.1**).

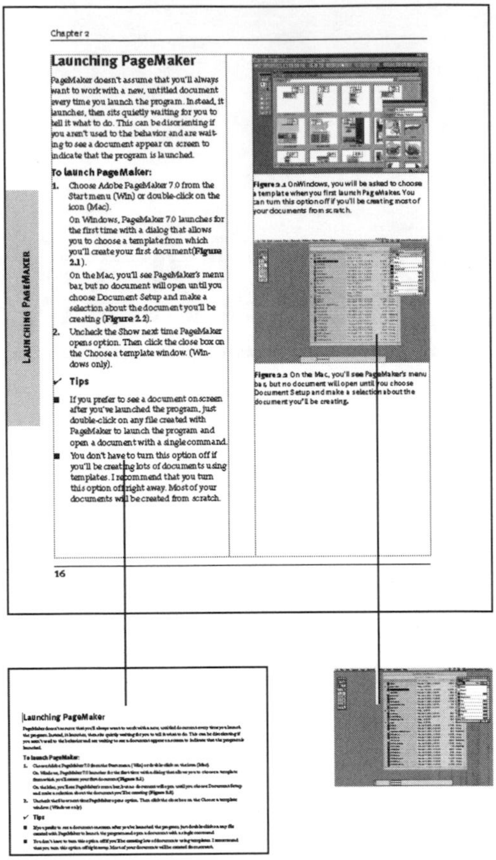

Figure 1.1 Text and graphics are each placed in a PageMaker file and then combined to form a layout page.

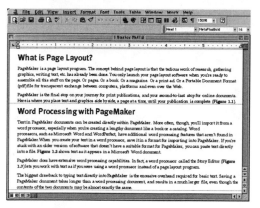

Figure 1.2 The text in this spread, as shown in Microsoft Word.

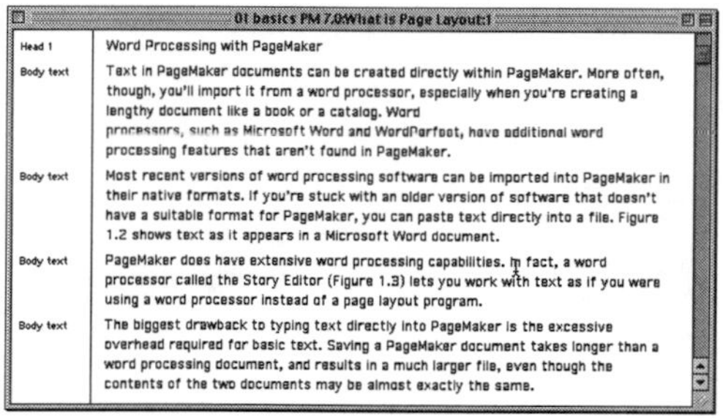

Figure 1.3 The text on this page, in PageMaker's Story Editor.

Word Processing with PageMaker

Text in PageMaker documents can be created directly within PageMaker. More often, though, you'll import it from a word-processing program, especially when you're creating a lengthy document like a book or a catalog. Word processors, such as Microsoft Word and WordPerfect, have additional word-processing features that aren't found in PageMaker.

Most recent versions of word-processing software can be imported into PageMaker in their native formats. If you're stuck with an older version of software that doesn't have a suitable format for PageMaker, you can paste text directly into a file. **Figure 1.2** shows text as it appears in a Microsoft Word document.

PageMaker does have extensive word processing capabilities. In fact, a word processor called the Story Editor (**Figure 1.3**) lets you work with text as if you were using a word processor instead of a page layout program.

The biggest drawback to typing text directly into PageMaker is the excessive amount of memory required to encode basic text. Saving a PageMaker document takes longer than a word processing document, and results in a much larger file, even though the contents of the two documents may be almost exactly the same.

Using Graphics with PageMaker

You can place graphics saved in a variety of file formats into your PageMaker document. All the popular formats are supported, including EPS, TIFF, BMP, WMF, JPEG, and GIF. You can create these graphics in other programs such as Adobe Photoshop or Adobe Illustrator. PageMaker even imports native Illustrator files.

Most of the images you see in this book, from screen shots to artwork, were edited in Adobe Photoshop before they were placed on each page. PageMaker can make limited modifications to placed images, such as cropping, scaling, rotating, and other effects. **Figure 1.4** shows what happens when a TIFF image is formatted in PageMaker. For more information on image control, please see Chapter 9.

PageMaker lets you create a limited variety of graphics by drawing basic shapes and lines and filling and stroking them with different colors. **Figure 1.5** shows several images created solely with PageMaker's drawing tools.

Figure 1.4 This photograph was placed in PageMaker, then PageMaker's Image Control dialog box was used to "stairstep" the grey levels.

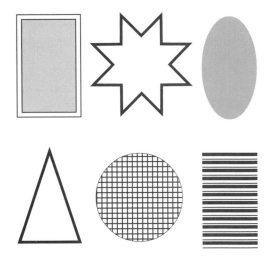

Figure 1.5 These images were created entirely within PageMaker using its built-in drawing tools.

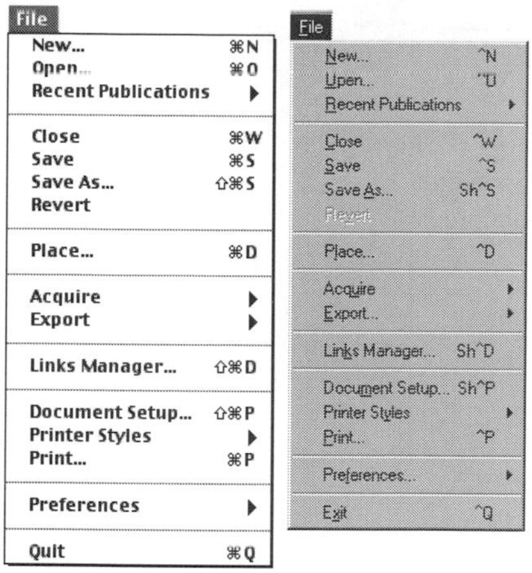

Figure 1.6 The File Menus for Mac and Windows.

The File Menu

The File menu (**Figure 1.6**) contains commands that allow you to manage your files. I'll discuss only those commands that may not be familiar to you from other programs, or those that behave a bit differently in PageMaker.

◆ **Recent Publications** contains a list of documents that you recently worked on.

◆ **Place** imports text and graphics files.

◆ **Acquire** is used to operate scanners and import images directly, with the addition of third-party software.

◆ **Export** is used to export text and graphics to files that can be used by other programs, and to change their format during the export. Also used to convert PageMaker documents to HTML or PDF formats.

◆ **Links Manager** manages all imported objects, from text to graphics. Keeps track of objects, type, location within the PageMaker document, and whether the source files have been renamed or moved since they were imported.

◆ **Document Setup** controls all aspects of the size and shape of your documents, including page numbers and numbering systems.

◆ **Printer Styles** defines styles and manages multiple printers and their settings.

◆ **Print** manages print jobs, including range of pages to print, landscape or portrait orientation, paper tray choices, color output, fonts, images, and any special features of your printer.

◆ **Preferences** controls graphics display, measurement systems, guides, font mapping, color management, online settings, trapping, and layout adjustments.

The Edit Menu

The Edit menu (**Figure 1.7**) contains basic editing commands.

◆ **Select All** behaves differently according to which tool is selected. With the text tool selected and the insertion point blinking in a text block, Select All selects all the text in the block containing the insertion point. With any other tool selected, Select All selects every item on the current page.

◆ **Deselect All** works just the opposite of the above, deselecting whatever has been selected.

◆ **Editions** lets you control linked documents, including whether they update automatically if they've been changed in their source programs. (Mac only)

◆ **Paste Multiple** is a souped-up paste function that works like a step and repeat command. Used to specify the number and offset of objects to paste from the clipboard.

◆ **Paste Special** changes the format of an object as it's exported from the Clipboard. Useful for translating text into graphics so you can apply special effects.

◆ **Insert Object** gives you access to other programs' libraries, like Microsoft's Clip Gallery or charts created in Excel.

◆ **Edit Story** displays the Story Editor, PageMaker's text editing module.

◆ **Edit Original** opens the program that created a text file or graphic so that you can make changes to the source.

◆ **Show Clipboard** shows the contents of the Clipboard. (Mac only)

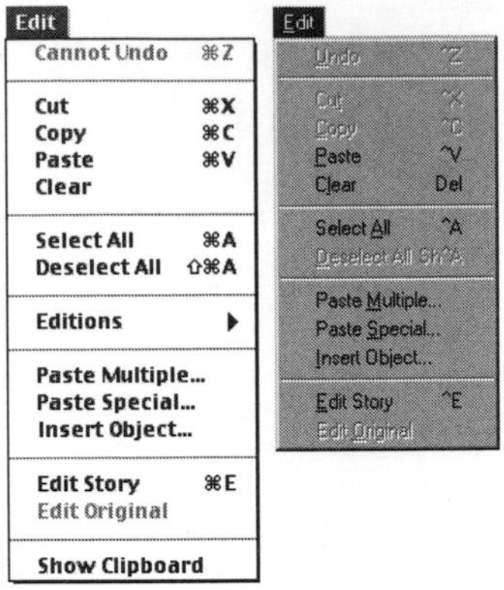

Figure 1.7 The Edit menus for Mac and Windows.

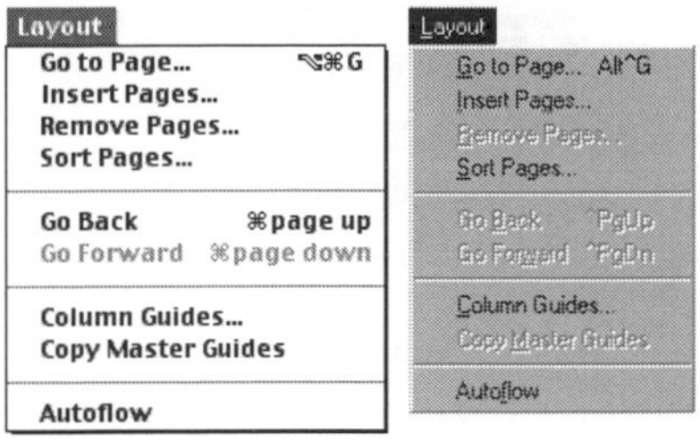

Figure 1.8 The Layout menus for Mac and Windows.

The Layout Menu

The Layout menu (**Figure 1.8**) organizes the commands that let you control how your layouts behave.

◆ **Go to Page** lets you type in the number of a specific page you want to see.

◆ **Insert Pages** increases your page count. You can control where the new pages are created: before the current page, after the currrent page, or when you have facing pages, in the middle of the current spread.

◆ **Remove Pages** deletes pages from your document, along with all the objects on those pages. Careful with this one!

◆ **Sort Pages** rearranges the order of the pages in your document. This can save time since you don't have to re-flow or make drastic changes to your text.

◆ **Go Back** takes you backward one page (or spread), the same as the Page Down key on your keyboard.

◆ **Go Forward** takes you forward one page (or spread), the same as the Page Up key on your keyboard.

◆ **Column Guides** controls the display of the column guides on your pages.

◆ **Copy Master Guides** copies the ruler guides from the Master Pages. Useful if you've moved the guides around on an individual page and need to reset them.

◆ **Autoflow** toggles the automatic flow of long text into a lengthy document. With Autoflow on, PageMaker uses the page margins and column guides to place text. It'll even create extra pages at the end of a document when necessary.

Chapter 1

The Type Menu

The Type Menu (**Figure 1.9**) contains all the commands that let you format text.

- **Leading** controls the amount of space between lines of selected text.

- **Type Style** applies styles to selected text. As a rule of thumb, you should only use styles with TrueType fonts. PostScript fonts usually have specially created bold, italics and other style fonts that should be used whenever they are available.

- **Expert Kerning** controls the space between pairs of text characters.

- **Expert Tracking** controls the space in between all the characters of longer passages of text.

- **Horizontal Scale** expands or contracts the width of individual characters.

- **Character** contains all the formatting commands available to change the appearance of individual text characters.

- **Paragraph** contains all the formatting commands available to change the appearance of paragraphs of text, such as space before or after a paragraph, rules (lines) before or after a paragraph, or how the lines within a paragraph of text break between columns or pages.

- **Indents/Tabs** changes the indents of a paragraph or controls the location of tabs. This dialog box is the only place you can control specialized tabs like leader characters and decimal tabs.

- **Hyphenation** turns hyphenation on or off, and controls how close to the end of a line PageMaker will try to insert a hyphen.

- **Alignment** controls paragraph alignment.

- **Style** applies paragraph-level styles.

- **Define Styles** creates and controls paragraph-level styles.

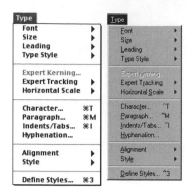

Figure 1.9 The Type menus for Mac and Windows.

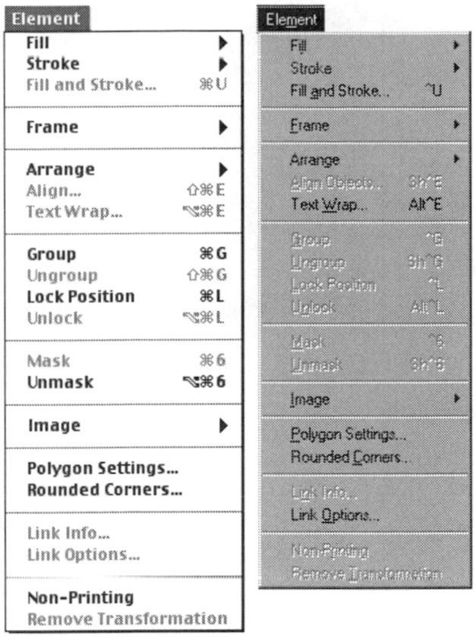

Figure 1.10 The Element menus for Mac and Windows.

The Element Menu

The Element menu (**Figure 1.10**) contains all the commands that let you control the graphic elements in your document.

◆ **Fill** controls what's inside the outline of objects drawn with PageMaker's tools.

◆ **Stroke** controls the stroke (or outline) of objects drawn with PageMaker's tools.

◆ **Fill and Stroke** contains all the Fill and Stroke options in a single dialog box.

◆ **Frame** controls the formatting of frames which hold text or graphics.

◆ **Arrange** lets you move objects in front of or behind other objects.

◆ **Text Wrap** determines how text and graphics interact with each other. They can overlap or text can "stay away" from graphics by a distance you specify.

◆ **Group** lets you combine several objects so they can be treated as a single object.

◆ **Ungroup** returns a grouped unit to individual objects.

◆ **Mask** crops a specific shape from a placed graphic.

◆ **Unmask** lets you undo a mask and return a graphic to its original shape.

◆ **Image** applies special effects to TIFF graphics placed in PageMaker.

◆ **Polygon Settings** changes the way the polygon tool draws objects.

◆ **Rounded Corners** controls the curve of corners made by the rectangle tool.

◆ **Link Info** keeps track of where a placed graphic's source file is stored.

◆ **Link Options** lets you store a graphic in a file or just insert a link to the original.

◆ **Non-Printing** codes an object so that it displays on screen, but doesn't print.

◆ **Remove Transformations** removes PageMaker-induced transformations applied to a graphic since it was placed.

The Utilities Menu

The Utilities menu (**Figure 1.11**) contains various commands for working with specialized PageMaker features.

◆ **Plug-ins** perform tasks like creating a drop cap, changing the case of text passages, creating a keyline around placed graphics, managing complex ruler guidelines, and tracing the various pieces of a placed story. Third-party developers also create plug-ins that can perform complex tasks like formatting data as it's imported from a database.

◆ **Find** searches for text. This command is only available in the Story Editor.

◆ **Find Next** finds the next instance of specified text. This command is only available in the Story Editor.

◆ **Change** searches for and replaces text. This command is only available in the Story Editor.

◆ **Spelling** accesses the spellchecker. This command is only available in the Story Editor.

◆ **Book** creates a book publication list that lets you manage processes like page numbering, generating a table of contents, indexing, and printing from a series of PageMaker files.

◆ **Index Entry** marks text for creating an index in a document.

◆ **Show Index** lets you preview the index before it is generated as a story.

◆ **Create Index** gathers all index entries and creates a story that can be placed in your document.

◆ **Define Colors** lets you create and edit colors for each document.

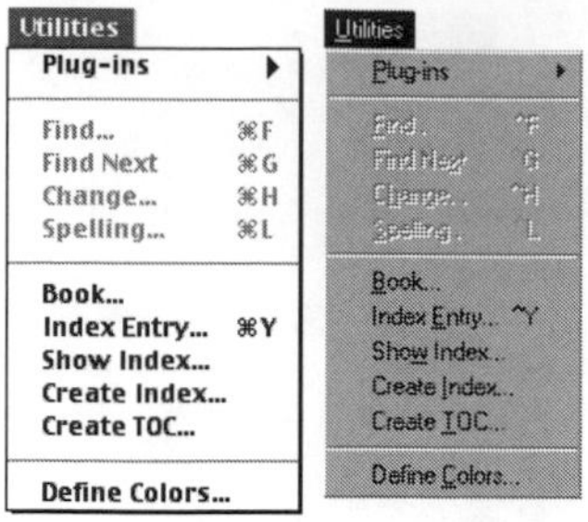

Figure 1.11 The Utilities menus for Mac and Windows.

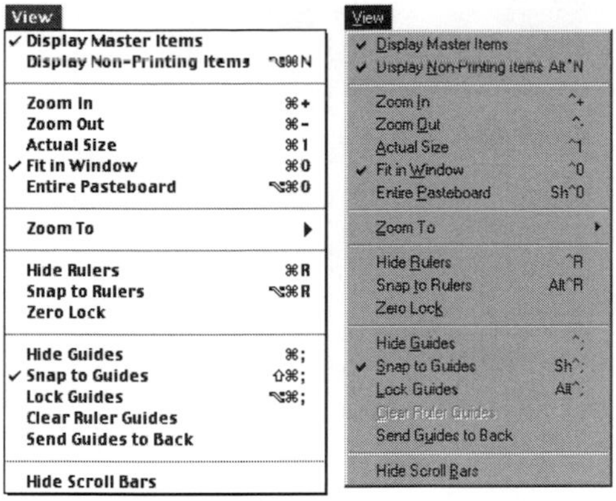

Figure 1.12 The View menus for Mac and Windows.

The View Menu

The View menu (**Figure 1.12**) lets you control how PageMaker displays your document.

◆ **Display Master Items** controls the display of items on the Master Page assigned to each page. When Master Items aren't displayed, they don't print.

◆ **Display Non-Printing Items** controls the display of non-printing items.

◆ **Fit in Window** displays the whole document in the window as large as it can be without cropping any printable area.

◆ **Entire Pasteboard** fits the entire pasteboard (which is approximately 48–by-48 inches) on your screen.

◆ **Hide Rulers** turns off the display of the page rulers. When the rulers are hidden, this command says Show Rulers.

◆ **Snap to Rulers** creates an invisible grid system whereby objects are pulled to increments on the ruler.

◆ **Zero Lock** locks the zero point where the horizontal and vertical rulers meet.

◆ **Hide Guides** suppresses the display of the guides you can drag from each ruler onto your document.

◆ **Snap to Guides** creates an invisible grid system whereby objects are pulled to the guides you create on your pages.

◆ **Lock Guides** prevents you from moving the guides you've created on the page.

◆ **Clear Ruler Guides** removes all the ruler guides from a page or spread at one time.

◆ **Send Guides to Back** can make it easier to work with these elements. By default, guides land on top of placed objects on your page. Sending them to the back makes them a tad harder to select accidentally.

◆ **Hide Scroll Bars** allows you to gain a little extra screen space by hiding the scroll bars. Trouble is, you lose your page icons, too.

THE VIEW MENU

The Window Menu

The Window menu (**Figure 1.13**) controls the display of the windows and palettes in the work area.

◆ **Tile** arranges all the open PageMaker documents so that you can see at least part of each file.

◆ **Cascade** arranges all the open PageMaker documents with their title bars slightly offset from one another, so that you can switch back and forth between them.

◆ **Hide Tools** suppresses the display of the toolbox. When the toolbox is hidden, the command says Show Tools.

◆ **Hide Control Palette** suppresses the display of the Control palette. When the palette is hidden, the command says Show Control Palette.

◆ **Hide Colors** suppresses the display of the Colors palette. When the palette is hidden, the command says Show Colors.

◆ **Hide Styles** suppresses the display of the Styles palette. When the palette is hidden, the command says Show Styles.

◆ **Hide Layers** suppresses the display of the Layers palette. When the palette is hidden, the command says Show Layers.

◆ **Hide Master Pages** suppresses the display of the Master Pages palette. When the palette is hidden, the command says Show Master Pages.

◆ **Hide Hyperlinks** suppresses the display of the Hyperlinks palette. When the palette is hidden, the command says Show Hyperlinks.

◆ **Plug-in Palettes** shows or suppresses the display of three Plug-in palettes: Data Merge, Library, and Scripts.

◆ **List of Open Documents** is a list of all the PageMaker documents you currently have open. A checkmark appears by the name of the active document.

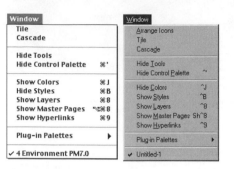

Figure 1.13 The Window menus for Mac and Windows.

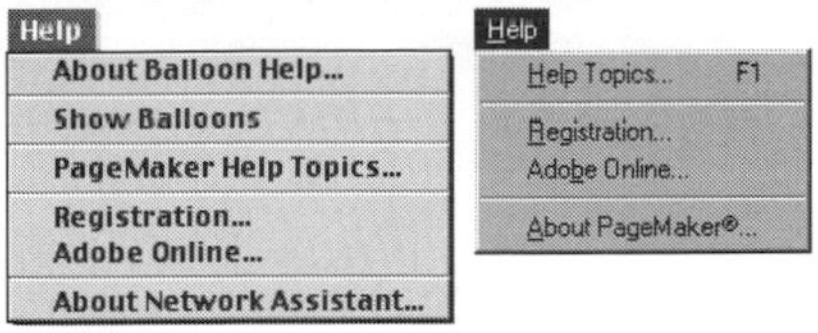

Figure 1.14 The Help menus for Mac and Windows.

The Help Menu

The Help menu (**Figure 1.14**) lets you access PageMaker's onboard help. This is the only menu that differs substantially between the Windows and Macintosh platforms.

♦ **About Balloon Help** provides an information screen for the Mac OS's contextual help flags. (Mac only)

♦ **Show Balloons** turns on the contextual help flags. These tiny flags look like cartoon character's talk balloons and contain a little information about the parts of your work environment that are common to all programs, or that belong to the operating system. (Mac only)

♦ **PageMaker Help Topics** (Mac) or **Help Topics** (Windows) offers a list of the major topics covered in PageMaker's onboard help.

♦ **Registration** helps you register your copy of PageMaker.

♦ **Adobe Online** is a clickable URL link to Adobe's Web site.

♦ **About PageMaker** brings up the title screen that you see when the program is launching.

THE HELP MENU

WORKING WITH FILES

There's no better way to get started using Adobe PageMaker than by looking at how to create new documents, save them, close them, and finally, how to open those documents you've created, saved, and closed.

The contents of this chapter are critical because you'll be doing these things every single time you use PageMaker. You might be tempted to skip this chapter if you're an advanced computer user. It's still a good idea to skim this chapter, since PageMaker does a few things differently than other programs. For instance, you can drag and drop text and/ or graphics from one document to another when you have more than one PageMaker file open at a time. Take the time to absorb this chapter fully; everything from this point on requires you to be very familiar with how to use PageMaker files.

In addition to the basics, I've included boatloads of tips on how to be as productive as possible while you're creating, saving, closing, and opening your documents.

Launching PageMaker

PageMaker doesn't assume that you'll always want to work with a new, untitled document every time you launch the program. Instead, it launches, then sits quietly waiting for you to tell it what to do. This can be disorienting if you aren't used to the behavior and are waiting to see a document appear on screen to indicate that the program is launched.

To launch PageMaker:

1. Choose Adobe PageMaker 7.0 from the Start menu (Win) or double-click on the icon (Mac).

   On Windows, PageMaker 7.0 launches for the first time with a dialog that allows you to choose a template from which you'll create your first document (**Figure 2.1**).

   On the Mac, you'll see PageMaker's menu bar, but no document will open until you choose File > Document Setup and make a selection about the document you'll be creating (**Figure 2.2**).

2. On Windows, uncheck the Show next time PageMaker opens option in the Document Setup dialog box. Then click the close box on the Choose a template window.

✔ Tips

- If you prefer to see a document onscreen after you've launched the program, just double-click on any file created with PageMaker to launch the program and open a document with a single command.

- You don't have to turn the Show next time PageMaker opens option off if you'll be creating lots of documents using templates. I recommend that you turn this option off right away. Most of your documents will be created from scratch.

Figure 2.1 On Windows, you will be asked to choose a template when you first launch PageMaker. You can turn this option off if you'll be creating most of your documents from scratch.

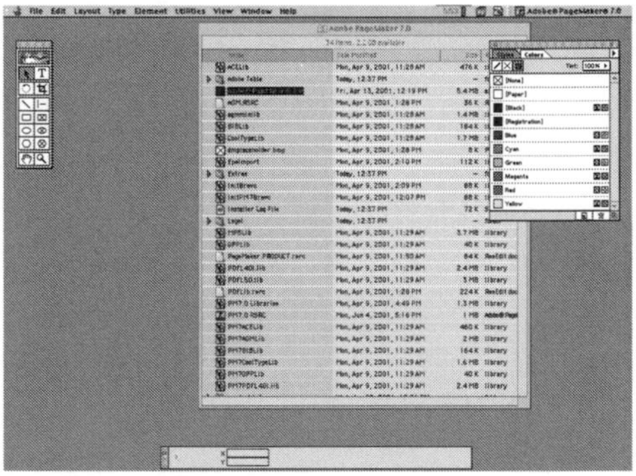

Figure 2.2 On the Mac, you'll see PageMaker's menu bar, but no document will open until you choose Document Setup and make a selection about the document you'll be creating.

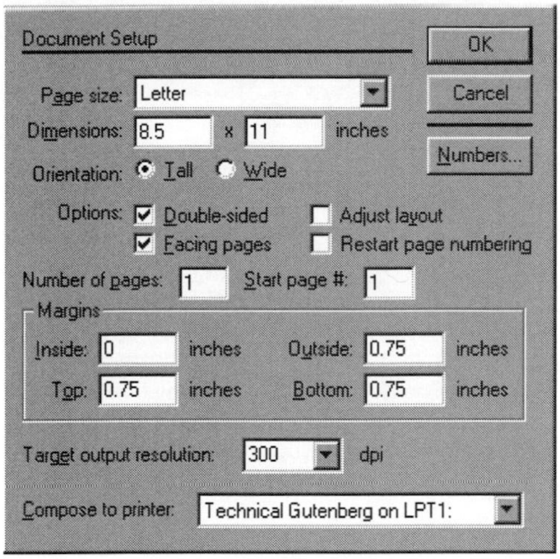

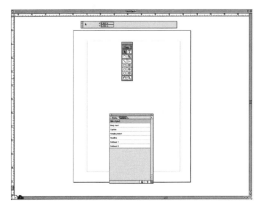

Figure 2.3 The Document Setup dialog box lets you set options for the dimensions, orientation and margins of each new document you create.

Creating a New Document

PageMaker asks you what you want it to do before blithely setting forth and creating a document. In other words, you'll see a dialog box and get a chance to make changes to the document's settings before PageMaker creates a new document for you.

To create a new document:

1. Choose File > New, or choose Ctrl+N (Win) or Command+N (Mac). This opens the Document Setup dialog box (**Figure 2.3**).

2. Enter the appropriate settings for your document in the Document Setup dialog box and click OK.

   A new document called *Untitled 1* will appear on your screen with the entire first page of the document displayed in the document window (**Figure 2.4**).

Figure 2.4 A new, untitled document.

The Document Setup Dialog Box

The Document Setup dialog box determines the way your document appears **(Figure 2.5)**. Here, I'll discuss some of the major controls. Step-by-step instructions for most tasks will follow on the next pages.

◆ **Page size** lets you select from several different predefined page sizes. Changing this pop-up menu automatically changes the values in the Dimensions text fields.

◆ **Double-sided** creates left and right pages, each of which appears separately when viewed in PageMaker.

◆ **Facing pages** shows left and right pages together on a spread. This option is only available when Double-sided is checked.

◆ **Adjust layout** is only available after the document has been created. This powerful option will reflow the text and inline graphics to fit a new page size.

◆ **Restart page numbering** only affects PageMaker documents used within book publications, and resets the page number to the Start page # value, regardless of its position within a book.

◆ **Number of pages** lets you specify the number of pages within your document. If you'll be using the Autoflow capabilities of PageMaker to add additional pages, keep the value at 1.

◆ **Start page #** is used when you have multiple files for a single document, i.e., one file per chapter in a book. Set numbers manually in each chapter, or use the Utilities > Book command and PageMaker will do it for you.

◆ **Target output resolution** sets the resolution of the final printout of your file.

◆ **Numbers** brings up the Numbers dialog box, where you can set the style of page numbers.

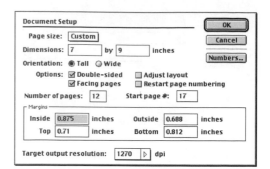

Figure 2.5 The Document Setup dialog box lets you set options for the dimensions, aspect and margins of each new document you create.

Dimensions

If you want a page size not listed in the Page size pop-up menu, enter the size of the page in these two text fields. Changing the values to something other than one of the preset values automatically changes the Page size pop-up menu to read "Custom." This helps prevent potential confusion after you've entered 18 inches by 4 inches (bumper sticker size), so that the Page size pop-up doesn't read "Letter."

Margins

The margin values set here are really margin guides, which can help you when you're designing your pages. The Inside and Outside text fields change to "Left" and "Right" when the Double-sided option is not checked.

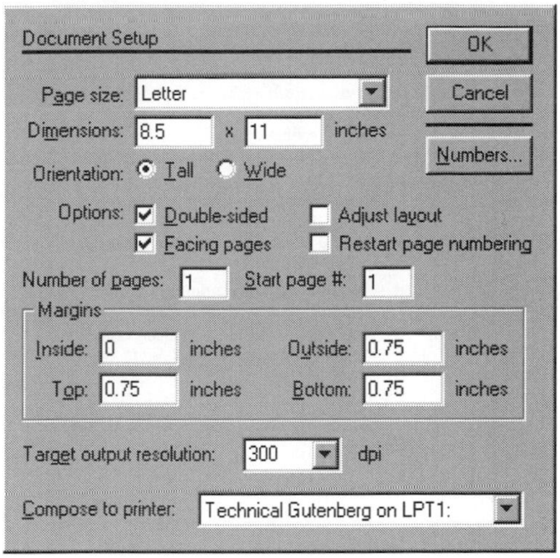

Figure 2.6 The Document Setup dialog box lets you set options for the dimensions, aspect and margins of each new document you create.

Setting a Document's Size

Normally, you'll set a document's size before you perform any other page layout task. PageMaker does allow you to change your document size after you've been working.

To set a document's size:

1. Choose File > New, or press Ctrl+N (Win) or Command+N (Mac). This opens the Document Setup dialog box (**Figure 2.6**).

    If the document has already been created, choose File > Document Setup, or choose Ctrl+Shift+P (Win) or Command+Shift+P (Mac).

2. Use the Page size pop-up menu to choose your page size.

    If the page size you want to use isn't listed, or if you want to create a page with dimensions that are different from the pop-up choices, enter the dimensions of the page into the Dimensions text fields.

3. Click the OK button.

    The document will be created (or changed) according to the settings you have chosen.

Adjusting Your Layout

There are several reasons why you may need to adjust your document setup during the layout process. You might find that the document has to be printed at a different size, forgoing the original settings. You might want to add a second document that is identical to the first except for its size. Whatever your reason, PageMaker makes it easy. Just open the Document Setup dialog box and change your document's dimensions. Then make sure to check "Adjust layout." PageMaker will reflow your text and rearrange your graphics. You'll find that it will do a pretty good job placing things just where you would have if you'd had to do the work yourself. However, you should plan to check out PageMaker's decisions. You will probably need to tweak the layout prior to printing.

Setting a Document's Margins

Margins behave differently in PageMaker than they do in some other programs. In most other programs, you can't place any object outside the page margins. In PageMaker, page margins are guidelines only. You can place text or graphics outside the pages margins you set. These margins act as guides to help you flow lots of text quickly, especially when you're using the Autoflow setting.

To set document margins:

1. Choose File > Document Setup, or press Ctrl+Shift+P (Win) or Command+Shift+P (Mac). The Document Setup dialog box will appear (**Figure 2.6**).

   If you haven't yet created a document, choose File > New or press Ctrl+N (Win) or Command+N (Mac).

2. In the Margins section, enter the four margin settings.

   These settings are the distances from the edge of the page. For instance, the Top text field determines how far the top margin is from the top edge of your document.

3. Click the OK button.

   Your document will reflect the margin settings (**Figure 2.7**).

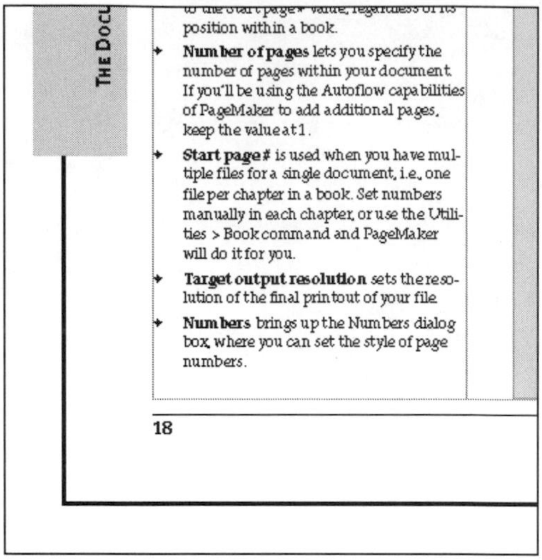

to the start page value, regardless of its position within a book.

◆ **Number of pages** lets you specify the number of pages within your document. If you'll be using the Autoflow capabilities of PageMaker to add additional pages, keep the value at 1.

◆ **Start page #** is used when you have multiple files for a single document, i.e., one file per chapter in a book. Set numbers manually in each chapter, or use the Utilities > Book command and PageMaker will do it for you.

◆ **Target output resolution** sets the resolution of the final printout of your file.

◆ **Numbers** brings up the Numbers dialog box, where you can set the style of page numbers.

18

Figure 2.7 This illustration is from the lower-left corner of a page, like one in this book. The light grey lines are the margin guides. The black lines represent the page boundaries. Notice that the page numbers appear outside the margin guides. The grey thumbtab even bleeds off the page.

Figure 2.8 The Save publication as dialog box allows you to create a name for a document or to change its name. You can also use this command to make a backup copy of your document in another location on your hard drive.

Saving a Document

I like to save my documents right after I've set the document dimensions. PageMaker does mini-saves each time you go from page to page within a document. These mini-saves can get you out of a jam if your system locks and you haven't remembered to do a "real" save in a while. But you have to have the document in a saved state before the mini-saves can work, so don't wait. Save right away.

To save a PageMaker document for the first time:

1. Choose File > Save or press Ctrl+S (Win) or Command+S (Mac).
   The Save publication as dialog box will appear (**Figure 2.8**).

   If you've previously saved the document, you won't see a dialog box. The Save command will overwrite your existing saved file, updating any changes you have made since the last time you saved.

2. In the Save publication as dialog box, type the name of the document you're saving.

   Be as descriptive as possible. The extension for Pagemaker 7.0 documents is .pmd. The Windows version of PageMaker adds it automatically. While it isn't necessary to use this extension on the Mac, it's a good idea to add it manually if the files will be shared cross platform.

3. Set the location where the file will be saved.

   By default, PageMaker will attempt to save your file in the PageMaker application directory. Don't let it do this. Instead, pick a directory (or create one) that contains other documents. I separate my files into clients and their projects.

4. Click the Save button.

Changing a Document's Name

You may need to change a document's name just to make a backup in the same folder as your original document. If so, use the method described below.

To change a document's name:

1. With the document open in PageMaker, choose File > Save or press Ctrl+S (Win) or Command+S (Mac).
   This saves the original document.

2. Choose File > Save As or press Shift+S (Win) or Command+ Shift+S (Mac).
   The Save Publication dialog box (**Figure 2.9**) will appear.

3. Type a different name or choose a different location for the file.

4. Click the Save button.

   The document is now saved and is retitled with the name you've just entered in the Save Publication dialog box.

   To continue working on the original document, follow the steps below.

5. Choose File > Close or press Ctrl+W (Win) or Command+W (Mac).
   The current document is closed.

6. Choose File > Open and locate the original file, then click the Open button.

   Or press Ctrl+O (Win) or Command+O (Mac).

   At this point you'll be working with the original file.

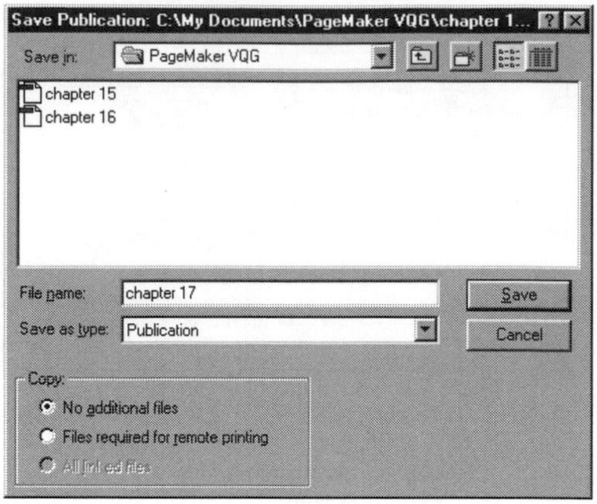

Figure 2.9 The Save Publication dialog box allows you to change a document's name or its location, or even both at the same time. This is especially useful for making backups of your files.

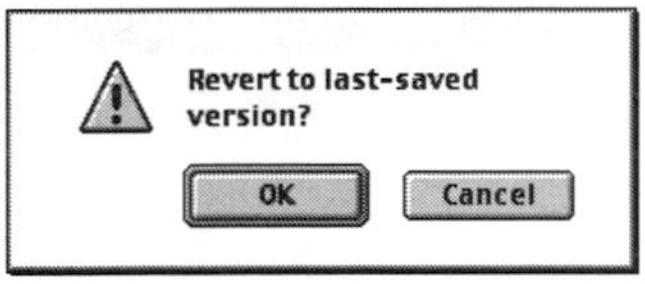

Figure 2.10 The Revert command is powerful and can often lose as much work as it saves.

Reverting to an Older Version of a Document

Sometimes a revert can save you lots of time. Maybe you've just made a series of changes that were wrong (for example, a Replace All in the Change dialog box). In this case, the undo command won't fix things. You'll have to use Revert to open the last version of your document.

To revert to the last-saved version of a document:

1. Choose File > Revert.

A dialog box will appear (**Figure 2.10**) asking if you really want to do this.

2. Click the OK button.

The document reverts back to however it was last saved.

✔ Tips

- This is a very powerful function and should be used with care. You always have one Undo available for most functions, so try that first if possible.

- The Revert command takes the document back to the state it was in when it was last saved. If that was some time ago, you might want to decide whether it will be take longer to re-create the work you've done since then, or to fix the recent work that you to want to undo.

Closing a Document

Closing a document allows you to remain in the program even though you've finished working with a particular file.

To close a document:

1. Choose File > Save.

   Always save your changes before closing. If you don't, you'll be presented with a dialog box that asks if you'd like to save your changes anyway (**Figure 2.11**). But saving before closing is a good habit to get into.

2. Choose File > Close or press Ctrl+W (Win) or Command+W (Mac).

   The document will close, and PageMaker will remain the active application.

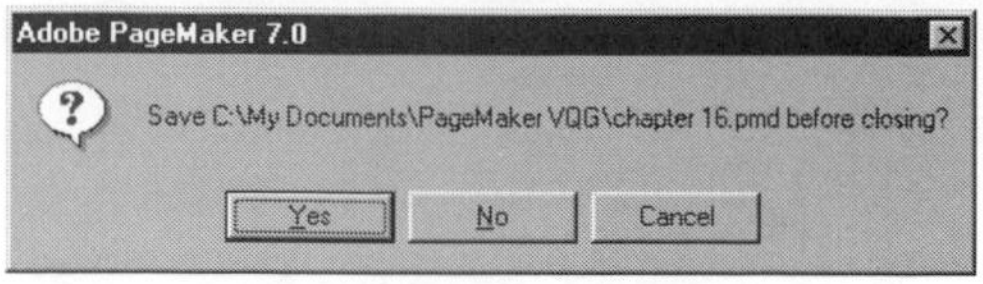

Figure 2.11 PageMaker protects you from accidentally losing your work. It will always ask you if you want to save your changes if you haven't saved manually when you close a document.

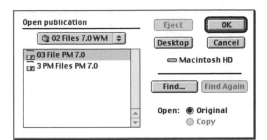

Figure 2.12 The Open dialog box gives you access to every folder on your local computer and every shared volume on your network. You can open a PageMaker document that "lives" anywhere on your network.

Opening a Document

You can open a new document to work on it, or to use items from that document. When more than one PageMaker document is open, you can drag and drop text or graphics from one file to the other.

To open a PageMaker document from within PageMaker:

1. Choose File > Open or press Ctrl+O (Win) or Command+O (Mac).

   The Open dialog box appears (**Figure 2.12**).

2. Locate the file you want to open.

3. Double-click on that file.

   The file will open in PageMaker.

✔ Tips

- If you open a document that was created in PageMaker 6.5, you will see a new, untitled document. Save this new document immediately. PageMaker converts the old file, leaving it intact. You can still work with the old document with an older version of PageMaker, if you need to.

- To work with files created in earlier versions of PageMaker, you'll have to launch them with an earlier version of the program. For instance, to work with a PageMaker 5.0 file, you'll have to first launch it in either version 6.0 or version 6.5. Then you can launch the 6.x version using PageMaker 7.0.

Quitting or Exiting PageMaker

Quitting or exiting a program removes it from the computer's RAM. You'll have to re-launch the program (which takes a lot of time) if you want to work on another PageMaker document. Don't use the Quit or Exit command to switch from one document to another. Use File > Close to close your document and File > Open to open the next document you want to work on.

To quit PageMaker:

◆ Choose File > Exit (Win) or File > Quit (Mac), or press Ctrl+Q (Win) or Command+Q (Mac).

  If no documents are open, PageMaker will quit instantly. If one or more unsaved documents are open, one dialog box per open unsaved document will appear asking if you want to save changes before closing (**Figure 2.13**). If you haven't made any changes to an open document, it will close automatically.

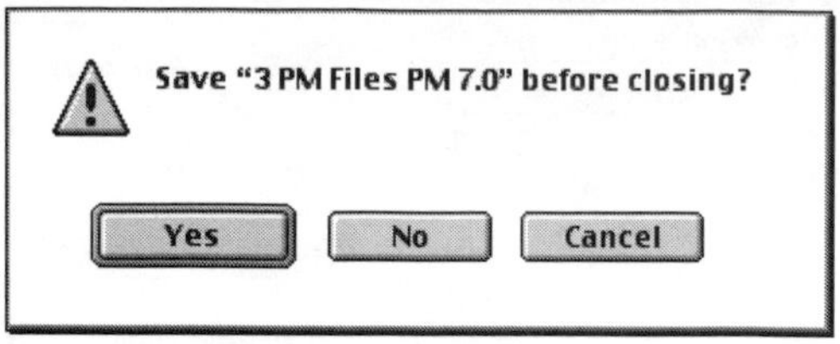

Figure 2.13 You'll see one copy of this dialog box for every unsaved document that's open when you quit or exit the program.

PAGEMAKER SCREEN

Adobe PageMaker is populated with palettes, menus, and dialog boxes, which contain powerful commands that let you control the design. The pasteboard in PageMaker is the electronic version of a conventional paste-up board. It is a fixed-size area that includes the document, objects that bleed off the document, and objects that lie totally outside of the document's boundaries.

After using PageMaker for a few months, you'll feel right at home in its world. But until then, this chapter is a guide to finding your way around without stumbling.

Viewing the Pasteboard

A conventional pasteboard is just a giant flat spot, usually a large tabletop, where objects are put while they're waiting to be waxed and pasted up. That's exactly what PageMaker's electronic pasteboard does. It's the "virtual green room" for your text and graphics to wait upon until they get to walk onstage. The pasteboard is a giant electronic background on which your layouts sit. You can use the pasteboard to store text and graphics that aren't ready to be placed in their final location within the document yet.

To view the pasteboard:

◆ Choose View > Entire Pasteboard

PageMaker shrinks your document down to a size where you can see the whole, amazing pasteboard (**Figure 3.1**).

Use the View > Zoom controls to increase or decrease the amount of the pasteboard you see.

✔ Tip

■ It's a good idea to take a look at the pasteboard when you're finishing up work on a file. You don't want to leave extra text and graphics lying on the pasteboard when it comes time to send the files off to the printer. All those extra items do nothing but bloat the size of your files.

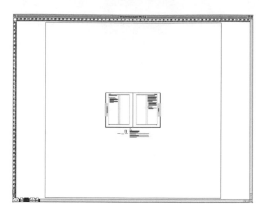

Figure 3.1 Here you can see just how big the pasteboard really is. You can see a few items placed on the pasteboard, just below the page spread. I use these when I need to paste in items like the checkmark and Tip headline that you see on this page.

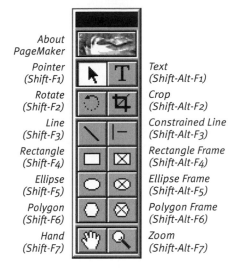

About
PageMaker

Pointer
(Shift-F1)

Rotate
(Shift-F2)

Line
(Shift-F3)

Rectangle
(Shift-F4)

Ellipse
(Shift-F5)

Polygon
(Shift-F6)

Hand
(Shift-F7)

Text
(Shift-Alt-F1)

Crop
(Shift-Alt-F2)

Constrained Line
(Shift-Alt-F3)

Rectangle Frame
(Shift-Alt-F4)

Ellipse Frame
(Shift-Alt-F5)

Polygon Frame
(Shift-Alt-F6)

Zoom
(Shift-Alt-F7)

Figure 3.2 The toolbox is the central storage for all the tools you'll need as you work with PageMaker. Learning and using the keyboard shortcuts will help you to be more efficient as you're working.

The Toolbox

The PageMaker toolbox contains all the tools used in PageMaker. The toolbox is normally visible, but it can be toggled off and on with a command in the Window menu.

You can also hide all palettes by pressing the Tab key while the Pointer tool is selected.

To show the toolbox:

◆ Choose Window > Show Tools.

The toolbox appears in front of your document window (**Figure 3.2**). If the toolbox was moved from its default position at the upper left of the document before it was hidden, it reappears at the same location the next time you show it.

✔ Tip

■ Choose Window > Hide Tools to hide the toolbox.

PageMaker's Screen

Figure 3.3 shows a typical PageMaker screen, with a PageMaker document open.

In addition to the pasteboard and toolbox, PageMaker offers a variety of other tools, including rulers, guides, and palettes, that let you organize your electronic workspace.

Everybody's work style is different. You'll want to experiment to find the combination of tools that best matches your work style. You'll also find that different documents, and even different parts of the design process, demand different setups. If you're just learning PageMaker, take the time to study these features so that you can use them effectively.

◆ **Rulers** appear at the top and left edges of the screen. Use them in combination with guides to create a design grid on the page.

◆ **Guides** are "pulled out" from the rulers. You can set up as many horizontal and vertical guides as you need.

◆ The **Styles Palette** organizes the commands that create, edit, and apply styles.

◆ The **Control Palette** changes its features depending on what object is selected. All available commands that affect an object are found in this palette.

◆ The **Colors Palette** organizes the commands that create, edit, and apply color.

◆ The **Master Pages Palette** organizes the commands that create, edit, and apply Master Pages and their elements.

◆ The **Layers Palette** organizes the commands that create, edit, and apply layers.

◆ The **Hyperlinks Palette** organizes the commands that create, edit, and insert hyperlinks.

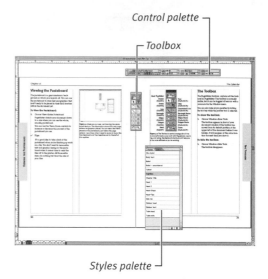

Control palette

Toolbox

Styles palette

Figure 3.3 This illustration is a screen shot of the previous spread. You can see how I like to arrange my work environment. The view is set to Fit in Window, so that it completely fills up the document window. The toolbox goes in the gutter between pages, with the Styles and Control palettes moved wherever there is a free space on the spread.

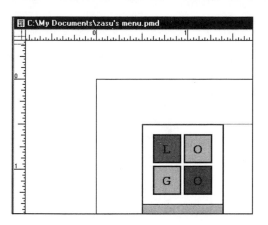

Figure 3.4 The rulers appear along the top and left edges of the screen. Notice that the zero point (or origin point) of the rulers intersects at the top left edge of the page. All measurements taken on these rulers refer to the top left corner of the page.

Showing Rulers

The rulers have several functions in PageMaker. They show the general size and position of objects in a document. The rulers display units in the selected measurement system.

The ruler origin (where the ruler starts measuring from) is in the upper-left corner by default. However, you can change the origin to any location on the pasteboard, so you can measure from a different location than the upper left.

To view rulers:

◆ Choose View > Show Rulers.

Rulers appear along the top and left sides of the document window (**Figure 3.4**).

✔ Tip

■ If you don't want the rulers showing when you work, choose View > Hide Rulers to hide the rulers.

Moving the Ruler Origin

If you need to measure or place something precisely, you can move the ruler origin from its default position. This makes it easier to get a quick measurement. Or you may prefer that your measurement reference start somewhere else than the upper-left corner of the page. Some designers like the zero point to be in the middle of a two-page spread so they can measure in positive numbers for the right page and in negative numbers for the left page.

To move the ruler origin:

◆ Click and drag from the ruler origin marker to a new location (**Figure 3.5**).

A pair of dashed lines appears on the rulers to help you place the zero point precisely.

When you release the mouse button, the ruler origin will be reset to the new location.

✔ Tips

■ Double-click on the ruler origin point to quickly reset the rulers to the upper-left corner of the document.

■ Choose View > Zero Lock to lock the rulers so that they aren't moved accidentally. The ruler origin point changes from two dotted lines to an empty square to indicate that the rulers are locked.

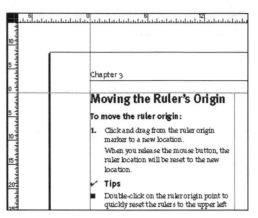

Figure 3.5 When you move the ruler's origin point, a pair of dashed lines help you line up the new origin point. In this illustration the origin point is being moved to the top of column one on the left page of the spread.

Dashed line

Pasta Text Frame

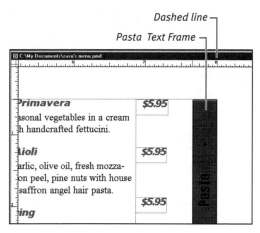

Figure 3.6 Notice the dashed lines in the rulers as the Pasta text frame is being moved. These lines indicate the object's position on the screen and its width. With Snap to Rulers turned on, PageMaker pulls each object toward the ruler increments. This feature helps you keep things lined up on your page.

Snapping to Rulers

PageMaker provides the Snap to Rulers feature to help you align objects while dragging or placing them. When Snap to Rulers is on, dragging or moving any object will force that object to align with a ruler marker. This way objects won't be a "hair" off.

To snap to ruler increments:

1. Choose View > Snap to Rulers.

   Ruler snapping is turned on.

2. Drag an object and release the mouse button.

   The object automatically snaps to a ruler marker (**Figure 3.6**).

✔ Tip

■ Use the General Preferences dialog box to change the default measurement system. The ruler redraws immediately with the new measurement system. The Snap to Rulers command will adopt these new markers next time you drag or place an object.

Changing the Default Measurement System

The default measurement system is inches. PageMaker lets you use five different systems: inches, decimal inches, picas, millimeters, and ciceros. The horizontal ruler reflects the measurement system that's set for the document, but you can have the vertical ruler working with a different system. For instance, with the system set in picas, you can still have the vertical ruler show inches, which is an easier system for some people to work with. Finally, the vertical ruler can have custom increments, expressed in points (**Figure 3.7**).

To change the default measurement system:

1. Choose File > Preferences > General.

2. Choose an item from the Measurements in pop-up menu.

3. Choose a measurement from the Vertical ruler pop-up menu.

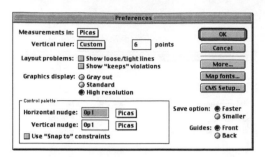

Figure 3.7 The General Preferences dialog box lets you change the measurement system for your document. In the settings above, I'm using picas for the main measurement system and a six-point increment in the vertical ruler.

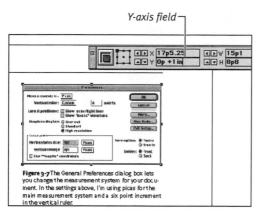

Y-axis field

Figure 3-7 The General Preferences dialog box lets you change the measurement system for your document. In the settings above, I'm using picas for the main measurement system and a six point increment in the vertical ruler.

Figure 3.8 The screen shot for the previous page is selected in this illustration. By typing "+ 1 in" in the y-axis field of the Control palette, I can move the screen shot down exactly one inch even though the vertical measurement in the document is picas.

Overriding Measurements

Most people prefer to work with inches, since they are the most familiar measurement system. However, type is generally measured in picas. Have your cake and eat it too with PageMaker by keeping the measurement system in inches, but overriding it temporarily to work with points and picas. Use the following list as a reference for overriding the measurement system:

◆ **Inches:** 1 in or 1"

◆ **Inches Decimal:** .1 in or .1"

A decimal inch is divided into tenths instead of halves, quarters or eighths.

◆ **Picas:** 1 p

Picas are normally used for typesetting measurements. There are six picas in one inch, making fractions of an inch much easier to express in picas than by using inch-based measurements.

◆ **Points:** p1 or 1 pt

There are 12 points in a pica, and 72 points in an inch. Points are used along with picas for typesetting measurements.

◆ **Millimeters:** 1 mm

◆ **Ciceros:** 1 c

Ciceros are a European version of North America's picas. However, they aren't easily divided into other measurement systems.

To override the measurement system:

1. In any text field where measurements are entered, type the appropriate suffix after the measurement (**Figure 3.8**).

   For instance, placing a *p* after a number designates a number as a pica.

2. Press Enter if you're using the Control palette or click OK if you're using a dialog box.

Working with Palettes

PageMaker groups many of its commands in a series of palettes to make your work more efficient. The main palettes are listed below:

◆ The Styles palette lets you apply paragraph styles to text and manage your style sheet. For more detail, see Chapter 7.

◆ The Colors palette lets you color objects, create, and manage color. For more detail, see Chapter 11.

◆ The Layers palette lets you create layers and move objects around on the layers. For more detail, see Chapter 14.

◆ The Master Pages palette lets you create and apply Master Pages. For more detail, see Chapter 16.

◆ The Hyperlinks palette lets you create and manage URLs for Web pages. For more detail, see Chapter 19.

To show a palette:

◆ Choose Window > Show [palette name] (**Figure 3.9**).
The palette appears (**Figure 3.10**).

✔ Tips

■ Palette commands change to "Hide" when the palettes are shown. Hide any palette with these commands.

■ Show and Hide the main palettes with keyboard shortcuts (**Figure 3.9**).

■ Display a palette's pop-up menu by clicking on the triangle in the upper-right corner of the palette.

■ Resize a palette by dragging the lower-right corner.

■ Move a palette by dragging its title bar.

Figure 3.9 The Window menu contains all the commands that let you show and hide PageMaker's extensive palette collection.

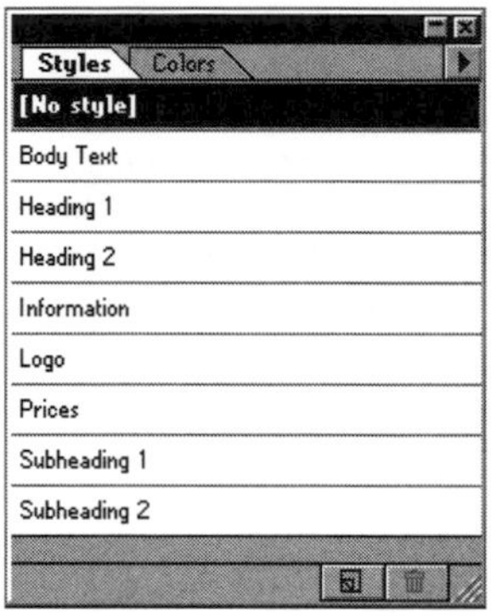

Figure 3.10 The Styles palette contains a list of all the styles that have been created in your document.

Working with the Control Palette

The Control palette is the workhorse of all palettes. Its features change based on the object that's selected on your layout.

If you have a text object selected with the pointer, the Control palette offers controls that allow you to move, resize, skew, flip, or rotate the text object as a unit. With the insertion point in a block of text, the Control palette allows you to change the font, size, style, leading, width, and other attributes of your type characters.

To show the Control palette:

◆ Choose Window > Show Control Palette. The Control palette appears (**Figure 3.11**).

✔ Tips

■ Choose Window > Hide Control Palette to hide the Control palette. Or press Ctrl+' (apostrophe) (Windows) or Command-' (Mac).

■ Ctrl +` (grave)/Command-` toggles between the Control palette and the active document.

■ Ctrl+Shift+~ (tilde)/Command-Shift+~ changes the Control palette from character view to paragraph view.

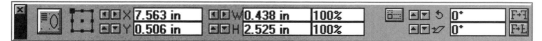

Figure 3.11 The Control palette changes its features based on the object you have selected. In this example, the Control palette is measuring a graphic object. Using the fields or the buttons by each field, you can move, reshape, rotate, flip, or skew the graphic.

Hiding All Palettes

Helpful as they are when you're working, all those palettes can get in the way when you're trying to imagine how your finished design will look.

To hide all palettes at once:

1. Make sure the Text tool is not selected in the toolbox. If it is, either click another tool or press Ctrl-Space/Command-Space to switch to the Pointer tool.

   The feature that hides all palettes doesn't work with the Text tool because the Tab key is used; when typing text, the Tab key inserts a tab.

2. Press the Tab key.

   All palettes (including the toolbox) will disappear.

✔ Tips

- Press the Tab key a second time to show all palettes at once.

- Hold down the Shift key while you press the Tab key to hide all the palettes except the toolbox.

- It's useful to be able to hide all the palettes at once, since PageMaker doesn't have a specific print preview command. When you want a print preview, press Tab to hide all the palettes. Then press Ctrl+; (semi-colon)/Command-; to hide your guides (**Figure 3.12**). That way, the screen looks almost like a real spread.

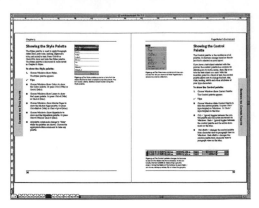

Figure 3.12 When you've finished a layout, it's helpful to remove all the distracting elements on your screen that won't print so you can see how well the layout works. In this illustration, all palettes have been hidden and the guides have been turned off.

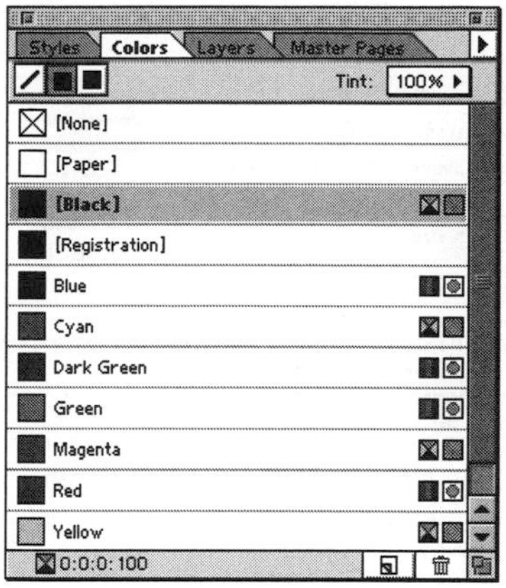

Figure 3.13 Some people find it helpful to dock all their palettes together in one place.

Combining Palettes

Some of PageMaker's palettes are paired by default. For instance, if you show the Styles palette, you'll see a shell that has both the Styles and Colors palette combined. The Styles palettes will be active since that's the command you chose.

If your work style demands a different combination of palettes, you can change them to suit yourself. And if you have an extreme case of screen real estate shortfall, you could even put all the palettes together in a single "shell." **Figure 3.13** shows four palettes in one shell.

To combine palettes:

1. Display all the palettes you want to combine on the screen.

2. Drag a palette *into* another palette and release the mouse button.

   You can tell a palette will be placed within another palette when the target palette gets a dark border around it.

   When you release the mouse button, the two palettes will be in one shell with tabs showing which palette is active.

✔ Tips

■ Activate an inactive tab by clicking on it.

■ The active tab is always white. Inactive tabs are grey.

Performing Mathematical Operations

PageMaker's number fields (anyplace in a palette or dialog box where you can type numerical text) let you perform basic mathematical operations. To make text six points larger, type +6 after the current value, then press Enter. To make text ten points smaller, type -10 after the current value, then press Enter (**Figure 3.14**).

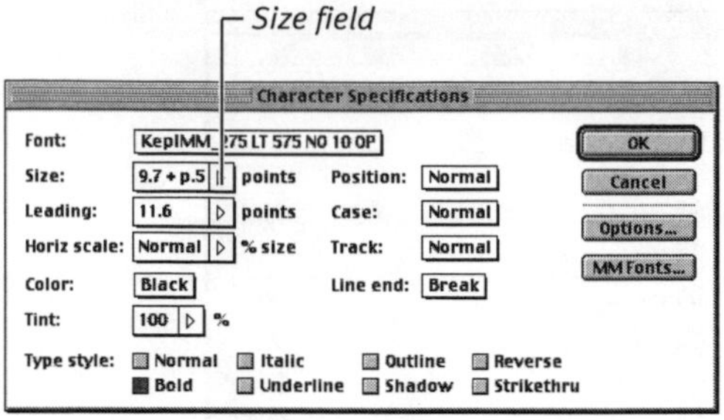

You can use multiple measurement types. For instance, if your measurement system is picas, you can add or subtract in inches or milli-meters. As long as you use PageMaker's abbreviations (see page 35), you can mix and match as many systems as you'd like. So to move an element two inches to the right, type +2 in after the entry in the text field.

But wait, there's more. Want to cut something to one third its size? Type /3 after the value. To make it three times as big, type *3 after the current value.

You can even use multiple operands (more than one plus, minus, division or multipli-cation) in a number field. The math follows the same rules as traditional math: It reads left to right, and multiplication and division are performed before addition and subtraction.

Change the order of the math by using parentheses around certain operands, such as (6+2)*3 instead of 6+2*3. The result of the first equation would be 24 (6 plus 2 equals 8, and 8 times 3 equals 24), while the result of the second equation would be 12 (2 times 3 equals 6, and 6 plus 6 equals 12).

✔ Tip

■ A few fields (those that format only type sizes) won't accept any measurement except points.

— Size field

Figure 3.14 You can use PageMaker's fields like mini calculators. Just type an operand and a number after the existing measurement in a field. In this illustration, we're adding five points to the type size of the selected text.

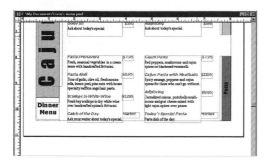

Figure 3.15 Your results may vary. This screen shot was taken on a 17" monitor running at 800 x 600 pixels. It appears slightly smaller than real life. Your Actual Size depends on two factors, the size of your monitor and the screen resolution you've chosen.

Viewing at Actual Size

You can view documents at multiple magnifications, from 25% to 400%. Viewing the document at a different magnification doesn't change the document itself, it only changes the way you see it. Though your text and images will look absolutely huge on screen when you're viewing your document at 400%, they haven't changed in size. They'll print the same regardless of your magnification. To actually make text and images larger or smaller, you'll need to scale them using the Control palette or through the appropriate dialog box.

Actual Size view helps you visualize how your document will look when it's printed, since with a screen resolution of 72 ppi, your document is precisely the same size on screen as it will be when it's printed. To get the most benefit from Actual Size, you may have to change your monitor's resolution. If your resolution is 1024 x 768 on a small monitor, you may find that Actual Size is quite small.

To view a document at Actual Size:

◆ Choose View > Actual Size.
  Or Ctrl+1/Command-1.

  If you have an item selected when you choose Actual Size, that item will be centered on your screen (**Figure 3.15**).

✔ Tips

■ Change the current view to Actual Size by double-clicking on the Zoom tool.

■ Choose View > Zoom In to increase the viewing size of the document.

■ Choose View > Zoom Out to decrease the viewing size of the document.

■ Choose View > Zoom To to see the available preset magnifications. A checkmark appears by the current zoom level.

Viewing at Fit in Window

Fit in Window view lets you see your document at the largest size that will fit completely within your screen. You'll probably spend most of your working time in this view.

If you're working on single-sided pages or a single-page document, only one page will fit in the window. If you're working with a spread, both pages will be fit to the screen size (**Figure 3.16**).

To change to Fit in Window view:

◆ Choose View > Fit in Window.

Or Alt+double-click the Hand tool in the toolbox (Win) or press Command-0 (Mac).

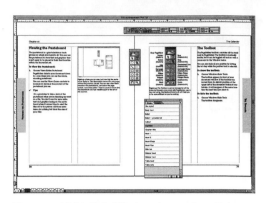

Figure 3.16 With Fit in Window chosen, PageMaker will make the document as large as it can, based on the size of your screen. This is the most useful of screen views and you'll probably spend most of your working time in Fit in Window view.

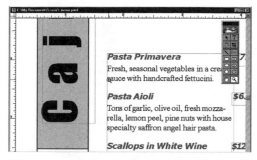

Figure 3.17 This illustration shows a document zoomed in to 200 percent. Notice that the Zoom tool is selected and the magnifying glass is in the center of the page. PageMaker centers the area on which you clicked in the new zoomed view.

Zooming One Step at a Time

The Zoom tool lets you zoom in and out of your PageMaker document. Each click with the Zoom tool takes you one step at a time through the preset zoom levels: 25%, 50%, 75%, 100%, 200% or 400%.

To zoom in one step at a time:

1. Choose the Zoom tool from the toolbox.

2. Click on the area you want to zoom to. That area will be enlarged by one increment (**Figure 3.17**). Continue clicking to keep zooming.

✔ Tips

■ To make the Zoom tool reduce instead of magnify, hold down the Ctr + Option keys (Win) or the Option key (Mac) while clicking. The Zoom icon changes to a minus sign to indicate reduction instead of magnification.

■ Ctrl++ (plus)(Win) or Command-+(Mac) zooms in.

■ Ctrl+- (minus)(Win) or Command--(Mac) zooms out.

Custom Zooming

Sometimes you need to see a small area of your document greatly enlarged. Or perhaps the preset zoom sizes don't meet your needs. You can make a custom zoom by dragging a selection rectangle with the Zoom tool.

To zoom in on a specific area:

◆ Using the Zoom tool, drag around the area you want to zoom to.

That area will fill the document window (**Figure 3.18**).

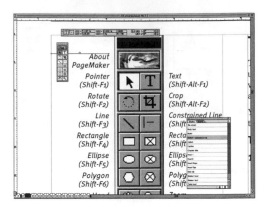

Figure 3.18 This illustration is a screen shot of Figure 3.2 magnified to fill a 20-inch monitor. It's helpful to zoom in extrememly close when you're trying to make fussy adjustments in a small space on the screen.

Hand tool

Pasta Primavera

Fresh, seasonal vegetables

sauce with handcrafted fett

Figure 3.19 The Hand tool lets you pan around your page. This method is far more accurate than using your scroll bars, particularly when the document is zoomed in.

Panning

Once you've zoomed in far enough, it becomes difficult to scroll a document around with just the scroll bars. A better way to navigate in a zoomed-in document is by panning.

To pan around a document:

1. Choose the Hand tool from the toolbox. Or press and hold the Alt key (Win) or the Option key (Mac) to access the Hand tool temporarily.

2. Click and drag within the document.

   The document moves around under the Hand tool (**Figure 3.19**).

   Notice that the screen doesn't redraw while you're still dragging. Sometimes, you'll drag a bit, then stop to let the screen refresh so you can see where you're going.

Setting a Document's Preferences

Any changes you make to one of PageMaker's Preference dialog boxes with a document open will affect only the currently active document.

◆ **Layout Problems** highlights problems that occur in justified type.

◆ **Graphics Display** changes the resolution at which graphics are displayed on screen. If you work with very large graphics, you can speed up your screen redraw speed by displaying graphics at a lower resolution.

◆ **Horizontal nudge** and **Vertical nudge** control how far an item will move when you use the arrow keys on your keyboard to "nudge" them.

◆ **Use Snap To Constraints** uses ruler increments for nudging objects.

◆ **Save Option** enables quick, incremental saves, but may create enormous files. Smaller is slower, but saves disk space.

◆ **Guides** can be created in front or back of your layout items. Guides are not as easy to select accidentally when they are sent to the back.

To change a document's preferences:

1. Choose File > Preferences > General, or Ctrl+K/Command-K.

2. Make the appropriate changes for your document and click OK (**Figure 3.20**).

3. Repeat for other Preference dialog boxes (Online, Layout Adjustment or Trapping).

✔ Tip

■ If you have several documents open at once, only the active document will be affected by changes you make.

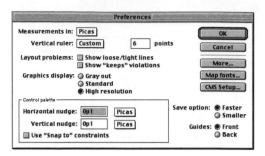

Figure 3.20 Changes made to Preferences when there is a document open affect only the currently active document.

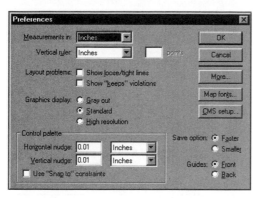

Figure 3.21 Changes made to Preferences with no documents open affect all future documents created by PageMaker.

Setting Application Preferences

If you make changes to PageMaker's preferences with no documents open, the new preferences will affect all new documents you create. The following preferences can be set application wide:

◆ Acquire source

◆ Document Setup

◆ Printer Styles

◆ All Preferences

◆ Column Guides and Autoflow on/off

◆ Most type options

◆ Element changes to fill and stroke

◆ Text Wrap options for new elements

◆ Polygon settings

◆ Rounded corner settings

◆ Link options

◆ Define Colors

◆ Viewable items (in the View menu)

◆ Various plug-ins

To change PageMaker's preferences:

1. Make sure there are no open documents.

2. Choose File > Preferences > General, or Ctrl+K/Command-K.

3. Make your desired changes to all appropriate Preference dialog boxes (**Figure 3.21**).

✔ Tip

■ Some preferences can't be set application wide. These commands will be greyed out when there are no documents open. Set these preferences individually in each new document.

Accessing More Preferences

PageMaker is so flexible that it can't fit all its preferences in a single dialog box. These options are available under More Preferences.

◆ **Greek Text Below** turns tiny type into grey bars when you're zoomed out on a layout.

◆ **Turn Pages When Autoflowing** lets you see each page when you're placing a long story with Autoflow. With Autoflow turned on, PageMaker makes new pages and places text using your margin and column guides. By default, PageMaker doesn't show you all this action. You'll just see the final page, with its text placed when the program is finished. With Turn Pages When Autoflowing is on, Page-Maker shows you each page as it is created and text is flowed onto it.

◆ **Story Editor** options control the font and size of text in the Story Editor. You can also have PageMaker reveal or suppress the display of paragraph symbols and style names.

◆ **Graphics** options lets you define how graphics are displayed in PageMaker and set the size at which an alert will occur when you're embedding graphics.

◆ **PostScript Printing** lets you define how much memory PageMaker allocates to printing PostScript graphics.

To access more preferences:

1. Choose File > Preferences > General, or Ctrl+K/Command-K.

2. Click on the More button.
   The More Preferences dialog box appears (**Figure 3.22**).

3. Make the appropriate changes.

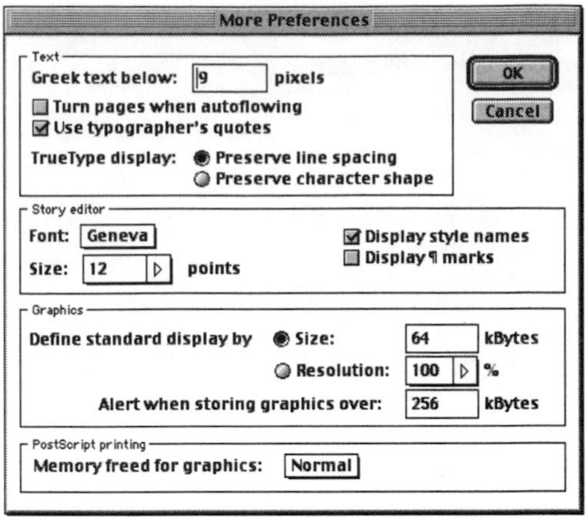

Figure 3.22 The More Preferences dialog box lets you change the way PageMaker's layout and printing functions work.

TEXT

One of Adobe PageMaker's greatest strengths is its ability to edit and manipulate type. You'll probably generate most of your text in standard word processing programs, but you'll want to use PageMaker's powerful text manipulation tools to do most of your text formatting.

PageMaker has all the usual text formatting capabilities—fonts, sizes, color, leading, paragraph indents—and then some. You can change the width of characters to fill a column of space in a headline. You can change the spacing between two individual characters or whole ranges of text. You can also add rules (lines) to paragraphs and specify that the lines stay with the text if it's reflowed.

PageMaker handles text using two different graphic metaphors: windowshades and frames. The windowshades are Adobe's own invention and will be familiar to experienced PageMaker users. Conversely, if you're migrating over from another program you may already be used to frames. PageMaker lets you mix and match windowshades and frames to your heart's content.

Accessing the Text Tool

PageMaker's Text tool is used for three main purposes:

◆ **Creating new text areas**

Text in PageMaker must exist inside a text block or a frame being used as a text block. Use the Text tool to create those text blocks.

◆ **Selecting text**

To make changes to existing text, text must first be selected with the Text tool.

◆ **Moving the insertion point**

The insertion point can be moved by clicking at the desired location within a text block.

To access the Text tool:

◆ Click on the Text tool in the toolbox, or press Shift+Alt+F1/Option+Shift+F1 (**Figure 4.1**).

✔ Tip

■ Set up a temporary toggle between the Pointer tool and any other tool by pressing Ctrl+Space/Command+Space. For example, if you press Command+Space while the Text tool is selected, PageMaker toggles back to the Pointer tool. Next time you press Command+Space, you'll get the Text tool.

Figure 4.1 The toolbox is shown with the Text tool selected.

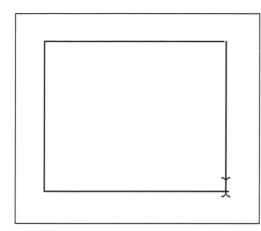

Figure 4.2 To create a text block of a specific size and shape, click and drag with the Text tool. If you just click and start typing without dragging first, you'll probably end up wasting time because you'll have to reshape the text block to fit your layout grid.

Creating Text Blocks

Make a text block when you want to create text in PageMaker.

To create a text block:

1. Click on the Text tool.

2. Click and drag diagonally on the pasteboard to draw a text block (**Figure 4.2**).

   As you drag, you'll see a rectangle appear onscreen. This represents the boundaries of the text block.

3. Release the mouse button.

   A blinking cursor will appear.

4. Type your text.

   You must type text at this point. If you click somewhere else or change tools, the text block you drew will vanish. PageMaker automatically deletes empty text blocks.

✔ Tip

■ To select a text block, click on it with the Pointer tool.

Changing a Text Block's Shape

When you select a text block with the Pointer tool, the block's boundaries become visible. These handles are called "windowshades" because you raise and lower them by clicking on the loops at the bottom of the block (**Figure 4.3**).

The text block has handles that allow you to change its shape. Drag the handles outward to make a text block wider. Drag them inward to make the block narrower. Raise and lower the loops to determine how much text is visible through the windowshades.

To change the shape of a text block:

1. Select the Pointer tool.

2. Click either the left or right handles on the bottom of the text block and drag.

    When you release the mouse button, the text in the text block will reflow to fit the new shape of the text block.

✔ Tips

■ Drag a text block with the Arrow tool to move it.

■ To rotate a text block, select the rotation tool, then click and drag on a text block's handle. Holding the Shift key constrains the rotation to 45-degree increments.

■ A red triangle in the bottom windowshade means there is more text in the story than is visible on the page. Drag the windowshade handle down to show more text.

■ A plus symbol in either loop means that part of the story has been placed somewhere else in the document.

■ An empty windowshade handle means there is no more text to flow.

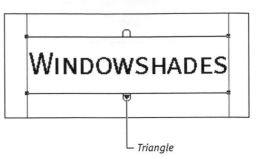

Triangle

Figure 4.3 The loops at the top and bottom of a text block give rise to the name "windowshades." You can change how much text is visible in each text block by raising or lowering the windowshades.

CHANGING A TEXT BLOCK'S SHAPE

Figure 4.4 The pointer changes to this shape when you click on a red triangle in a windowshade. Click in the upper-left corner of a page or column to place text with this icon.

Creating Linked Text Blocks Manually

Units of text in PageMaker are called "stories." Stories can be only a single character or hundreds of pages long. You may need only one text block to display a complete story, or hundreds. No matter how long a story is, or how many text blocks are needed to display it, the story remains "threaded" together.

Text blocks can be linked together so that a story flows from one column to another and from one page to another. If you make a change in the first text block, the text in all subsequent linked blocks reflows to reflect that change. You can select text in multiple linked text blocks simply by dragging the Text tool from one text block to another.

To create linked text blocks:

1. Drag the bottom windowshade up until a red triangle appears.

   Release the mouse button to see the red triangle.

2. Click the red triangle on the windowshade to load text.

   Your cursor will change into the loaded text icon, which looks like the upper-left corner of a document page (**Figure 4.4**).

3. Click and drag somewhere else in your document to create a new text block linked to the first one.

   When you release the mouse button, the text will reflow into the area you dragged.

   Create additional linked text blocks by repeating steps 1 through 3 for each new linked text block you need.

✔ Tip

■ If you get a loaded text icon and then decide you don't need it, just click on the Pointer tool. This dumps the text back into the story without unthreading it.

Creating Linked Text Blocks Automatically

When you're placing long passages of text in a document, it may take a very long time to place a column of text, click on the red triangle to load the text again, then move to a new location and dump another column of text. PageMaker can handle all this tedium for you with the Autoflow option.

With Autoflow turned on, you'll click to place text just as you would manually. But the icon changes to indicate that the text will flow automatically (**Figure 4.5**).

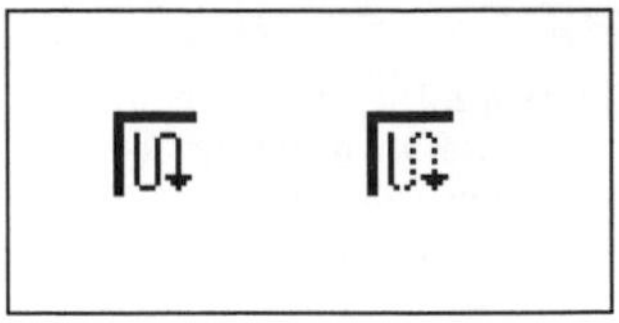

To automatically connect several text blocks:

1. Choose Layout > Autoflow.

2. Drag the bottom windowshade up until the red triangle appears.

3. Click the red triangle in the windowshade to load text.

   Your cursor will change into a page corner containing a squiggly arrow (**Figure 4.5**).

4. Click in the upper-left corner of the page or column into which you want the long story to begin flowing.

   When you release the mouse button, the text will flow into the column you clicked and into any additional columns it needs.

✔ Tip

- Place text semi-automatically by holding down the Shift key while you click to place the text. The icon changes from the solid curved line pictured above to a partly dashed line. Text will flow from the top of the page or column where you click and will stop at the bottom page margin. The text icon remains loaded, so that you can just click in the next column where you want to flow your text.

Figure 4.5 The icon on the left is the Autoflow loaded text icon. Place lengthy passages of text with this icon. The icon on the right is the Semi-Autoflow loaded text icon.

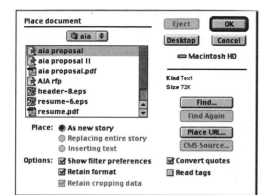

Figure 4.6 The Place document dialog box lets you choose which text file will be imported. In this shot, text options are shown because a text document is highlighted.

Placing Text

PageMaker lets you insert text that was created in another program, such as a word processor, into a PageMaker document. When you bring text into PageMaker this way, you are 'placing' text.

To place text in a PageMaker document:

1. Choose File > Place, or Ctrl+D/ Command+D.

   The Place document dialog box will appear (**Figure 4.6**).

2. Locate the document that contains the text you want to place, select it, and click OK.

   The pointer changes into the loaded text icon.

3. Click in the upper-left corner of a page or column to place the text.

   The text will be placed on the page.

✔ Tips

- If Autoflow is turned on, the text will flow into as many columns as necessary, adding pages as needed.

- If Autoflow is turned off, the text will stop flowing at the bottom of the column in which you clicked.

- You can ignore column and page margins if you want to. Click and drag to make the text flow into the text block you 'drew' with the loaded text icon.

- To place text in a text block that's already been flowed, use the Text tool to click in a text block at the location where you want the additional text inserted. Then choose File > Place and select the Inserting text option in the Place dialog box.

Changing Import Options

When you place text, you can modify the import options used to bring in the text. Filter options are specific to the type of document you'll be importing. Most of the time you can ignore these options, but occasionally they are necessary. For instance, if you're placing a delimited file from a database or spreadsheet, it may be useful to tell PageMaker whether to read tagged text codes or to ignore them.

To change import filter options:

1. Choose File > Place, or Ctrl+D/ Command+D.

   The Place document dialog box appears.

2. Find the document that contains the text you want to place, and select it.

3. Check the Show Filter Preferences check box, then click OK.

   The Import Options dialog box appears for the file you selected.

   Figure 4.7 shows the Microsoft Word filter preferences. Preferences for other formats will vary.

4. Make the appropriate changes and click OK to implement them.

   The text is imported according to the settings you made in the Import Options dialog box.

✔ Tip

■ PageMaker can read certain program-specific tags, like table of contents and indexing tags. Some options also let you decide how PageMaker converts some types of formatting such as tabs or line-breaks.

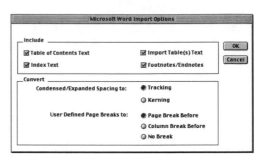

Figure 4.7 The Import Options dialog box will offer different options depending on the type of document you are placing.

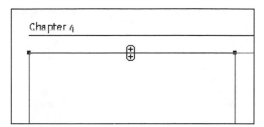

Figure 4.8 This illustration shows an empty text block. Notice that the top and bottom handles each have plus symbols in them. This indicates that there are other blocks before and after the empty text block. When you empty a text block before deleting it, the story remains intact. But if you delete a text block that has text showing in it, you will also delete the text.

Deleting Text Blocks

When you place lengthy passages of text in linked text blocks, the story is 'threaded' into each block. You can lose parts of your story if you delete a text block without reflowing the text first. Be sure to follow the steps outlined below to insure the integrity of your story when you delete an unneeded text block.

To delete a text block:

1. Click on the text block with the Pointer tool to select it.

2. Drag the lower windowshade handle up to close the text block completely (**Figure 4.8**).

3. Click anywhere else on the document to deselect the text block.

   Deselecting an empty text block causes PageMaker to delete it automatically.

✔ Tip

■ A text block may contain text that you want deleted. In this case, you can select the text block and press the Delete key on your keyboard. The text block and all the text within it will vanish. Take care using this method, however: PageMaker will not warn you before deleting the text block and its text.

Selecting Text

To format text after it's been placed, select it first. PageMaker has several shortcuts you can use to select different amounts of text.

To select an entire story:

1. With the Text tool selected, click once in a text block.

2. Choose Edit > Select All, or Ctrl+A/ Command+A.

   All text in the story (even if it is distributed among multiple linked text blocks) will be selected (**Figure 4.9**).

✔ Tips

- You can't select multiple stories within PageMaker at the same time.

- Double-click on a word to quickly select the whole word.

- Double-click and drag to add whole words to your selection.

- Triple-click in a paragraph to quickly select the whole paragraph.

- Triple-click and drag to add whole paragraphs to your selection.

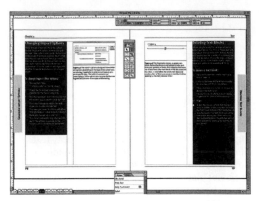

Figure 4.9 All the text in linked text blocks is highlighted when you choose Edit > Select All. Notice that in this illustration only the main text is included in the selected story. Headers, footers and captions are in their own separate stories.

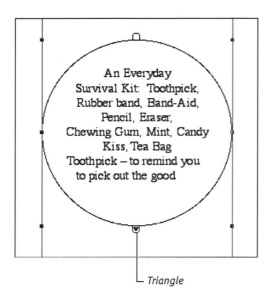

Triangle

Figure 4.10 Text is placed in a circle drawn with PageMaker's Circle Frame tool. Notice the triangle in the lower handle, which means that part of the story has not yet been placed.

Placing Text in a Frame

In addition to using text blocks to organize and hold stories, PageMaker also allows you to use frames to hold text. The frame tools look like regular drawing tools, except that they have x's in them.

As with text blocks, you can click and drag to create a frame, then begin typing to create small bits of text within PageMaker. More often, though, you'll place text that's been created in another program into your Page-Maker document. You can place text into frames, then link them together just as you do with text blocks.

To place text in a frame:

1. Draw a frame with one of PageMaker's Frame tools (a rectangle, oval, or hexagon with an 'x' in it).

Make sure the object remains selected.

2. Choose File > Place, or Ctrl+D/ Command+D.

The Place dialog box will appear.

3. Locate the document that contains the text you want to place, select it, and click OK.

The pointer changes to the loaded text icon.

4. Click in a frame to place the text in it.

The text will be placed in the frame (**Figure 4.10**).

✔ Tip

■ A red triangle at the bottom of a frame indicates that part of the story has not yet been placed. Either make the frame larger, or create another frame and link it to the first so that all the text in the story will be visible.

Linking Frames Containing Text

With long passages of text, a single frame may not be large enough to hold an entire story. Just as with text blocks, you can link frames together so that an entire story is visible. When you change a linked frame's size or shape, text will adjust and reflow into subsequent frames.

To link frames containing text:

1. Draw a second frame with the Frame tool of your choice.

2. Click the first frame to select it.

3. Click on the red triangle to load the text icon (**Figure 4.11**).

4. Click the second frame.

   PageMaker flows the text into the second frame.

   Repeat steps 1 through 3 until the entire story is visible. The last frame's handle will be empty when all the text has been placed.

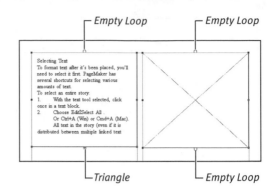

Figure 4.11 The frame on the right is awaiting text that will be flowed from the frame on the left.

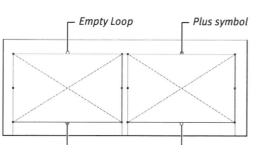

Figure 4.12 These two empty text blocks are linked together. The top handle of the frame on the left is blank, indicating that the story will begin in this frame. A plus symbol in a loop of a text frame indicates that it is linked to another frame.

Linking Empty Frames

In some ways, frames are more versatile than text blocks. You can link frames even if they don't yet contain text. When you place text in linked frames, PageMaker flows text automatically until it has filled all the linked frames.

To link empty frames:

1. Draw frames on each page where you want text to flow.

2. Click the bottom handle of the first frame. The pointer changes to a chain icon.

3. Click the next frame in the series. The handles change to indicate the frame's linked status (**Figure 4.12**).

4. Repeat steps 1 through 3 until you've linked all the frames you need to link.

✔ Tips

■ You can 'trace' the linked frames in your document by highlighting a frame, then choosing Element > Frame > Next Frame or Element > Frame > Previous Frame. PageMaker will highlight the next frame in the series, even going to another page if necessary.

■ Unlike text blocks, text frames can be deleted without losing the text they contain. PageMaker reflows text from a deleted frame into the story's other frames.

Attaching Text to a Frame

Perhaps you've created text in a text block, but you want to convert it to a frame. This is useful for sidebars, where you want to have a colored background for your text. With a frame, the text and fill can be moved and resized as one unit, which makes edits easier.

To attach text to a frame:

1. Draw the frame of your choice using one of PageMaker's Frame tools.

2. Select the text block you want to insert in the frame.

3. Click the frame while pressing the Shift key.

   Both elements will be selected (**Figure 4.13**).

4. Choose Element > Frame > Attach Content, or Ctrl+F/Command+F.

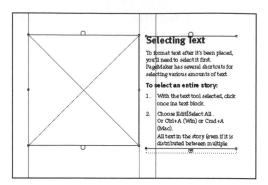

Figure 4.13 This block of text on the right will be attached to the frame on the left with the Element > Frame > Attach Content command.

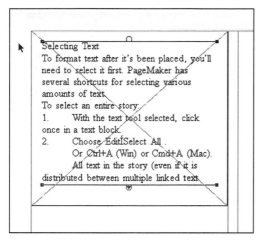

Figure 4.14 Text can be separated from a frame and will become a separate object that can be formatted independently from the frame. Once it's separated, the text becomes a text block that lands on top of the frame, as in the illustration above.

Separating Text from a Frame

Once text has been attached to a frame or flowed inside it, you can separate the text and frame.

To separate text from a frame:

1. Click the frame with the Pointer tool.

2. Choose Element > Frame > Separate Content, or Ctrl+F/Command+F.

   The frame and its text become separate objects (**Figure 4.14**).

Setting Frame Options

You can align text within a frame and set how far text is inset from the frame's edge using the Frame Options dialog box.

To set frame options:

1. Click a frame to select it.

2. Choose Element > Frame > Frame Options, or Ctrl+Alt+F/ Command+Option+F.

   The Frame Options dialog box appears (**Figure 4.15**).

3. Make the appropriate changes and click OK.

✔ Tip

■ Frames are especially helpful when you're using shaded boxes for text. Use the Element > Fill and Stroke dialog box to set a solid fill of 10 or 15 percent. Fills that are darker than this can make your text hard to read.

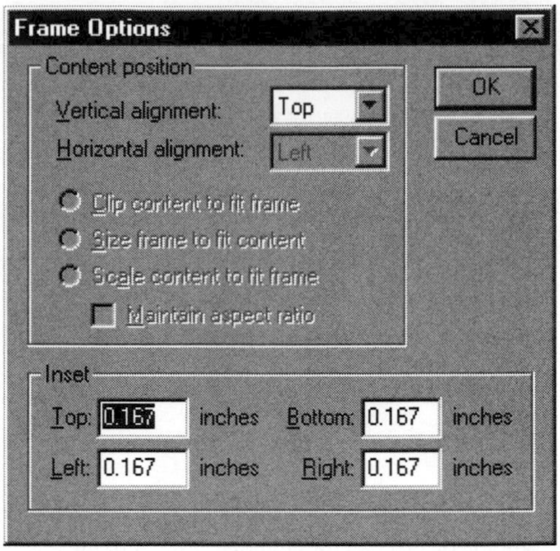

Figure 4.15 Change the position of text within a frame using the Frame Options dialog box. Set vertical and horizontal alignment and inset here.

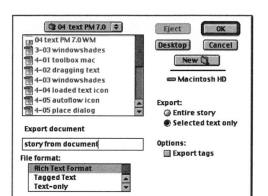

Figure 4.16 You can export text created in a PageMaker document so that it can be used in other software programs. The Export dialog box lets you name the exported file and set options for its contents and file format.

Exporting Text

You can take text out of PageMaker and export it to other applications. Just make sure that you export it into a file format that's appropriate for the program in which you want to use the text. Refer to the other program's manual to see which file formats it supports.

To export text:

1. Select the text you want to export.

2. Choose File > Export > Text.
   The Export Document dialog box appears (**Figure 4.16**).

3. Type a name for the text file you're exporting.

4. Choose a file format from the list of formats.

5. If you want to export the entire story, choose that option. Otherwise, leave the Selected text only option selected.

6. Click Save.
   The text is exported to a file.

Controlling Hyphenation

Hyphenation is turned on by default. In a justified paragraph, PageMaker calculates how to make each line match the width of the lines above and below it. You can control how the program makes its decisions about hyphenation, or you can turn it off altogether:

◆ **Manual only**

Hyphenated words occur only when you manually break them using Ctrl+Shift+Hyphen/Command+Shift+Hyphen.

◆ **Manual plus dictionary**

Words are hyphenated manually, or as they are found in PageMaker's dictionary.

◆ **Manual plus algorithm**

Words are hyphenated manually, or they can be broken according to PageMaker's built-in hyphenation algorithm.

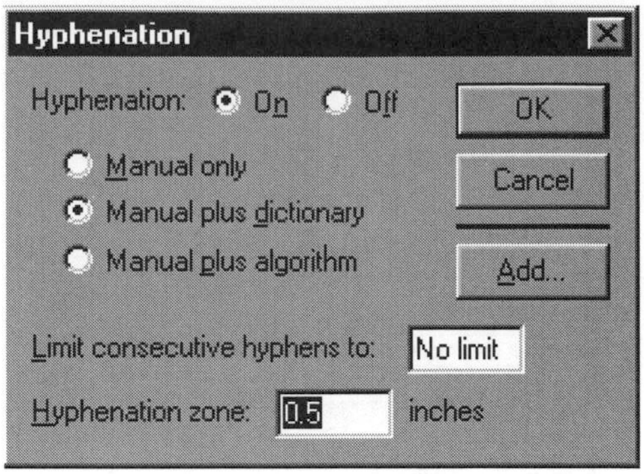

To control hyphenation:

1. Choose Type > Hyphenation.

   The Hyphenation dialog box appears (**Figure 4.17**).

2. Change the options or turn hyphenation off.

3. Click OK.

   The hyphenation options are changed for the selected text, or for all new text blocks if no text was selected.

✔ Tip

■ Hyphenation should be used sparingly. It is a little harder to read text when it's hyphenated. Thin columns of text will require more hyphenation. You may find that adjusting your layout to make the columns slightly wider will also help make your text more legible.

Figure 4.17 Turn hyphenation off and on or control the way it works with the Hyphenation dialog box.

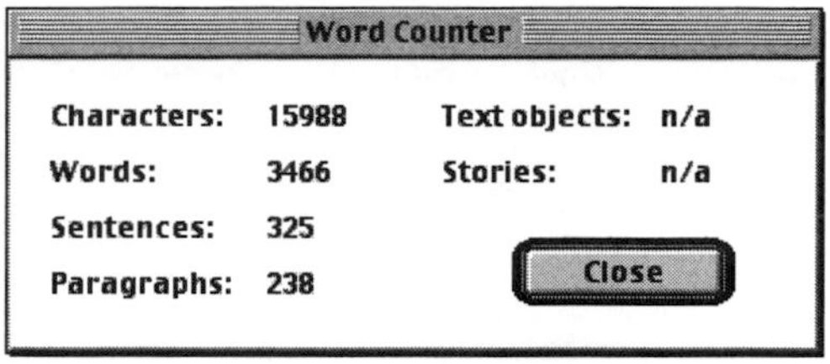

Word Counter

Characters:	15988	Text objects:	n/a
Words:	3466	Stories:	n/a
Sentences:	325		
Paragraphs:	238	[Close]	

Figure 4.18 The Word Counter dialog box gives you feedback on the number of characters, words, sentences and paragraphs in a selected passage of text.

Counting Words

PageMaker has a feature that allows you to count the number of words in selected text.

To count the words in a text block:

1. Click a text block to select it.

2. Choose Utilities > Plug-ins > Word Counter.

   PageMaker displays a box providing information about your document (**Figure 4.18**).

✔ Tip

- Use various text-selection techniques to quickly specify the amount of text in which PageMaker is to count the words.

Checking Spelling

PageMaker's spelling tools are similar to a spelling checker in most word-processing programs. The main difference is knowing how to get the Spelling command to appear in the menu. You have to view a story in Page-Maker's Story Editor in order to make the spelling commands appear in the Edit menu.

To check spelling:

1. Click the text block in which you want to check spelling.

2. Choose Edit > Edit Story, or Ctrl+E/Command+E.

   The Story Editor window for that text block appears (**Figure 4.19**).

3. Choose Utilities > Spelling, or Ctrl+L/Command+L.

   The Spelling dialog box appears (**Figure 4.20**).

4. Click Start.

   The spell checker finds the first word that has been spelled incorrectly.

5. Click on the correctly spelled version of the word in the list box of suggested correct spellings.

6. Click Replace.

   The word is replaced with the correctly spelled version of the word, and the next misspelled word is highlighted.

7. Replace each successive misspelled word with the correctly spelled version until the Spelling check complete message appears in the Spelling dialog box.

8. Close the Spelling dialog box.

9. Close the Story Editor window.

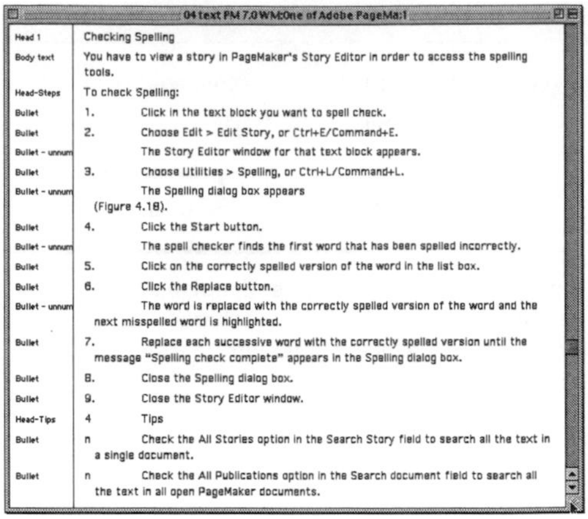

Figure 4.19 PageMaker's Story Editor allows you access to common word-processing utilities, like spell checking and searching.

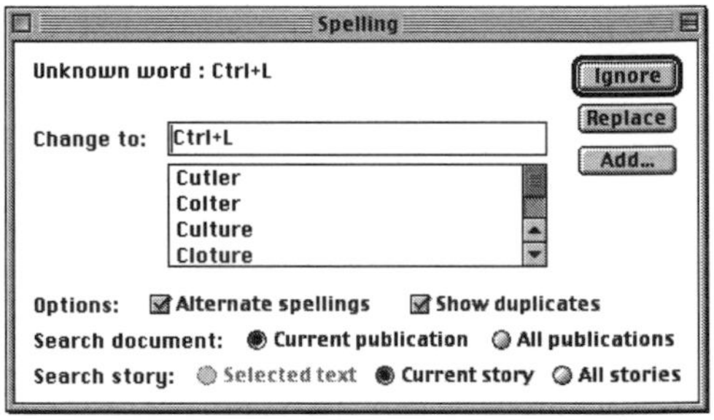

Figure 4.20 PageMaker's Spelling dialog box lets you check spelling within selected text only, within the current story or in all stories in a document.

✔ Tips

- If a word doesn't appear in the list of correctly spelled words, type it in the Change to field, then click Replace.

- A word may be spelled correctly, even though PageMaker has flagged it for change. If this happens, just click Ignore.

- If you frequently use a words that are used in a specialized trade, or even typical words like street names or people's names, you may find that you're spending lots of time telling PageMaker to ignore correctly spelled words. Next time PageMaker flags one of your specialized words, click the Add button. The word will be added to PageMaker's dictionary and it won't be flagged in the future.

- Check the All Stories option in the Search Story field of the Spelling dialog box to search all the text in a single document.

- Check the All Publications option in the Search document field of the Spelling dialog box to search all the text in all open PageMaker documents.

Finding Text

PageMaker has standard search features that allow you to find text in a document without laboriously reading each word of text. You can search within selected text in a single text block, search through the entire current story, or search all stories in a document. You can even search all open documents, which is helpful if you're working on chapters of a book that are stored in separate documents.

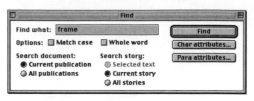

Figure 4.21 Use the Find dialog box to enter search criteria for text in your document.

To find specific text in a text block:

1. Select the text block in which you want to find a word.

2. Choose Edit > Edit Story, or Ctrl+E/Command+E.

   The Story Editor window for the story appears.

3. Choose Utilities > Find, or Ctrl+F/Command+F.

   The Find dialog box appears (**Figure 4.21**).

4. Type the word, phrase, or other sequence of characters you want to find in the Find what text field.

5. Click the Find next button.

   The text you specified (if it occurs in the text block) will be highlighted in the Story Editor.

✔ Tips

- View the text you specifed in the context of your layout by choosing Edit > Edit Story with the text highlighted. PageMaker will close the Story Editor window and go to the page in which the text occurs.

- For details about the Char attributes and Para attributes buttons, see the sections on Replacing Text with Character Formats and Replacing Text with Paragraph Formats later in this chapter.

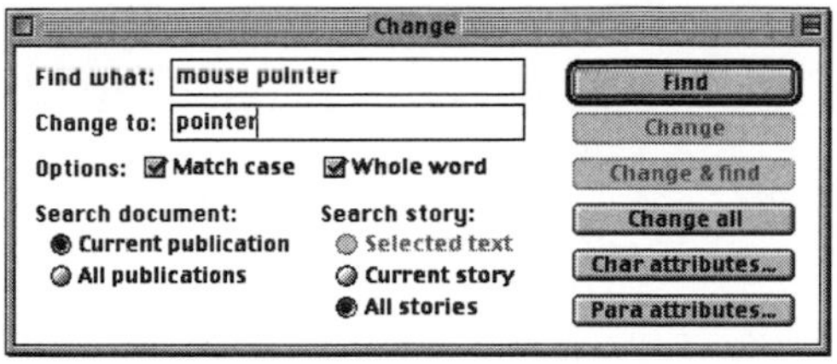

Figure 4.22 Type the word, character string or phrase you're looking for in the Find what field and the replacement text in the Change to field of the Change dialog box.

Replacing Text

If the style rules for your document change in the middle of production, don't worry. You can use PageMaker's Change command to change all instances of 'mouse pointer' to 'pointer.'

To replace text:

1. Select the text block in which you want to replace text.

2. Choose Edit > Edit Story, or Ctrl+E/ Command+E.

   The Story Editor window for the story appears.

3. Choose Utilities > Change, or Ctrl+H/ Command+H.

   The Change dialog box appears (**Figure 4.22**).

4. Type the word or character string you want to replace in the Find what field.

5. Type the replacement text in the Change to field.

6. Click the Find button.

   The text (if it occurs in the text block) is highlighted in the Story Editor.

7. Click the Change button.

   The highlighted text will be replaced with the Change to text.

✔ Tips

■ Type two spaces in the Find what field and a single space in the Change to field to replace those pesky double spaces some typists put between sentences.

■ Use special characters to replace extra paragraph or tab symbols. Type ^t^t in the Find what field and ^t in the Change to field to replace multiple tab characters. Type ^p^p in the Find what field and ^p in the Change to field to replace multiple paragraph symbols.

Replacing Text with Character Formats

PageMaker lets you replace fonts, point sizes, or almost any text formatting that it can apply to text. This feature is very useful when you need to be sure that you've formatted all related text in the same way. For example, this book uses Zapf Dingbats for the symbol that precedes the bulleted tips. I can search my document for all incidents of the letter 'n' where it occurs as a whole word and change it to Zapf Dingbats. I could also change the formats of text without regard to the text itself. For instance, I could search for all italic text and change it to bold.

To replace text with specific formats:

1. Select the text block in which you want to replace character formats.

2. Choose Edit > Edit Story, or Ctrl+E/Command+E.

   The Story Editor window for the story appears.

3. Choose Utilities > Change, or Ctrl+H/Command+H.

   The Change dialog box appears.

4. Type the text you want to replace in the Find what field.

5. Type the replacement text in the Change to field.

6. Click on the Char attributes button.

   The Change Character Attributes dialog box appears (**Figure 4.23**).

7. Set the attributes for the characters you want to find.

8. Set the attributes for the replacement character format.

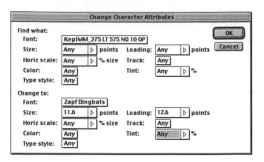

Figure 4.23 The Change Character Attributes dialog box lets you search for and replace all instances of text that have been formatted a specific way. In the illustration above, the dialog box is set to find all text formatted with the body text font for this book.

9. Click the Find button.

The word (if it occurs in the text block) is highlighted in the Story Editor.

10. Click the Change button.

The highlighted word is replaced with the text and formatting you specified.

✔ Tips

■ Check the All Stories option in the Search Story field of the Change dialog box to search all the text in a single document.

■ Check the All Publications option in the Search document field of the Change dialog box to search all the text in all open PageMaker documents.

■ Save time by clicking the Change All button. But only use Change All if you're certain that every instance of text that's been formatted as you indicated in the Find what field should be changed without your approval. PageMaker makes all the changes without showing you each instance of text. The Undo command won't work on text that's been edited with Change All, so be careful.

Replacing Text with Paragraph Formats

You can also replace paragraph formatting features with PageMaker's Change function. For instance, you may have realized that you used the wrong style to format all headlines of a specific type. PageMaker can find and reformat them automatically. The text in the paragraphs will not be changed; only the formatting for the paragraph will change.

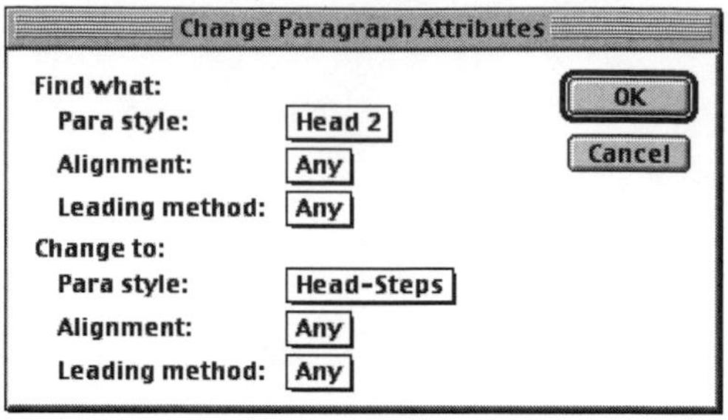

To replace text with specific formats:

1. Select the text block in which you want to replace text.

2. Choose Edit > Edit Story, or Ctrl+E/ Command+E.

   The Story Editor window for the story appears.

3. Choose Utilities > Change, or Ctrl+H/ Command+H.

   The Change dialog box appears.

4. Click on the Para attributes button.

   The Change Paragraph Attributes dialog box appears (**Figure 4.24**).

5. Set the attributes for the paragraphs you want to find.

6. Set the attributes for the replacement paragraphs.

7. Click the Find button.

   The paragraph (if it occurs in the text block) is highlighted in the Story Editor.

8. Click the Change button.

   The highlighted paragraph is replaced with the formatting you specified.

Figure 4.24 The Change Paragraph Attributes dialog box lets you search for and replace all instances of paragraphs formatted in specific way. With these settings, all paragraphs formatted with Head 2 style will be reformatted with Head-Steps style.

✔ Tips

■ Check the All Stories option in the Search Story field of the Change dialog box to search all the text in a single document.

■ Check the All Publications option in the Search document field of the Change dialog box to search all the text in all open PageMaker documents.

■ Save time by clicking the Change All button. But only use Change All if you're certain that every instance of text that's been formatted as you indicated in the Find what field should be changed without your approval. PageMaker makes all the changes without showing you each instance of text. The Undo command won't work on text that's been edited with Change All, so be careful.

CHARACTER FORMATTING

When we talk about characters in Adobe PageMaker, we're talking about letters, numbers, and anything else you can type with a single keystroke.

In this chapter, we'll talk about the kinds of character-level formatting you can apply to text. These are the more common means of formatting text—fonts, point sizes, leading, style, color. We'll also discuss some less common, but still useful, means of formatting characters—position, case, track and tint.

Character attributes can be formatted by any of several methods: using the Character Specifications dialog box, the Type menu, the Character Control palette, or by using a keyboard command.

Formatting Characters with the Type Menu

You can change many aspects of a character's formatting. You can change the font, the size, the style, the color, and even the width of a character. For just a single change, say, changing the bullet character in a sentence to a special font, using the Type menu (**Figure 5.1**) is probably the quickest method.

To format characters with the Type menu:

1. Select the characters to be formatted.

2. Choose Type > Font > [your font].

Or choose Size or Leading or Style from the Type menu to set any of these format details.

✔ Tip

■ If you work with lots of fonts, you'll want at least one type utility. ATM Deluxe lets you activate fonts on a per document basis, which saves you from having to scroll through a long list of fonts you aren't currently using. Adobe Type Reunion puts font families together in a program's font menus, and even places your most commonly used fonts at the top of the menu to make them conveniently accessible.

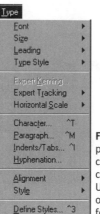

Figure 5.1 The Type Menu provides quick access to all character-level formatting commands in PageMaker. Use the menu when you are only applying one kind of formatting to a bit of text.

Applying Type Styles

The Style submenu contains the most commonly used character formatting commands. Bold and Italics are the most common formats of all. Other programs that allow formatting just fatten the characters for bold and slant them a little for italics. Often the printed results are less than stellar.

If you get squirrely results from your printer when you're using bold and italics from the Style menu, check to see whether a bold or italics version of the font you're using is installed on your computer. If not, either install the fonts or use a different font.

In general, it's best to apply styles from the Font menu, that is, actually choose a Bold or Italics version of the font instead of applying a style. You'll get better results.

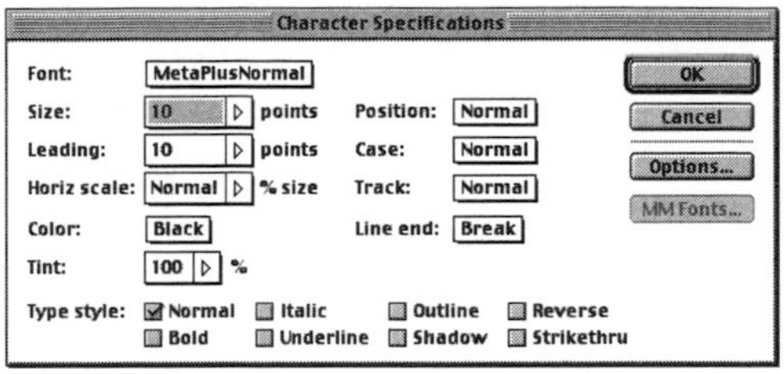

Figure 5.2 The Character Specifications dialog box organizes most of the formatting commands that you can apply to text. You also have access to optional formatting, like Superscript controls and Small Cap Size from the Options button in the dialog box.

Formatting Characters with the Character Specifications Dialog Box

The Character Specifications dialog box organizes most of the formatting commands that are applicable to text. Only the kerning command, which applies to character pairs, is not available in this dialog box.

Some of the less frequently used commands, like Superscript controls and Small Cap Size, are found nowhere else in the program. Use the Character Specifications dialog box when you want to apply several types of formatting to a single selection of text, or when you need access to the optional formats.

To format characters with the Character Specifications dialog box:

1. Select the characters to be formatted.

2. Choose Type > Character, or Ctrl+T/ Command+T.

   The Character Specifications dialog box appears (**Figure 5.2**).

3. Make the appropriate changes in the dialog box, then click OK.

✔ Tips

- If you find yourself making the same few character-level formatting changes over and over again, investigate using Styles. Styles organize complex sets of formats and let you apply them all at once with a single click. See Chapter 7 for more information about Styles.

- Keyboard Shortcuts are covered in Appendixes A and B.

FORMATTING WITH THE CHARACTER DIALOG BOX

Formatting Characters with the Control Palette

For sheer efficiency, the Control palette can't be beat when you're heavily into text-formatting mode. The palette floats on top of your work and can be moved wherever it's most convenient. Best of all, once you activate the palette you can tab from field to field without using the mouse, which can be the biggest time-saver of all.

When you view the Control palette, its default is the Character view (**Figure 5.3**). Its tools change to reflect the item that's selected.

To modify character attributes using the Character Control palette:

1. Choose Window > Show Control Palette if the Control palette isn't showing (**Figure 5.3**).

2. Select the characters you want to modify.

3. Make the appropriate changes in the Control palette.

✔ Tip

■ Select from the Control palette's font list by typing in the Font area the first few characters of the name of the font you want to use. Press the Enter key to apply the change when the correct font is displayed.

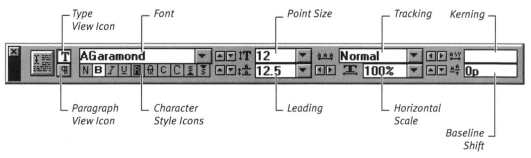

Figure 5.3 The Control palette is especially useful when you're doing lots of formatting. It is always available, floating on top of your work area. Also, you can activate its controls via the keyboard instead of using the mouse.

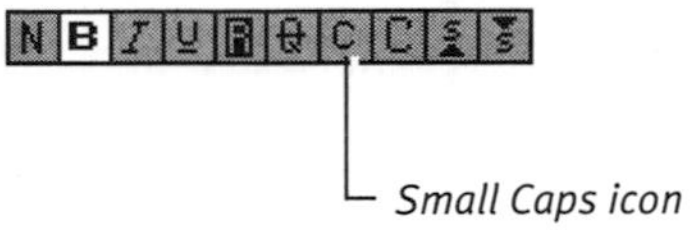

NB*IU*Bⓒ*CⒸ*≜* *

— *Small Caps icon*

Figure 5.4 The styles section of the Character panel of the Control palette. Small Caps are easier to read than regular upper-case text and can be toggled off and on without the need to retype text.

Using Small Caps

Most people are familiar with basic character styles like Underline and Strikethrough. But Small Caps is not as well understood. It's a useful format that can emphasize small bits of text, like headlines, as in this book's chapter headlines and the thumb tab on the edge of this page.

The Small Caps option offers two main benefits over just pressing the Caps Lock key and typing away. First, you can turn Small Caps off and on. If you change your mind, you don't have retype the text you want to change. Second, Small Caps are a little easier to read than a line of All Caps. Your readers will thank you for making the text more legible.

To use Small Caps:

1. Choose Window > Show Control Palette if the Control palette isn't currently showing.

2. Select the characters you want to change to small caps.

3. Click the small caps icon on the Character view of the Control palette (**Figure 5.4**).

   If the styles icons aren't showing in the Control palette, click on the uppercase 'T' icon on the palette to view them.

✔ Tip

■ To change the size of small caps, choose Type > Character, then click the Options button in the Character Specifications dialog box. The default is 70 percent of the point size of the current text.

Changing Case

You may sometimes use text that has been created by someone else. Such text may have been typed in all caps or in title case (with the first letter of each word capitalized). Fortunately you don't have to retype this text just to change the case. Instead, use automatic case changing to change the characters permanently to normal upper- and lower case.

To change case:

1. Use the Text tool to select the characters you want to change.

2. Choose Utilities > Plug-ins > Change Case (**Figure 5.5**).

   The Change Case dialog box appears.

3. Select a case option that's appropriate for your text.

4. Click OK.

   Note the Apply button. If you aren't sure which case you want, make a selection, then click Apply to audition the new look. Click OK when you've made your choice.

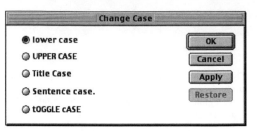

Figure 5.5 The Change Case plug-in permanently changes the case of selected text.

XML H_2SO_4

Figure 5.6 The 'TM' above is set in superscript. The digits in the chemical formula are set in subscript.

Subscript icon

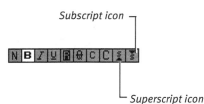

Superscript icon

Figure 5.7 The styles section of the Control palette.

Using Superscript and Subscript

Superscript and subscript are opposite sides of one formatting coin. Text is made smaller and moved a preset distance from the baseline (the imaginary line that the bottom of most characters rests on) (**Figure 5.6**).

Superscript is used to shrink characters and to raise them slightly above the baseline. It is often used for footnotes and special symbols that appear within text.

Subscript is like superscript except that it moves the text slightly below the baseline. Subscript text is often used for chemical notations.

To superscript text:

1. Select the characters you want to change.

2. Click the Superscript icon (**Figure 5.7**) on the Character view of the Control palette. Or click the Subscript icon, if appropriate.

✔ Tip

■ Change the size or location of superscript or subscript text by choosing Type > Character, then clicking on the Options button in the Character Specifications dialog box. The default size setting is 58.3 percent of the point size of the current text. The default offset position is 33.3 percent above or below the baseline of the current text.

Using Horizontal Scaling

PageMaker lets you make the characters in your text wider or thinner by using Horizontal Scale. You can make letters as skinny as 5 percent or as wide as 250 percent of their original width.

Of course, these extreme adjustments should only be made when there's a compelling reason, such as slightly changing the width of type to make it fit in a column, or in order to give headline type a special look (**Figure 5.8**).

To change horizontal scale:

1. Select the characters you want to adjust.

2. On the Character view of the Control palette, click the field identified by a T with a double-ended arrow under it (**Figure 5.9**).

3. Type a new value in the text box.

4. Press Enter.

✔ Tips

- Use the horizontal scale's nudge icons for more precise control.

- You can also access Horizontal Scale from the Type menu.

Huge Sale Today!

Figure 5.8 The headline above is set at a relatively small type size for a headline—18 point. But using the Control palette's nudge controls for horizontal scaling, I can give the text emphasis by making it fit the column width precisely.

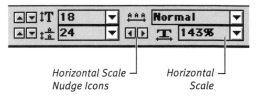

Horizontal Scale ⌐   Horizontal ⌐
Nudge Icons   Scale

Figure 5.9 The Horizontal Scale icons and field on the Character view of the Control palette.

USING HORIZONTAL SCALING

Come to our Grand Opening on May 25th.

Figure 5.10 Give text an old-fashioned feel of quality by setting ordinals with a slight baseline shift.

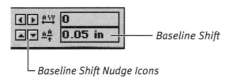

Baseline Shift

Baseline Shift Nudge Icons

Figure 5.11 The Baseline Shift field and its nudge controls on the Character view of the Control palette.

Using Baseline Shift

Baseline shift moves characters up or down from the baseline. However, unlike superscript or subscript, baseline shift preserves the point size of the text (**Figure 5.10**).

To change baseline shift:

1. Select the characters you want to move up or down from the baseline.

2. Click the Baseline Shift field, in the lower-right corner of the Character view of the Control palette (**Figure 5.11**).

3. Type in a value for the distance you want the characters to move up or down. Type a positive number to move text above the baseline, or a negative number to move text below the baseline.

   You can specify increments as small as one-tenth of an inch.

4. Press Enter.

   The selected characters move up or down according to the amount you specified.

✔ Tips

- Change the default size of Baseline Shift by choosing Type > Character, then clicking on the Options button in the Character Specifications dialog box. The default setting is zero.

- Use the Baseline Shift's nudge icons for more precise control.

Adjusting Leading

Leading is the distance between the baselines of consecutive lines of type (**Figure 5.12**). The greater the leading value, the more space appears between individual lines of text. The default value for leading is 120 percent of the text's point size.

To adjust leading:

1. Select the characters you want to adjust.

   Although you can adjust the leading of individual characters in a line of text, you'll normally select whole paragraphs at a time, in order to avoid the look of type set on a bumpy road.

2. Click in the Leading field in the Character view of the Control palette (**Figure 5.13**).

3. Type in the leading value you want.

4. Press Enter.

✔ Tips

- The leading value affects the entire line containing the selected characters. Lines below the formatted line are moved down by the same amount as the leading value.

- Use the Leading nudge icons for more precise control.

- You get points for knowing the following bit of trivia: The word 'leading' rhymes with 'shedding,' and is named for the tiny lead pipes typesetters used to place between rows of type in the days of movable-type presses.

Then I passed to a Master

Who is higher in repute,

Trusting to find justice

At the world's root.

Figure 5.12 The text set above has "loose" leading. It is 14-point type set on 35-point leading. Typesetters refer to this as 14/35 and it's often read as "fourteen on thirty-five." 14/35 represents spacing of two-and-a-half times the point size.

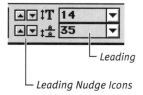

Leading

Leading Nudge Icons

Figure 5.13 The Leading field and nudge icons on the Character view of the Control palette.

Talking
Talking

Figure 5.14 The first word is set normally, with no kerning. The second word has been kerned .04 of a point between the "Ta" and the "al." I also kerned slightly (only .02 each) between the "in" and the "ng." Notice that the spacing seems more even than in the unkerned version.

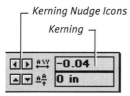

Kerning Nudge Icons

Kerning

Figure 5.15 The Kerning field and nudge icons on the Character view of the Control palette.

Kerning

Kerning changes the space between any pair of characters. In passages of body text, you wouldn't kern type because it's just too small to be a visual problem. But in headlines, where type is much larger, ungainly white spaces can develop between pairs of letters.

Some characters demand this treatment, such as a capital 'T' in front of any lowercase letter without an ascender or a descender (**Figure 5.14**). Ascenders are the parts of a letter, for example the tops of the 'l' and the 'k' that extend higher than the rest of the lowercase letters. Descenders are the parts of letters that dip below the baseline.

There is no menu command for pair kerning. Use the Control palette or the keyboard shortcuts outlined below.

To kern letter pairs:

1. Click between the two letters you want to kern.

2. Press Ctrl+Backspace/Command+Delete to remove space between the letters. Continue until you get the look you want.

3. Press Ctrl+Shift+Backspace/Command+ Shift+Delete to add extra space between letters or to undo kerning.

✔ Tips

■ Use the Kerning nudge icons on the Control palette to precisely adjust kerning (**Figure 5.15**).

■ Get a book on typesetting to learn which letter pairs most often need kerning. *Stop Stealing Sheep and Find Out How Type Works*, by Erik Spiekermann and E.M. Ginger, is an excellent reference.

Adjusting Tracking

Tracking adjusts space between all the characters in a word, a line, a paragraph, or even an entire story. Be careful how you use tracking, though, as it overrides the letter spacing that font designers build into their characters. If you alter the built-in tracking too much or over too large an amount of text, legibility is sacrificed (**Figure 5.16**). Instead, use tracking to alter the space in small sequences of text. For instance, if you are setting a phrase in small caps in the body of a paragraph, loosening the tracking for the phrase may make it easier to read.

To adjust tracking:

1. Select the characters for which you want to change the tracking.

2. Choose a tracking setting from the Tracking pop-up menu on the Character view of the Control palette (**Figure 5.17**).

   The space between the selected characters will change.

✔ Tip

- The title of the type reference book mentioned above, *Stop Stealing Sheep and Find Out How Type Works*, is said to come from an old story about the heralded but gruff type designer who exclaimed that any man who would letterspace type would also steal sheep. (Letterspacing is another term for tracking long passages of text.)

  Though probably apocryphal, the story is meant to caution against using tracking as a shortcut for choosing a font that works with your design grid. If you find that you need to adjust tracking frequently to make lines fit your columns, you should either adjust your layout or use a different font.

Superscript is a text format used to make characters smaller and to raise them up above the baseline. It is often used for footnotes and special symbols that appear within text.

Superscript is a text format used to make characters smaller and to raise them up above the baseline. It is often used for footnotes and special symbols that appear within text.

Figure 5.16 The first paragraph above is not tracked. the second has Very Tight Tracking applied. The text takes up less space, but legibility is compromised.

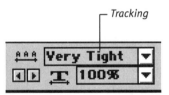

— *Tracking*

Figure 5.17 The Tracking pop-up list on the Control palette has six predefined tracking amounts: No Track, Very Loose, Loose, Normal, Tight and Very Tight.

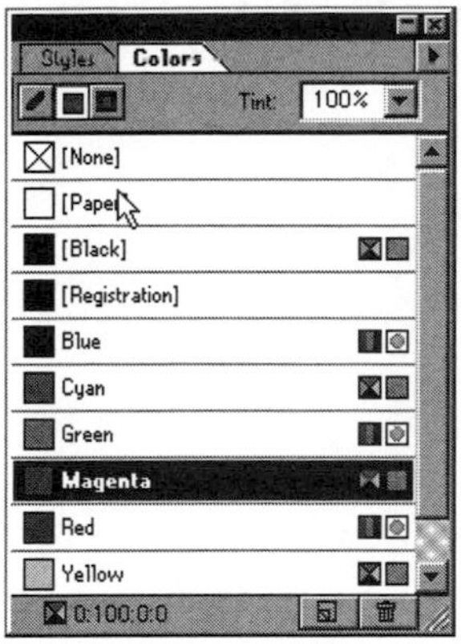

Figure 5.18 Use the Colors palette to apply colors to selected passages of text.

Changing Text Color

With a multi-color print job, or if you're designing for the Web, you'll want to consider what colors to use on the page. Your design may look livelier if you choose a text color other than black.

To color characters:

1. Select the text you want to color.

2. Display the Colors palette by choosing Window > Show Colors (**Figure 5.18**), or Ctrl+J/Command+J.

   The Colors palette appears.

3. Click the color you want to apply to the selected text.

   The characters change to the color you selected in the palette.

   Using color is discussed in more detail in Chapter 11.

✔ Tip

■ The colors you apply to text can make your publication sink or swim. Colors that don't contrast well with your paper stock will be hard to read. The smaller your body type, the more pronounced this effect will be. Choose a bright, contrasting color for body text. Save the outrageous colors for headlines or other limited bits of text.

Adding Tints to Text

You can tint any text color from 0% (white) to 100% (the actual color). This is a great way to give the illusion that a printed piece contains more colors than it actually does.

To tint characters:

1. Select the characters you want to tint.

2. Display the Colors palette by choosing Window > Show Colors (**Figure 5.19**), or Ctrl+J/Command+J.

   The Colors palette appears.

3. Choose a tint percentage from the Tint pop-up menu at the top of the palette.

   The characters change to the tint you selected in the menu.

✔ Tips

■ Be careful not to tint type too much. Pale text is very hard to read, particularly when it's set in small point sizes.

■ Do a test print before your final output to make sure you like the tints. Don't forget that a tinted red turns pink, which may not project the image you want.

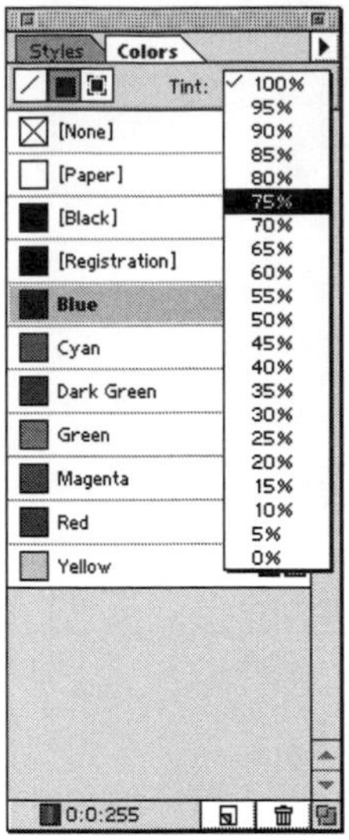

Figure 5.19 The Tint control appears near the top right of the Colors palette. Use tints with care; they wash out under 50% and text may become illegible.

Paragraphs and Tabs

To understand how paragraph formatting works in Adobe PageMaker, it's helpful to look at how the program defines a paragraph. Basically, a PageMaker paragraph is any number of characters that appear between successive paragraph symbols. So a paragraph may consist of only a single character (the paragraph symbol itself) or thousands of characters.

When you apply paragraph-level formats to any character within a paragraph, the paragraph is formatted as a whole unit. This can be disconcerting if you aren't expecting it, so be prepared. On the other hand, this function will save you time since you don't have to select a whole paragraph to apply paragraph-level formatting. Just click anywhere in the paragraph, apply your formatting, and you're done.

The major paragraph-level formats are: styles, indents, space before, space after, alignment, tabs, and rules. Other less frequently used options include widow and orphan control, page and line breaks, dictionaries, word and letter spacing, and leading defaults.

Applying Paragraph Formats with the Menu

When you have only one paragraph-level formatting change to make, it's fastest to use the Type menu if you don't have the Control palette visible. The most common paragraph formatting option accessed through the menu is alignment.

Text can be set so that the text block is flush left (like most of the text in this book), flush right, centered, justified, or force justified. Keyboard shortcuts for alignments are even quicker than the menu.

- **Align Left** is Ctrl+Shift+L/ Command+Shift+L.

- **Align Center** is Ctrl+Shift+C/ Command+Shift+C.

- **Align Right** is Ctrl+Shift+R/ Command+Shift+R.

- **Justify** is Ctrl+Shift+J/ Command+Shift+J.

- **Force Justify** is Ctrl+Shift+F/ Command+Shift+F.

To apply paragraph formats with the Type menu:

1. Click anywhere in the paragraph you want to format, or select any amount of text within the paragraph.

2. Choose Type > Alignment, or Type > Type Style > [your style] (**Figure 6.1**). The format will be applied to the paragraph you selected.

Figure 6.1 The Type menu provides quick access to all the character-level formatting commands in PageMaker. Use the Type menu when you are applying only one kind of formatting to a bit of text.

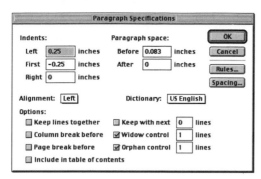

Figure 6.2 The Paragraph Specifications dialog box organizes almost all the formatting commands that you can apply to a paragraph of text. The only item missing is Styles, which has its own dialog box.

Applying Paragraph Formats with the Dialog Box

The Paragraph Specifications dialog box is the nerve center for most paragraph-specific controls and formatting. While paragraph controls are also found in the Type menu and the Paragraph Control palette, the Paragraph Specifications dialog box contains everything needed for general paragraph formatting.

Certain formatting commands, like applying rules or widow and orphan control, are only available in the Paragraph Specifications dialog box.

To apply paragraph formats with the dialog box:

1. Click anywhere in the paragraph you want to format or select any amount of text within the paragraph.

2. Choose Type > Paragraph, or Ctrl+M/ Command+M.

   The Paragraph Specifications dialog box appears (**Figure 6.2**).

3. Make the appropriate changes in the dialog box, then click OK.

   The formats you selected will take effect.

Applying Paragraph Formats with the Control Palette

The Paragraph Control palette includes the most commonly used paragraph controls. Because it floats above your work space, it can be the quickest and most convenient method for applying paragraph formats. The Control palette changes options based on the item selected. When you select text, or a text block, you'll see one of the Control palette's two sets of text-formatting panels, either text or paragraph. The panel icons toggle the Control palette back and forth between panels (**Figure 6.3**).

To apply formats with the Paragraph Control palette:

1. Choose Window > Show Control Palette or Ctrl+' (apostrophe)/Command+'.
   The Control palette appears.

2. If the Control palette doesn't look like the one in **Figure 6.3**, click the Paragraph Attributes button (¶).

3. Make the appropriate changes.

4. Press Enter.
   The changes you made will take effect.

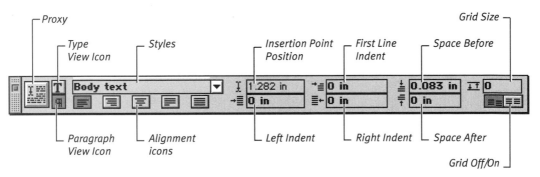

Figure 6.3 The Paragraph view of the Control palette offers the quickest and most convenient method for applying paragraph formats to text.

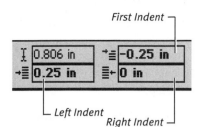

First Indent

Left Indent

Right Indent

Figure 6.4 The paragraph indent fields are grouped on the Paragraph Control palette. Note that the icons give you clues about each field. You can apply all three types of formats to a paragraph with a few keystrokes.

Applying Indents

Every paragraph has three indent controls:

◆ **Left Indent** controls how far from the left edge of the text block the left side of the text is aligned.

◆ **Right Indent** controls how far from the right edge of the text block the right side of the text is aligned.

◆ **First Indent** controls how far the first line of a paragraph is set in from the left indent.

All indent values are initially set at 0 (zero) by default.

To apply indents:

1. Choose Window > Show Control Palette or Ctrl+' (apostrophe)/Command+'. The Control palette will appear.

2. If the Control palette doesn't look like the one in **Figure 6.3**, click the Paragraph Attributes button (¶).

3. Place your cursor anywhere within the paragraph.

4. Click in the Left Indent field on the Control palette. Enter the value by which you want to indent the left edge of the paragraph text (**Figure 6.4**).

5. Press the Tab key to highlight the First Indent field. Enter the value by which you want to indent the first line of the paragraph.

6. Press the Tab key to highlight the Right indent field. Enter the value by which you want to indent the right edge of the paragraph.

7. Press Enter. The changes you specifed will take effect.

APLYING INDENTS

Applying Hanging Indents

In a hanging indent format, the first line of a paragraph sticks out to the left of succeeding lines (**Figure 6.5**). You can set hanging indents by specifying a negative (minus) value for your first line indent. This setting obviously can't exceed the positive value of the left indent.

For instance, in a paragraph with a left indent of 1p, you could set a hanging indent of -1p (using a hyphen to indicate the minus sign). In this case, the first line of the paragraph would be even with the left edge of the text block, but the rest of the paragraph would align 1p right from the left edge.

To create a hanging indent:

1. Choose Window > Show Control Palette. If necessary, click the Paragraph Attributes button (¶).

2. Click to place the insertion point in the paragraph you want to change.

3. Type a value in the Left Indent text field in the Paragraph Control palette.

   In order to set a hanging indent, you must have a left indent greater than 0 (zero).

4. Press Tab, and enter a negative number in the First Line Indent text field.

   You can enter a number value less than or equal to the positive number entered as the left indent. Entering the inverse of the left indent (if the left indent is 3p6, you would enter -3p6) will result in the first line of the paragraph beginning at the left edge of the text block.

5. Press Enter.

✔ Tip

■ Choose Type > Indents/Tabs to create hanging indents visually. See **Figure 6.6** for details.

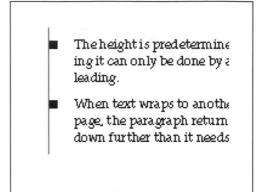

Figure 6.5 The paragraphs illustrated above use hanging idents to "hang" their bullets on the margin. A tab after the bullet lines up the first line of actual text with the left indent that's been specified.

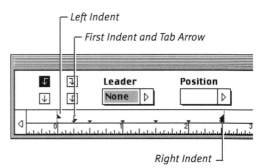

Figure 6.6 The Indents/Tabs ruler is a visual representation of the paragraph you're formatting. The dotted lines on the right and left represent the width of the text block.

Paragraphs

You can add space between par.
using additional paragraph retu
ing the Paragraph Spacing cont
space before or after a paragrap

Let's get one thing straight righ
additional paragraph returns is

Figure 6.7 By using space between paragraphs, you have more control over white space than you would have by just pressing the Return key a few times. Spacing can be set as a percentage of point size, which is more typical than having a white space that's as high as the text.

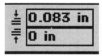

Figure 6.8 The Space Before and Space After fields in the Paragraph Control palette.

Applying Space Between Paragraphs

Let's get one thing straight right away: Using additional paragraph returns is a bad thing. It may seem easier (heck, you're just whacking the Enter key, after all), but if you ever have to go back to that document to edit it, you'll be sorry. There are two problems with using paragraph returns to add space between paragraphs:

◆ The height is predetermined, and you can only change it by adjusting the leading.

◆ When text wraps to another column or page, the paragraph return may push it down further than it needs to go, causing layout problems.

On the other hand, you can easily apply paragraph spacing by clicking in the Paragraph Control palette and then typing in the spacing you want. When you use the Paragraph space commands, you have more control over how the white space in your text appears on the page (**Figure 6.7**).

To add space between paragraphs:

1. Choose Window > Show Control Palette. If necessary, click the Paragraph Attributes button (¶).

2. Click in the paragraph you want to change.

3. Click in the Space Before or Space After text fields in the Control palette and enter the amount of space you'd like in each (**Figure 6.8**).

   If you can't see these fields, click on the Paragraph Attributes button (¶) on the Control Palette.

4. Press Enter.

Creating Paragraph Rules

PageMaker lets you place rules (lines) above or below each paragraph. Use rules to make underlined table headings or for colored boxes behind white or light-colored text. When you make rules instead of using the drawing tools to create separate lines, the rules flow along with your text if you move the text block or edit your text (**Figure 6.9**).

To create a paragraph rule:

1. Click to place the insertion point in the paragraph you want to add a rule to.

2. Choose Type > Paragraph or Ctrl+M/ Command+M.

3. Click the Rules button in the Paragraph Specifications dialog box.
   The Paragraph Rules dialog box appears.

4. Check the Rule above paragraph option in the Paragraph Rules dialog box, and change any settings that are appropriate.

5. Click the Options button.
   The Paragraph Rule Options dialog box appears.

6. Set the offset distance of the rule from the top of the paragraph.
   Offset refers to the amount of space between the text and the rule.

7. Enter an offset value and click OK three times to dismiss all the dialog boxes.

✔ Tips

- Hold down the Shift key (Win) or the Option key (Mac) while you click OK to exit several dialog boxes at once.

- Set large rules above and below a line of text, then use the Paragraph Rules Options to move their position to create a background block for reversed text. See **Figure 6.10** and **Figure 6.11** for details.

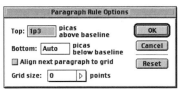

Senate Rejects Bush Nominee

Senate Rejects Key Nominee

Figure 6.9 This illustration shows two uses of paragraph rules. In the first example, a simple rule was applied below the paragraph. In the second example, heavy rules (12 points each) above and below the text form a black background for reversed text.

Paragraph Rules

☐ **Rule above paragraph**
Stroke style: `1 pt ────`
Stroke color: `Black`
Tint: `100` ▷ %
Stroke width: ○ Width of text ● Width of column
Indent: Left `0` picas Right `0` picas

☑ **Rule below paragraph**
Stroke style: `4 pt ████`
Stroke color: `Black`
Tint: `100` ▷ %
Stroke width: ○ Width of text ● Width of column
Indent: Left `0` picas Right `0` picas

[OK] [Cancel] [Options...]

Figure 6.10 The Paragraph Rules dialog box shows the settings for the first line of text in **Figure 6.9**.

Paragraph Rule Options

Top: `1p3` picas above baseline
Bottom: `Auto` picas below baseline
☐ Align next paragraph to grid
Grid size: `0` ▷ points

[OK] [Cancel] [Reset]

Figure 6.11 This illustration of the Paragraph Rule Options dialog box shows the optional settings for the second line of text in **Figure 6.9**.

WASHINGTON (AP) - Solid Democratic opposition sank President Bush's choice to lead federal product safety efforts Thursday, dealing the administration its first nomination defeat and stirring partisan rancor on Capitol Hill.

The Senate Commerce Committee cast a 12-11 party-line vote not to recommend Mary Sheila Gall for confirmation as chairwoman of the Consumer Product Safety Commission.

It was a setback for Bush that left the White House mulling how it might still elevate Gall or quickly replace her as a

Figure 6.12 These three paragraphs have different spacing formats applied. The top paragraph has default spacing and the middle paragraph uses only letter spacing. The bottom paragraph uses only word spacing.

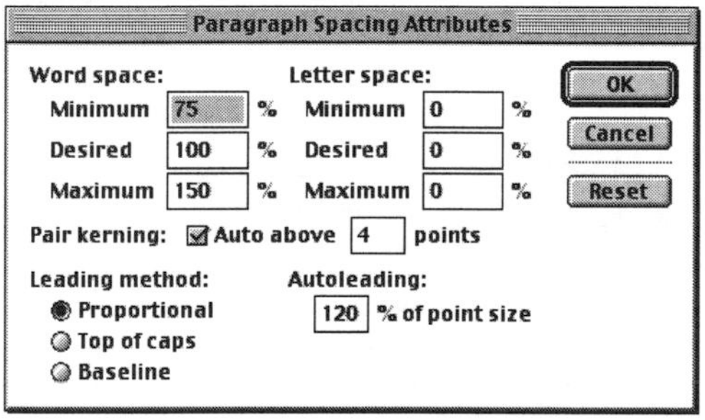

Figure 6.13 The Paragraph Spacing Attributes dialog box above shows the settings for the third paragraph of text in **Figure 6.12**.

Using Paragraph Spacing

PageMaker lets you control how space is added (or removed) in justified paragraphs. There are two primary types of spacing:

- ◆ **Word space** controls the width of the space bar character, which determines the amount of space between words.

- ◆ **Letter space** controls the amount of space around each letter.

You can specify either or both controls. The typographer who designed your fonts has optimized the width of each letter and built in kerning pairs for specific sets of letters so that they always look nice together. But when text is justified, the increased (or decreased) space can look odd (**Figure 6.12**). By allowing PageMaker to adjust letter space, you can improve the look of justified text. However, spacing can be distracting, if it isn't done correctly. Use these commands with care.

To control paragraph spacing:

1. Click to place the insertion point in the paragraph you want to change.

2. Choose Type > Paragraph.
   The Paragraph Specifications dialog box appears.

3. Click the Spacing button.
   The Paragraph Spacing Attributes dialog box appears (**Figure 6.13**).

4. Enter spacing changes into the dialog box.

5. Click OK twice to dismiss both dialog boxes.

✔ Tip

- ■ Always do test prints before you finalize a print job. Spacing is not always accurately displayed on your monitor. When in doubt you should trust only the printout.

Controlling Widows and Orphans

A widow is the first line of a paragraph that falls at the bottom of a column (**Figure 6.14**). An orphan is the last line of a paragraph that falls at the top of a column (**Figure 6.15**).

PageMaker has built-in controls that allow you to specify how many lines of text from a paragraph can fall at the bottom or top of a column. To control widows and orphans, PageMaker moves a line (or more, depending on your settings) from one column into the next one.

To control widows and orphans:

1. Click in the paragraph in which you want to control widows and orphans.

   In most cases, you'll want to select all the text in a story to prevent widows and orphans throughout.

2. Choose Type > Paragraph.

   The Paragraph Specifications dialog box appears.

3. Check the Widow control and Orphan control check boxes and enter the smallest number of lines that you'll allow at the bottom (widows) and top (orphans) of any column of text (**Figure 6.16**).

   I usually keep both settings at 3, so I never have less than three lines of a paragraph at the top or bottom of a column.

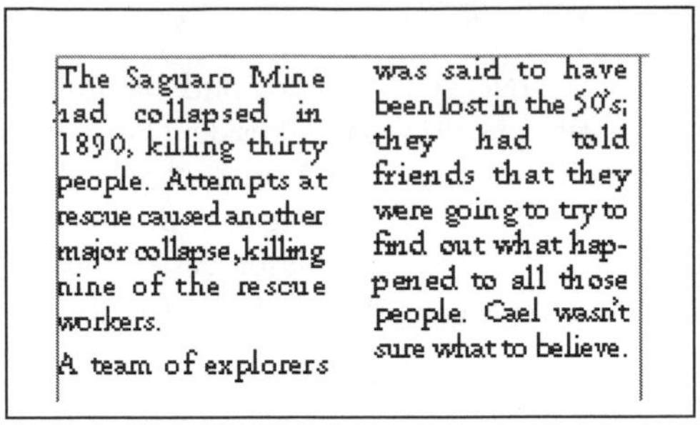

The Saguaro Mine had collapsed in 1890, killing thirty people. Attempts at rescue caused another major collapse, killing nine of the rescue workers.

A team of explorers

was said to have been lost in the 50's; they had told friends that they were going to try to find out what happened to all those people. Cael wasn't sure what to believe.

Figure 6.14 The last line of column one is a widow.

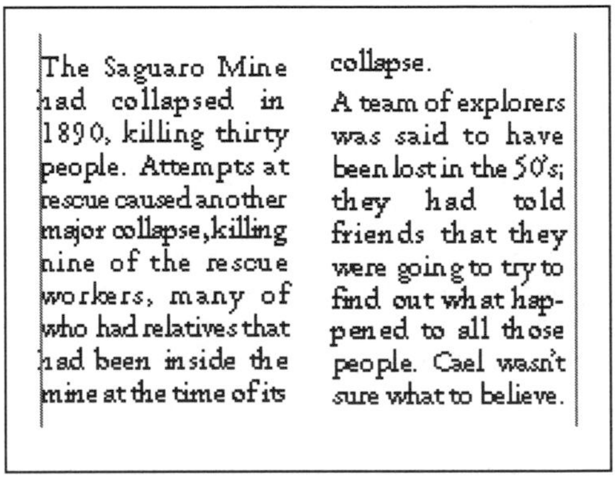

The Saguaro Mine had collapsed in 1890, killing thirty people. Attempts at rescue caused another major collapse, killing nine of the rescue workers, many of who had relatives that had been inside the mine at the time of its

collapse.

A team of explorers was said to have been lost in the 50's; they had told friends that they were going to try to find out what happened to all those people. Cael wasn't sure what to believe.

Figure 6.15 The first line of column two is an orphan.

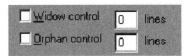

Figure 6.16 A part of the Paragraph Specifications dialog box (near the bottom right), where you control widow and orphan line breaks.

Applying Tabs

Tabs are used to space type horizontally in a column. You can also use tabs to create 'columns' of text within a text block.

By default, tabs are set at every half-inch from the left edge of the text block. These default tabs are flush left, meaning that type is aligned to the left of the tab stop.

When you create a new tab stop, all the default tab stops to the left of the 'custom' stop are erased.

To apply a custom tab:

1. Click to place the insertion point in the paragraph you want to format with tabs.

2. Choose Type > Indents/Tabs (**Figure 6.17**).
   The Idents/Tabs ruler appears.

3. Set tabs in the proper locations in your column of text.

4. If you aren't sure if your tabs are set correctly, click the Apply button first to see your line of text formatted. When you click Apply, the text is formatted in the background, but the ruler remains in place so you can make adjustments.

5. Click OK when the text is set correctly.

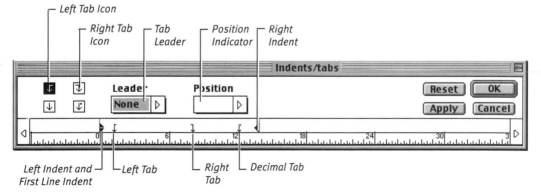

Figure 6.17 The Indents/tabs ruler is a visual representation of paragraph indents and tabs commands.

Understanding Tab Types

PageMaker employs four different tab types: left, right, center, and decimal.

◆ **Left tabs** align text flush left with the tab, so that the text expands to the right.

◆ **Right tabs** align text flush right with the tab, so that text expands to the left.

◆ **Center tabs** align text so that it is centered at the tab stop.

◆ **Decimal tabs** align text or numbers with the first decimal point within the characters. If there is no decimal, they act as right tabs.

You can of course mix tab types. **Figure 6.18** shows text formatted using each of the four tab types.

To apply tab types:

1. Click to place the insertion point in the paragraph you want to format with tabs.

2. Choose Type > Indents/Tabs.

3. Use the ruler to set tabs in the proper locations within your column of text. Click the icon for the type of tab you want to apply.

4. Click OK.

✔ Tip

■ If you aren't sure if your tabs are set correctly, click on the Apply button first to see your line of text formatted. When you click on Apply, the text is formatted in the background, but the ruler remains in place so you can make adjustments. Click OK when the text is formatted properly.

City	Pop.	Elevation
Bell Town	320	1200.32
Bézier	11,500	600.20
Burgundy	390	1632.60
Swordshire	509	3021.04
Centura	82	380.62

Figure 6.18 All four tab types were used to create this table. Center tabs were used for the headings. left tabs were used for the cities, right tabs for the population figures and decimal tabs were used for the elevations.

UNDERSTANDING TAB TYPES

The Verde Diner

Fish $5.00

Fish and Chips $6.50

Chips $1.50

Potatoes (Make your own chips).......... $1.00

Tater Tots.. $2.00

Figure 6.19 Tab leaders help you line up items of text when it's formatted in tables across a column.

Applying Tab Leaders

Tab leaders (pronounced 'leeders') are strings of characters that fill the space before tabs. Any tab type can include a tab leader, and any character can be specified as a tab leader.

Typically, you'll find tab leaders in a table of contents, on menus, or in any other list where items on the same line may be spaced far away from one another (**Figure 6.19**). A line of periods is the most frequently used kind of tab leader.

To create a tab leader:

1. Click to place the insertion point in the paragraph you want to contain the tab leader.

   If you want to format multiple paragraphs at once, select part of every paragraph that needs to be formatted.

2. Choose Type > Indents/Tabs.

   The Indents/Tabs ruler appears above the current column.

3. Drag a tab onto the ruler at the position where you want it to appear.

4. From the Tab Leader pop-up menu, select the character you want to use, or type in a custom character.

5. Click OK.

✔ Tip

■ Format tab leaders with any character attributes you want. Select the leaders and change the font, size or style.

STYLES

Styles are the most useful text-formatting tool a new user can latch onto. They can help you format your documents more efficiently, and make sweeping changes to a document with a few keystrokes.

Styles can also automate the formatting of text, even if you're typing it from scratch in Adobe PageMaker. For example, you can create and define a headline style that switches automatically to body text style when you type a return.

Styles are applied to paragraphs, but they can contain both character-level and paragraph-level formatting. All of PageMaker's text-formatting commands can be attached to a style and applied to text with a single click.

Styles are created, edited, deleted, and applied using the Styles palette. We'll discuss these techniques and more in this chapter.

The Styles Palette

The Type menu allows you to create and apply styles. But you will likely do most of your work with styles using the Styles palette.

Styles are listed alphabetically in the main pane of the palette. This list of all the styles used in a document is called a style sheet.

The triangle at the upper right of the Styles palette lets you access a pop-up menu for creating, deleting, duplicating, and importing styles (**Figure 7.1**). You can also change the way the palette gives you feedback, including icons that indicate a style override and styles that have been imported from another PageMaker document.

To access the Styles palette:

◆ Choose Window > Show Styles or Ctrl+B/ Command+B.

The Styles palette appears.

✔ Tips

■ A plus symbol beside a style name indicates that the style of the currently selected text has been overridden (i.e., additional formatting that is not included in the style definition has been applied to the text).

■ A disk icon beside a style name indicates that the style was imported along with placed text.

■ The Styles palette is usually the most convenient place to view your list of styles. However, you can also view and apply them by choosing Type > Type Style and by using the Style pop-up menu on the Control palette.

Pop-up menu triangle

Figure 7.1 The Styles palette centralizes all the commands you need for working with and managing your styles. In this illustration, the pop-up menu indicates that the Styles palette is set to display Overridden icons and Imported icons.

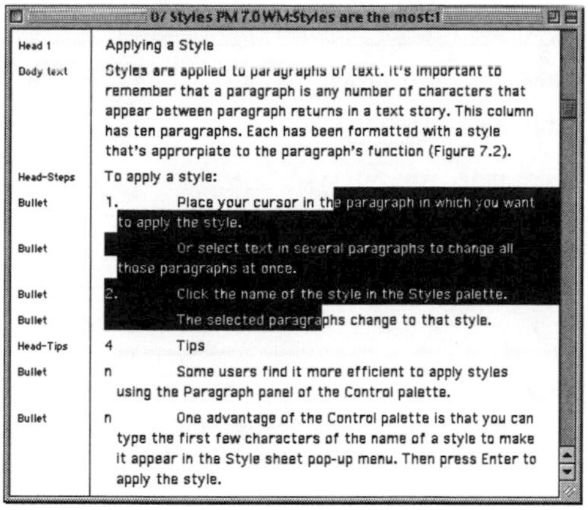

Figure 7.2 The Story Editor displays the name of styles that have been applied to paragraphs in a story.

Applying a Style

Styles are applied to paragraphs of text. It's important to remember that a 'paragraph' means any number of characters that appear between paragraph returns in a text story. This column has 11 paragraphs. Each has been formatted with a style that's appropriate to the paragraph's function (**Figure 7.2**).

To apply a style:

1. Place your cursor in the paragraph to which you want to apply the style.

   Select text in several paragraphs to change all those paragraphs at once.

2. Click the name of the style in the Styles palette.

   The paragraphs you selected change to that style.

✔ Tips

- Some users find it more efficient to apply styles using the Paragraph panel of the Control palette.

- The Control palette lets you type the first few characters of a style's name to make it appear in the Style pop-up menu. Then press Enter to apply the style.

- Notice the selection in **Figure 7.2**. Four paragraphs were selected together in order to apply the Bullet style to them as a unit. Only parts of the first and last paragraphs need to be selected because styles format entire paragraphs, not individual characters of text.

Defining a New Style

Once you've experimented with your text and have it formatted just the way you want, you can convert these format settings into a style that you can quickly apply to other text.

To define a new style based on existing text:

1. Highlight the text you want to use as a style.

2. Choose Type > Define Styles, or Ctrl+3/ Command+3.

   The Style Options dialog box appears.

3. Click New.

   The Style Options dialog box appears (**Figure 7.3**).

4. Type a name for the new style.

   Be as descriptive as you can. For instance, use names like Headline, Body Text, or Caption. Establishing a strong naming convention will make it easier for you to recall the function of each new style.

5. Click OK.

   The new style appears in the Styles palette.

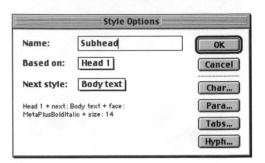

Figure 7.3 The Style Options dialog box lets you assign a name to your new style. In this case, the new style will be used as a subhead and is based on the style called Head 1.

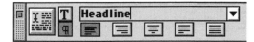

Figure 7.4 Type over the name of the current style in the Paragraph panel of the Control palette to create a new style almost instantly.

Figure 7.5 PageMaker asks you if you want to create a new style when you've typed over the name of a style in the Control palette.

Defining a New Style with the Control Palette

Use the Control palette to create styles quickly even if the Styles palette isn't showing. The paragraph display of the Control palette lists the current style. Type over the current style name to immediately create a new style.

To define a new style with the Control palette:

1. Highlight the text you want to use as a style.

2. Click the Style pop-up menu in the Control palette (**Figure 7.4**).

3. Click and drag to select the name in the text box.

4. Type a name for the new style. Be as descriptive as you can.

5. Press Enter. An alert dialog box appears. Confirm that you want to create a new style (**Figure 7.5**).

6. Click OK. The new style appears in the style sheet.

Modifying a Style

One of the most powerful features of PageMaker's Styles function is the ability to change the definition of a style, which in turn reformats every paragraph in your document that's been formatted with that style. It's a blazingly fast way to redesign a document.

To modify an existing style:

1. In the Styles palette, double-click the name of the style that you want to modify (**Figure 7.6**).

    The Style Options dialog box appears.

2. Click one of the buttons along the right side of the Style Options dialog box.

    The corresponding dialog box will appear. For instance, clicking the Char button opens the Character Specifications dialog box, with settings for that style (**Figure 7.7**).

3. Make your changes and click OK.

    This returns you to the Style Options dialog box.

4. Click OK.

    All paragraphs formatted with the style you just edited will be updated throughout the document.

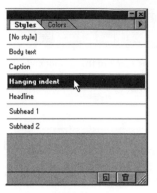

Figure 7.6 Double-click a style's name to edit it.

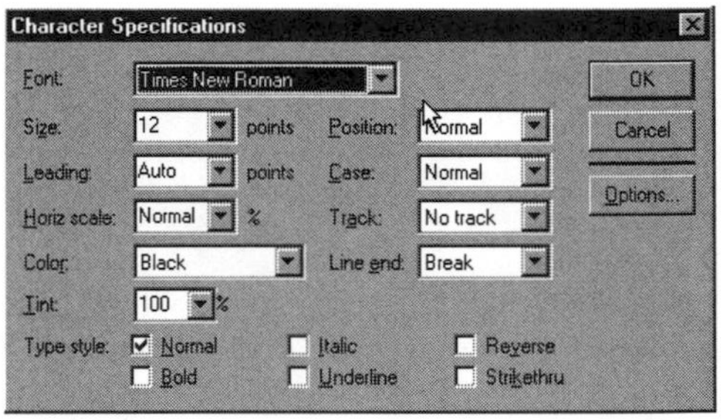

Figure 7.7 The Character Specifications dialog box.

New Style icon —

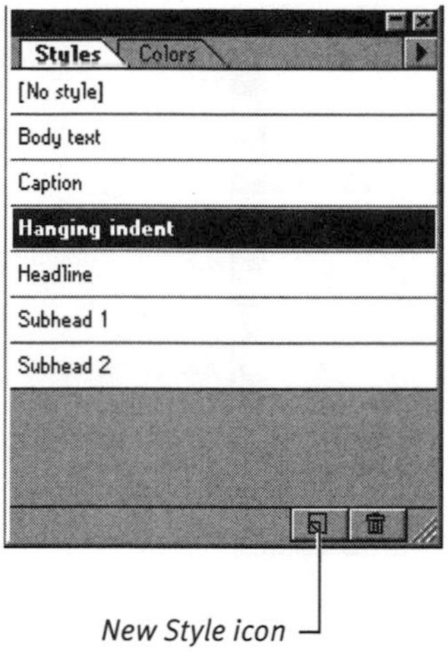

Figure 7.8 Drag a style to the New Style icon in the Styles palette to quickly duplicate an existing style.

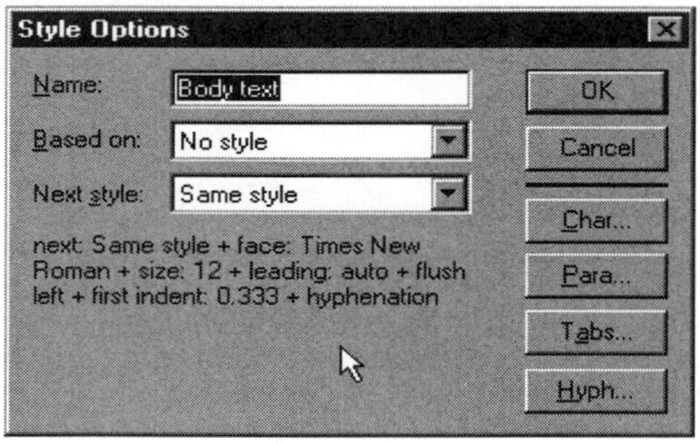

Figure 7.9 The Style Options dialog box.

Duplicating a Style

When you're creating a style sheet, you'll often find that you need a new style that's nearly the same as an existing style. It's usually fastest to duplicate the existing style, then edit it.

To duplicate an existing style:

1. In the Styles palette, drag the style name down to the New Style icon (**Figure 7.8**).

   When you release the mouse button, the Style Options dialog box appears, with the style name and the word 'copy' after it in the Name text field (**Figure 7.9**).

2. Rename the duplicate style.

   You could keep the name 'style copy' but this probably won't be descriptive enough to help you remember where to apply the style later.

3. Click OK.

   The new style is added to the Styles palette.

DUPLICATING A STYLE

Deleting a Style

There are several reasons you may want to delete a style. You may have created it in error and don't need it cluttering up the Styles palette. Or you may have placed text that also imported a foreign style into your style sheet. To avoid applying an imported style accidentally, it's best to delete it.

To delete an existing style:

1. Drag the name of the style you want to delete down to the trash can icon at the bottom of the Styles palette (**Figure 7.10**).

   When you release the mouse button, a dialog box asks you to confirm that you want to delete the style (**Figure 7.11**).

2. Click Delete.

   The style is removed from the list.

✔ Tip

■ Use care when deleting styles that have been applied to text. Paragraphs formatted with a style retain their formatting when a style is deleted. However, the paragraph will not have a style attached to it. It is better to use styles consistently throughout a document, because you won't be able to rely on style modifications to reformat paragraphs that have no style attached to them.

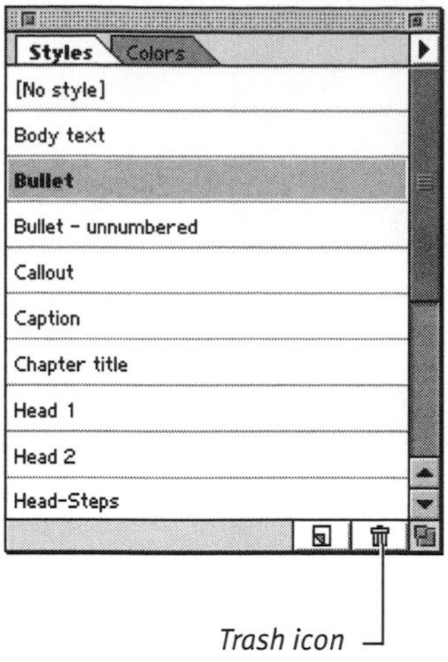

Trash icon

Figure 7.10 Drag a style to the Trash icon to delete it.

Delete style "subhead"?

Cancel   Delete

Figure 7.11 PageMaker asks you to confirm that you want to delete a style. If you change your mind, you can click Cancel and the style will be preserved.

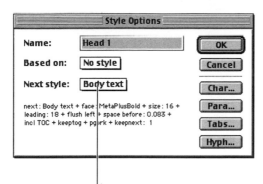

Next style pop-up menu

Figure 7.12 Use the Next style option when defining styles so PageMaker will apply styles to your text as you're typing it. In the example above, Body text is automatically applied to the paragraph after every Head 1 you type in the document.

Cascading Styles

Another powerful capability of styles allows you to switch to another style when you type a Return. This allows you to set up a series of styles that will be applied automatically as you type within PageMaker.

Cascading (sequenced) styles were used to create this book. Most pages have the same series of paragraph styles: headline, body text, step headline, and the steps themselves.

I frequently take advantage of cascading styles by typing a line of headline text, applying the Head 1 style to the text, then pressing Return. PageMaker automatically chooses the Body Text style for the new paragraph, even before I've typed a single character. After I type the headline for a set of steps, PageMaker applies the Step style for me. The Next style option allows you to create this sequence.

To set up cascading style sheets:

1. In the Styles palette, double-click the style you want to cascade into another style.

   The Style Options dialog box for that style appears (**Figure 7.12**).

2. From the Next style pop-up menu, select the style you want to cascade to.

3. Click OK.

   The style will cascade to the next style when you are typing text.

Basing Styles on Other Styles

The Based on option in the Style Options dialog box allows you to base a style on another style. In addition to the obvious benefit of ensuring that styles have similar attributes, the Based on option lets you make changes to several styles at once.

Here's how it works: Let's say that my Body text style is the first style I create. The next style I create is the Bullet style, which is just like the Body text except it includes a hanging indent. If the Bullet style is based on Body text, I can edit both styles just by changing the format for Body text.

To base a style on another style:

1. In the Styles palette, double-click the style you want to base on another style.

   The Style Options dialog box appears.

2. Choose a style from the Based on pop-up menu (**Figure 7.13**).

3. Click OK.

   The first style is now based on the style selected in the pop-up menu. Any changes to the based-on style will be reflected in the style you just modified.

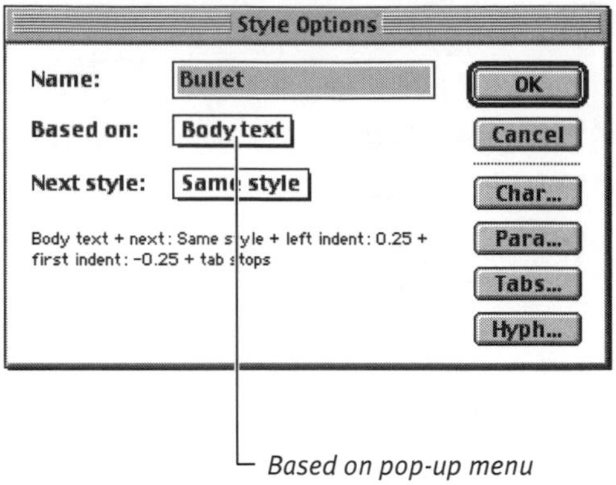

— *Based on pop-up menu*

Figure 7.13 If you base one style on another, you get two modifications for the price of one. In the style illustrated above, Bullet will take any changes made to the Body text style because it is based on it.

Figure 7.14 A dialog box will ask you to confirm that you want to replace one style with another before the styles are merged.

Merging Styles

You can merge two styles together to make your style sheet less cluttered and easier to understand. When you merge two styles, all text that has one style applied to it will automatically have a new style applied instead.

For instance, say I am using two styles, one called Body Text and the other called Basic Text. If I decide that both styles should have the same attributes as Body Text, I can merge Basic Text with Body Text, keeping only the Body Text style. After the merge, all the text that was formerly Basic Text will be formatted as Body Text.

To merge two styles:

1. In the Styles palette, double-click the style that contains the attributes you now want to use for both styles.

   The Style Options dialog box appears.

2. Rename the style with exactly the same name as the style you want to merge it with, and click OK.

   Warning! The case of your style name matters in this instance. PageMaker will be perfectly happy to give you one style called bullet and another called Bullet.

   A dialog box will ask if you really want to replace the style (**Figure 7.14**).

3. Click OK.

   The styles are merged.

✔ Tip

■ The tricky thing about merging styles is predicting the outcome. Remember that you'll get the preferred attributes with the name of the less-preferred style.

Importing Styles

You can use styles created in other PageMaker documents by importing a style sheet into your current document. This is very useful when you're publishing periodicals or if you just want to use the same styles throughout all the publications you create.

To import styles from other PageMaker documents:

1. Choose Import Styles from the Styles palette pop-up menu (**Figure 7.15**).

2. Click the Import button in the Style Options dialog box.

   A dialog box appears allowing you to choose the PageMaker document from which you want to import styles (**Figure 7.16**).

3. Select the file that contains the style sheet you want to import and click Open (Win) or OK (Mac).

   If the file you selected has styles with the same name as those in the current document, a warning dialog box appears. This dialog box asks if you want to copy over your existing styles (**Figure 7.17**).

4. Click OK.

   The new styles are imported from the document you selected.

✔ Tip

- Remember that letter case matters in style names. PageMaker will import a style named body text without overwriting an existing style called Body Text, or even Body text.

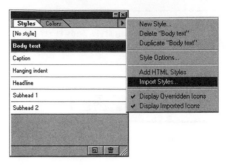

Figure 7.15 You can save time creating new styles by importing existing style from another PageMaker document.

Figure 7.16 The Import styles dialog box.

Figure 7.17 PageMaker asks you to confirm that you want to copy over your existing styles before it imports a style sheet.

Importing Styles When Placing Text

When you bring styled text into PageMaker, any styles it includes are added to your style sheet.

Use any of the following methods to bring styled text into a PageMaker document:

- ◆ Place text with the File > Place command.

- ◆ Paste text in a text block from a document created in an application that supports styles.

- ◆ Drag text into a document from a document created in an application that supports styles.

Styled text brings its styles along with it. When styles are imported along with text, duplicate styles are not overwritten. Imported styles that have the same name as existing styles in a PageMaker document will have an asterisk added after their names. In these cases, you can use the Merge technique on page 115 to simplify your style sheet.

✔ Tip

- ■ If you want styled text imported into your document, but don't want the style sheet to be included, there is a work-around solution you can use if the source document was created by PageMaker. Open the source document and select all the text in the story you want to place in the document you're working on. Click No Style in the Styles palette. The text retains its formatting, but no styles will be imported.

Changing the Default Style

The default style in your document is the style that's automatically applied to text when you create a new text block. To change the default style, switch the Pointer tool (ensuring that no text is selected), then click on the style you want to use as the default style.

Each new text block you create will have the style of your new default.

DRAWING

Adobe PageMaker includes several drawing tools that comprise most of the toolbox. These tools can be used for simple tasks, like creating background screens, or more complex touches, like creating special graphical elements including stars and polygons.

There are four main drawing tools: a Line tool, a Rectangle tool, an Ellipse tool, and a Polygon tool. The two-dimensional shape tools also come in a frame version: That is, they draw shapes that can be filled with text. The frame tools are marked with an 'x' in their centers.

Every object created in PageMaker can be modified, edited, filled, and stroked with color.

Drawing Lines

PageMaker has two Line tools (**Figure 8.1**). The first one creates a straight line at any orientation. The second is a Constrained Line tool that draws lines only at increments of 45 degrees.

You can control the way a line will look before you draw it by double-clicking the Line tool and changing the settings in the Custom Stroke dialog box (**Figure 8.2**).

To draw a line:

1. Select the Line tool from the toolbox.
   The cursor changes to a crosshair.
2. Click and drag on the document to draw your line.
   As you drag, a line appears.
3. Release the mouse button and the line will be drawn and selected, with sizing handles on either end (**Figure 8.3**).
   Move or resize the line by clicking and dragging the handles, if necessary.

✔ Tip

- You don't need to waste time switching to the Constrained Line tool, because the regular Line tool will behave the same way if you press the Shift key as you draw.

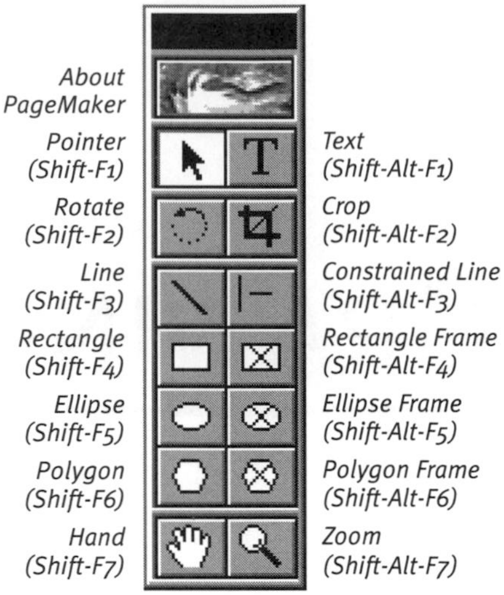

About PageMaker
Pointer (Shift-F1)
Text (Shift-Alt-F1)
Rotate (Shift-F2)
Crop (Shift-Alt-F2)
Line (Shift-F3)
Constrained Line (Shift-Alt-F3)
Rectangle (Shift-F4)
Rectangle Frame (Shift-Alt-F4)
Ellipse (Shift-F5)
Ellipse Frame (Shift-Alt-F5)
Polygon (Shift-F6)
Polygon Frame (Shift-Alt-F6)
Hand (Shift-F7)
Zoom (Shift-Alt-F7)

Figure 8.1 The Toolbox contains all PageMaker's drawing tools.

Custom Stroke
Stroke style:
Stroke weight:
0.5
points
OK
Cancel
Transparent background
Reverse

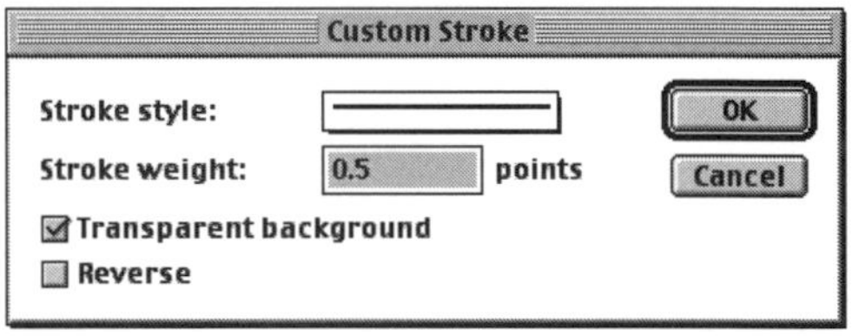

Figure 8.2 The Custom Stroke dialog box lets you change the way a line will appear. You can change the width of the line and select from preset stroke styles.

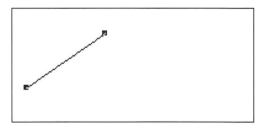

Figure 8.3 After you draw a line, it remains selected so you can resize it, move it or change its angle.

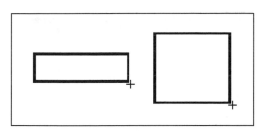

Figure 8.4 These rectangles are captured at the moment they are being drawn. Notice the crosshair at the bottom left of each shape. Pressing Shift while you draw constrains the rectangle to a perfect square, as on the right.

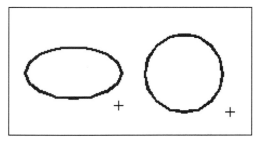

Figure 8.5 These ellipses are captured at the moment they are being drawn. Notice the crosshair at the bottom left of each shape. Pressing Shift while you draw constrains the ellipse to a perfect circle, as on the right.

Drawing Rectangles or Ellipses

PageMaker includes tools for drawing rectangles and ellipses. Both shapes are drawn using the same technique.

To draw a rectangle:

1. Choose the Rectangle tool from the toolbox.
   The cursor changes to a crosshair.

2. Click and drag anywhere on the screen.
   As you drag, a rectangle appears.

3. Release the mouse button when the rectangle is the desired size (**Figure 8.4**).

✔ Tips

- Press the Shift key while you're drawing to constrain the shape to a square. Make sure you keep the Shift key pressed when you release the mouse button; if you release the Shift key first, the square will change to a rectangle.

- Draw an ellipse by choosing the Ellipse tool, then following steps 2 and 3 above (**Figure 8.5**).

- Press the Shift key while you're drawing with the Ellipse tool to constrain the shape to a circle.

- If you drag outside the edge of the page, the document will scroll to allow you to extend the shape.

Drawing a Rounded-Corner Rectangle

Rounded rectangles let you vary the shapes you use in your documents. They appear less formal and can lend a friendly look to your publication.

To draw a rounded-corner rectangle:

1. Double-click the Rectangle tool in the toolbox.

   The Rounded Corners dialog box appears (**Figure 8.6**).

2. Choose a corner setting from the preset shapes.

3. Click and drag anywhere on the screen.

4. Release the mouse button when the rectangle is the desired size.

   Press the Shift key as you draw to constrain the shape to a rounded-corner square.

✔ Tip

■ The Rounded Corners dialog box won't change a rectangle that's already been drawn. In other words, you can't convert a square-corner rectangle to a rounded one. You'll have to delete the existing rectangle and draw a new one.

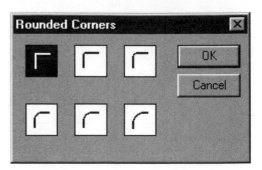

Figure 8.6 The Rounded Corner dialog box lets you choose from six predefined rounded-corner shapes when you are drawing a rectangle.

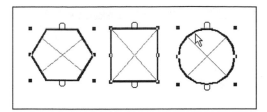

Figure 8.7 The three major frame shapes—polygon, rectangle, and circle.

Drawing Frames

Although frames are drawn with drawing tools, they differ from other objects in two main ways:

- ◆ A frame can hold either text or graphics content.

- ◆ Text frames can be threaded together to hold a long text story.

Frames can be used as placeholders when you're designing periodical publications, like newspapers, newsletters, or magazines.

You can distinguish an empty frame from a normal graphic object because the empty frames display a non-printing 'x' in their centers (**Figure 8.7**).

To draw a frame:

1. Choose the Frame tool of your choice from the toolbox.

    The cursor changes to a crosshair.

2. Click and drag anywhere on the screen.

    As you drag, the frame appears.

3. Release the mouse button when the frame is the desired size.

✔ Tip

- ■ You can draw an irregularly shaped frame using the manual drawing technique described on page 125.

Drawing a Polygon Automatically

The Polygon tool has two different drawing modes, depending on how you use the tool. If you click and drag as you do with other drawing tools, PageMaker automatically draws a closed shape that's been predefined in the Polygon Settings dialog box. See the next page for details on drawing an irregularly shaped polygon.

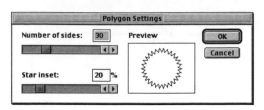

Figure 8.8 The Polygon Settings dialog box lets you create a shape with any number of sides from 3 to 100.

To draw a polygon automatically:

1. Double-click the Polygon tool in the toolbox.

   The Polygon Settings dialog box appears (**Figure 8.8**).

2. Drag the Number of Sides slider or enter the number of sides, and click OK.

   Choose any number between 3 and 100. The upper limit is 100 because at that point, the sides are so small that the shape will look like a circle.

3. Click and drag anywhere on the screen.

   A polygon appears as you draw.

4. Release the mouse button when the polygon is the correct size.

   Press the Shift key as you draw to constrain the sides of the polygon so that they are equal in length.

✔ Tips

- To draw a triangle, enter 3 for the Number of sides in Polygon Settings. To draw an equilateral triangle, press the Shift key as you draw.

- Use the Star Inset setting to create star shapes. You can make a simple five-pointed star or a complex starburst like the one shown in **Figure 8.8**.

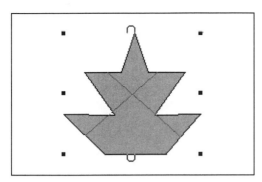

Figure 8.9 Click (don't drag) with the Polygon tool to create an irregularly shaped frame, like this one. Notice that the loop at the top of the frame appears to be unfinished. Don't worry, this is normal PageMaker behavior and it won't change the way the frame works.

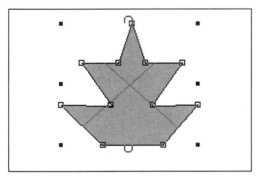

Figure 8.10 Double-click with the Pointer tool on a finished polygon to reshape it. A handle appears at each corner point. Drag the handles to modify the drawing.

Drawing a Polygon Manually

If you click in the publication with the Polygon tool, it creates a series of anchor points that define an irregular shape (**Figure 8.9**).

To draw a polygon manually:

1. Click the Polygon tool in the toolbox.

2. Click (don't drag) on your document. A point appears.

3. Move the cursor and click again. A line appears between the two points.

4. Continue clicking to create the lines and angles that make up your shape.

5. When you want to close the object, click on the first point you entered. A large square handle appears that closes the shape.

✔ Tips

■ Edit an irregular polygon by double-clicking on it with the Pointer tool and moving the handles that appear (**Figure 8.10**).

■ Leave an irregular polygon shape open by double-clicking on the final point you want to draw. This technique may not appear to work if the shape is set to display a fill. In this case, you may need to set the object's fill and color to none. See page 128 for details on changing an object's fill.

Changing an Object's Size

Once an object has been created, you may need to resize it. All graphic objects in PageMaker have handles that allow you to resize them.

To change the size of an object:

1. Choose the Pointer tool in the toolbox.

2. Click the object you want to resize. The sizing handles appear around the object (**Figure 8.11**).

3. Click and drag any one of the sizing handles.

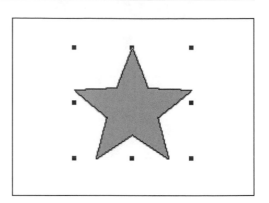

Figure 8.11 Every graphic object has handles around it that allow you to resize it. If an object's handles aren't visible, use the Pointer tool to select it.

Sizing Handles

Any shape drawn in PageMaker will have sizing handles on its edges and corners that allow you to reshape the object. If you drag a handle on the sides of an object, you'll be changing its width. If you drag a handle on the top or bottom of an object, you'll change its height. Save time by dragging a corner handle, which changes width and height at the same time.

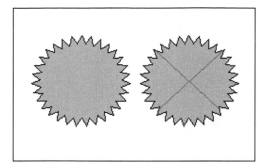

Figure 8.12 The object on the right was created with the Polygon tool, then converted to a frame to act as a container for text or graphics.

Changing an Object into a Frame

Perhaps you've drawn an object and then realized that you want to place text or a graphic in the object. You can do so by converting an existing object into a frame.

To change an object into a frame:

1. Choose the Pointer tool in the toolbox.

2. Click the object you want to change to a frame.

   The object is selected.

3. Choose Element > Frame > Change to Frame.

   The shape preserves its fill, line weight, and other object attributes (**Figure 8.12**).

✔ Tips

- Convert a frame to a normal graphic object by selecting the frame and choosing Element > Frame > Change to Graphic.

- If you want to convert a frame that already contains text or a graphic to a normal graphic object, you need to first choose Element > Frame > Separate Content.

Chapter 8

Changing Fills

PageMaker can fill any of its two-dimensional objects with any of a variety of different fill patterns. Each fill can be colored and tinted in any way you like. See Chapter 11 for more information on colors and tints.

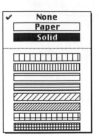

Figure 8.13 The Fill menu contains preset fills that you can apply to a two-dimensional object created with Page-Maker's drawing tools.

To choose a preset fill:

1. With the Pointer tool, select the object(s) you want to fill.
2. Choose Element > Fill > and the pattern you want to use.

   The Fill submenu appears (**Figure 8.13**).

   The object(s) are filled with the pattern you chose.

✔ Tip

- Use this technique to change the default fill of all new objects you draw. Make sure that no object is selected, then choose a new fill for the default.

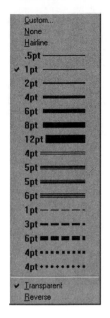

Figure 8.14 The Stroke menu contains a list of widths that can be assigned to any object drawn with PageMaker's drawing tools.

Changing Strokes

A stroke is the line on the outside edge of any drawn object. You can change the stroke of objects using the Stroke command.

To choose a default stroke:

1. With the Pointer tool, select the object(s) whose strokes you want to change.

2. Choose Element > Stroke > and the stroke you want to use.

    The Stroke submenu appears **(Figure 8.14)**.

    The object(s) are stroked with the new style.

✔ Tip

■ Use this technique to change the default stroke of all new objects you draw. Make sure that no object is selected, then choose a new style for the default.

Changing Fill and Stroke

If you're changing the fill and stroke of an object, it is more efficient to use the Fill and Stroke dialog box than the menus because the dialog box gives you access to both commands.

The dialog box also lets you color and tint both fills and strokes.

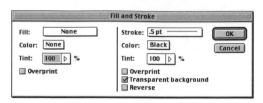

Figure 8.15 The Fill and Stroke dialog box contains options for coloring both the boundaries and interiors of objects.

To change fill and stroke at the same time:

1. With the Pointer tool, select the object(s) you want to modify.

2. Choose Element > Fill and Stroke, or Ctrl+U/Command+U.

   The Fill and Stroke dialog box appears (**Figure 8.15**).

3. Change the options in the Fill and Stroke dialog box, then click OK.

   The object is filled and stroked with the options you chose.

✔ Tip

■ Use this technique to change the default fill or stroke of all new objects you draw. Make sure that no object is selected, then choose a new fill or stroke for the default.

Transparencies and Reverses

Choose a transparent background if you want objects placed behind a patterned stroke to show through the spaces in the pattern. If you don't choose transparency, the spaces in the pattern are opaque.

Choose Reverse to draw a paper-colored outline of a shape on a contrasting black, shaded, or colored background.

CHANGING FILL AND STROKE

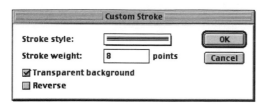

Figure 8.16 The Custom Stroke dialog box lets you apply one of a list of predefined stroke styles in combination with a stroke weight you type in.

Figure 8.17 A line drawn with the custom settings used in **Figure 8.16**.

Creating Custom Strokes

In addition to the default stroke settings (selected from either the Stroke menu or from the Fill and Stroke dialog box), you can define your own custom settings.

To create a custom stroke:

1. Select the object whose stroke you want to customize.

   If no object is selected, the changes will affect all strokes created after you define the custom stroke setting.

2. Choose Element > Stroke > Custom.

   The Custom Stroke dialog box appears (**Figure 8.16**).

3. Make any changes you want in the Custom Stroke dialog box and click OK.

4. The selected object's stroke will match the settings in the Custom Stroke dialog box (**Figure 8.17**).

✔ Tip

■ Use this technique to change the default stroke of all new objects you draw. Make sure that no object is selected, then create the custom stroke that you want as the default.

PLACING IMAGES

Everybody's heard the old bromide that a picture is worth a thousand words. And it's certainly true that few publications seem complete without pictures and other graphics.

Once graphics are in place, PageMaker allows you to crop, size, colorize, and use Photoshop's powerful filters on your placed images.

Supported File Formats

PageMaker supports several file formats for placed images. File types include:

◆ PICT

◆ TIFF

◆ EPS

◆ GIF

◆ WMF (Windows)

◆ EMF (Windows)

The two main types of graphics that can be placed into PageMaker are pixel-based art and vector-based art.

Pixel-based art (**Figure 9.1**) is created from thousands of pixels (tiny dots of color or tone) in each image, which when viewed together represent a shape, an object, a person, a landscape, and so on. On your computer screen, photographic images are always pixel based. Pixel-based artwork is generated by scanners, digital cameras, and software such as Adobe Photoshop and Corel Painter.

Vector-based artwork (**Figure 9.2**) is created from colored shapes, which can be made to represent almost anything. Vector artwork is used for logos, illustrations, and typography. Vectors are created by applications such as Adobe Illustrator or Macromedia FreeHand. One advantage of vectors is that they can be resized without any loss of quality—unlike pixel-based art, which can suffer when enlarged.

While pixel-based art can stored in any of the file types listed above, vector-based artwork can only be stored in PICT or EPS files.

Figure 9.1 This pixel-based graphic is a photograph that has been edited using Adobe Photoshop.

Figure 9.2 This vector-based image is a logo created in Adobe Illustrator. It was placed in PageMaker in its native Illustrator format.

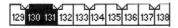

Figure 9.3 Click on the page icon to go to the page on which you want to place an image.

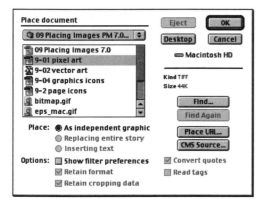

Figure 9.4 The Place document dialog box changes its Place and Option choices based on the item that's selected in the file list.

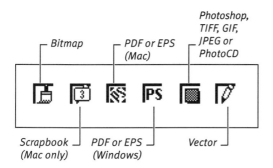

Figure 9.5 The Pointer tool changes shape to help indentify the file format of the graphic you're placing.

Placing Images

When you place a graphic, the pointer changes shape to indicate the type of graphic format being placed.

To place an image:

1. Use the page icons at the bottom-left edge of your screen to go to the correct page (**Figure 9.3**).

2. Choose the Pointer tool from the toolbox.

3. Choose File > Place or Ctrl+D/ Command+D.

   The Place document dialog box appears (**Figure 9.4**).

4. Navigate to the image you want to place and click OK.

   The cursor changes to the Place cursor (**Figure 9.5**).

4. Click anywhere in the document.

   The image will be placed with the upper-left corner at the spot where you clicked.

✔ Tips

- If you know that an image needs to be a specific dimension, you can click and drag with the loaded icon. The graphic will fill the space you clicked and dragged. Hold the Shift key down while you click on one of the corner handles to repair any distortion that may have occurred when the graphic was placed.

- If you have chosen the Text tool and are in a text block when you choose File > Place, the graphic will appear as an inline graphic, meaning that it is part of the text block and will reflow along with the text.

Wrapping Text

How images interact with text is a fundamental design choice for every publication. If you placed a text block on top of an image, you might let the image show through the lines of text. With the right image, this could be a very nice effect. But you can also set a text wrap for any image. That is, you can make a boundary around the image that causes text blocks to wrap around the image (**Figure 9.6**).

To wrap text around a graphic:

1. Select an image.

2. Choose Element > Text Wrap.

   The Text Wrap dialog box appears (**Figure 9.7**).

3. Click the middle Wrap option icon.

   The right icon is not available unless you customize the text wrap.

4. Click on a Text Flow option.

   The left icon jumps text over an image and continues the text on the next page or column. The middle icon jumps text over an image and continues on the same page, but no text flows to the left or right of the image. The right icon lets text flow on all four sides of an image.

5. Enter Standoff values for the image's boundary. Standoff is how far away from an image the text will stay.

6. Click OK.

   The boundary (a dotted line) appears around the image at the distance you specified for Standoff.

✔ Tips

- Text wraps work across layers, unless you select Wrap text on same layer only.

- Select text blocks with the Pointer tool, then choose Element > Group. Now you can set a Text Wrap for a text block.

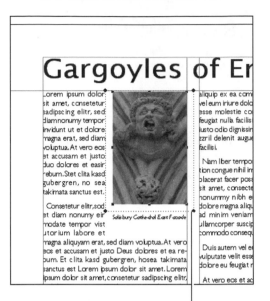

Text Wrap boundary ⌐

Figure 9.6 This image has a one pica standoff on the left, right, and bottom. There is no standoff on the top, so that the headline can flow normally.

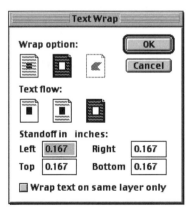

Figure 9.7 The Text Wrap dialog box lets you specify the wrap option, text flow, and standoff.

⌐ Irregular Text Wrap boundary

Boundary handle ⌐

Figure 9.8 Click on the image boundary to create a new handle. Then drag the handle or a line segment to customize the boundary's shape.

Customizing Text Wrap

A plain, four-sided text wrap is fine for regular graphics. But suppose your image has an irregular shape? To lend an air of informality to your publication, set a custom text wrap.

To customize the text wrap around a graphic:

1. Apply text wrap normally.

2. With the object selected, click on the boundary where you want a new handle to appear.

3. Customize the boundary to fit your image by dragging handles or line segments.

   The irregular boundary changes to reflect the shape of your image (**Figure 9.8**).

✔ Tips

- Text will reflow each time you move a handle or line segment. Hold down the spacebar while you're customizing the boundary to keep text from reflowing until you're finished.

- Press Shift as you drag to constrain movement to vertical or horizontal.

- Restore a regular text wrap to an irregularly wrapped image by choosing Element > Text Wrap and selecting the middle Wrap option.

- Pay attention to how an irregular text wrap affects your text margins. The eye can deal with ragged right margins because they're so common. But ragged left margins are a challenge to read because the eye loses the rhythm that's set up with a constant left margin. Be considerate of your readers and try to leave the left margins fairly straight (**Figure 9.8**).

CUSTOMIZING TEXT WRAP

Moving Placed Images

Images can be moved on the page, or even from page to page within a document once they've been placed.

To move a placed image:

1. Choose the Pointer tool from the toolbox.

2. Click the image you want to move and drag it to a new location.

   As you drag, an outline of the image area (always a rectangle no matter the shape of the graphic) appears under your cursor (**Figure 9.9**).

3. When the image is where you want it to be, release the mouse button.

   The image appears in the new location.

✔ Tips

- Click and hold for a second before you begin dragging an image. A ghosted image appears that will help you align the image in its new location (**Figure 9.10**).

- There are two ways to move an image to another page. Cut and paste the image from one page to another or drag the image off the page onto the pasteboard where it can wait until you're ready to place it on another page.

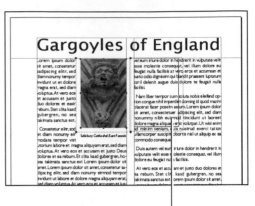

Outline of image

Figure 9.9 You'll only see an outline of the image as you drag it across your screen. The image redraws when you release the mouse button.

Figure 9.10 If you click and hold for a second before you begin dragging an image, you'll see the image as you move it.

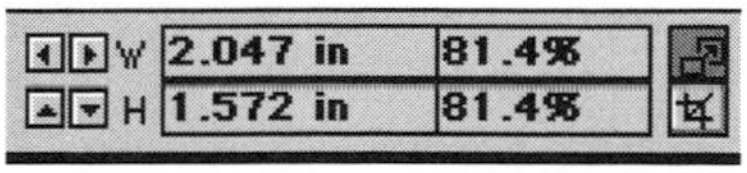

Figure 9.11 The Control palette lets you resize images in several ways. Use the nudge icons to resize an image very precisely or you can type specific widths or percentages in the resizing fields.

Resizing Placed Images

An image created in another program is often the wrong size for use in your publication. You can resize the graphic by clicking and dragging its sizing handles, but this can distort the image. Instead, use the resizing features of the Control palette to maintain the image's proportions as you resize it. Using the Control palette to modify objects is discussed in more detail in Chapter 13.

To resize a placed image:

1. Choose the Pointer tool from the toolbox.

2. Click the object you want to resize.
   Sizing handles appear around the object.

3. Enter a specific width and height for your image in the Width and Height fields of the Control palette (**Figure 9.11**).
   See Chapter 3 for more information about using arithmetic in the Control palette.

4. Press Enter.
   The image will be resized.

✔ Tips

■ Whenever possible, resize the graphic in its source file. Printing will be quicker if PageMaker doesn't have to do all the math necessary to resize a graphic while it's trying to render a document to a printer.

■ If distortion occurs while you're resizing an image, you can repair it by pressing the Shift key while you click an image's corner handle. Just wait a moment and PageMaker will redraw the image to its original proportions.

■ Press the Shift key while you're dragging on the corner handle of an image. This constrains the image resize to its original proportions. The image won't distort when you resize it using this method.

Cropping Placed Images

Sometimes an image includes too much extra space around the important bits of the image. Or maybe you've got a portrait with too many distracting elements around your subject's head. You can use PageMaker's Cropping tool to trim the edges of a placed image.

Think of cropping as placing a mat on top of an image. If the window in the mat is smaller than the image, only part of the image will be visible. Once you've got the mat cut to the right shape, you can move the image around underneath the mat to display just the part of the image you want. PageMaker does the same thing electronically, except instead of a mat, it uses a 'bounding box.'

To crop an image:

1. Choose the Cropping tool from the toolbox.

2. Click the image you want to crop.

3. Place the Cropping tool over a handle so that the handle shows through the middle of the Cropping tool (**Figure 9.12**).

4. Click and drag to resize the bounding box.

5. Use the Cropping tool to drag the image around under its bounding box so that the section of the image you want is visible.

   Figure 9.13 shows an image before and after it has been cropped.

✔ Tip

■ Whenever possible, crop the graphic in its source file. Printing will be much quicker if PageMaker doesn't have to do all the math necessary to crop a graphic while it's trying to render the document to a printer.

Figure 9.12 Place the Cropping tool over the handle of the graphic so the handle is visible through the tool.

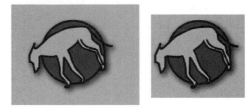

Figure 9.13 The image on the left is the original. The image on the right has been cropped to eliminate too much dead space.

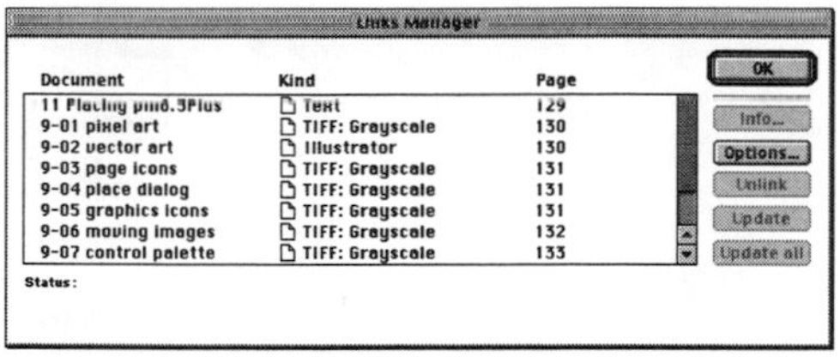

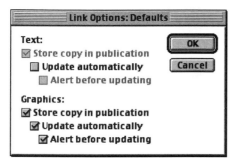

Figure 9.14 The Links Manager dialog box gives you information about all the objects placed in your document. The image's name, kind and the page number on which the object has been placed are listed.

Figure 9.15 The Link Options dialog box lets you embed an image in your document. Choose Store copy in publication to embed an image in your document.

Embedding an Image

Linked images are the default in PageMaker documents. Linking an image puts a proxy of the image in your PageMaker document. You can crop, resize, move, and rotate the image, but the source image is unaffected. The original image file for all linked images must accompany the PageMaker document when you give the file to someone else to print or modify.

You have to jump through a few hoops to embed an image. Embedding an image makes it a part of the PageMaker document. Each embedded image makes the document file larger by the amount of the placed image's size, while linked images take up only a fraction of their real size in the document file.

If you don't feel constrained by disk space, or the transferral of files that may reach multi-gigabyte proportions, you may want to embed images in the document instead of linking them.

To embed an image:

1. Place an image into your document.

2. Choose File > Links Manager, or Ctrl+Shift+D/Command+Shift+D.
   The Links Manager dialog box appears (**Figure 9.14**).

3. Click the image you want to embed.

4. Click the Options button.
   The Link Options dialog box appears (**Figure 9.15**).

5. Click the Store copy in publication check box.

6. Click OK in both dialog boxes.
   The placed image will be embedded in the document.

Changing the Graphics Display

PageMaker has three different display settings for graphics that are placed in documents:

◆ **Standard** means the graphic appears at screen resolution, which looks great until you zoom in on an image.

◆ **High resolution** looks the same as Standard at 100 percent, but once you zoom in, the image retains its quality. High resolution can slow PageMaker dramatically if many images are placed in the document.

◆ **Gray out** makes all images that are not selected display in gray, providing previews that are extremely zippy, and bearable even on slower computers. Of course, the trade-off is that you don't see the real image of your page, which can make it challenging to finalize your design.

To change the graphics display:

1. Choose File > Preferences > General, or Ctrl+K/Command+K.

   The Preferences dialog box appears (**Figure 9.16**).

2. Choose one of the three Graphics display options.

3. Click OK.

   All graphics in the document are affected by the change.

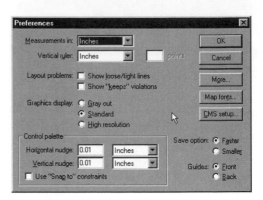

Figure 9.16 Use the Preferences dialog box to control your Graphics display options.

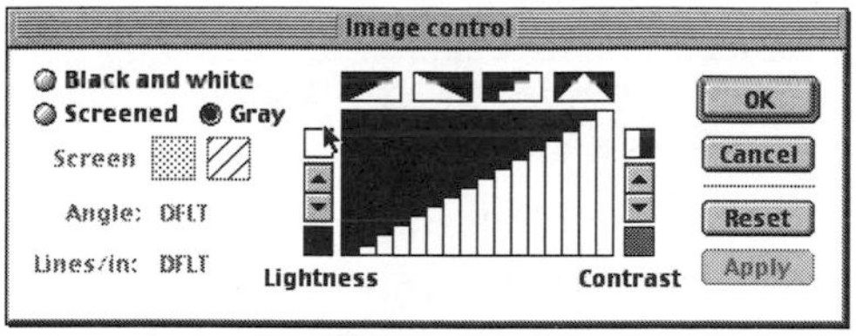

Figure 9.17 The Image Control dialog box on the Mac.

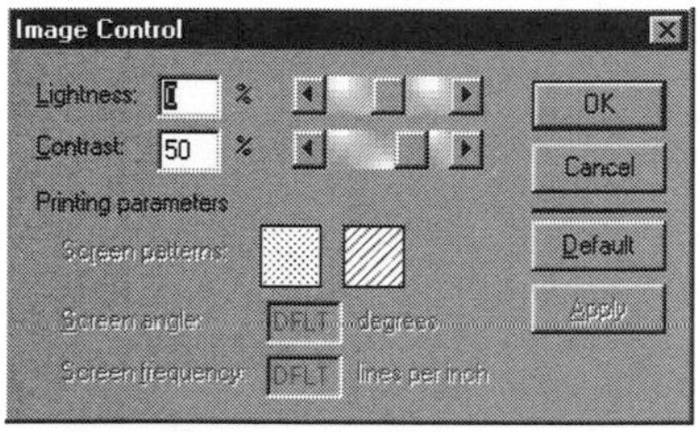

Figure 9.18 The Image Control dialog box on Windows.

Mac Image Control Options

In the Mac OS, there are also these options:

◆ **Black and white** is automatically selected if the selected graphic is a 1-bit, paint-type image.

◆ **Screened** changes the shape of the dots that are used to make the image if the image is black and white

◆ If **Gray** is selected for a gray-scale TIFF image, the screen ruling selected in the Color printing dialog box will be used when you print. To specify a different screen ruling, select Screened and enter a value in the Lines/In box.

◆ **Gray-level patterns** lets you choose from two different patterns. Click on a icon to select it.

Using Image Control

You can modify grayscale bitmap images in the following ways:

◆ **Contrast** makes objects lighter or darker in relation to their background.

◆ **Lightness** adjusts the overall percentage of light areas in the image.

◆ **Screen pattern** lets you specify a line screen for special effects.

If you are printing to a PostScript printer, you can also customize the following items:

◆ **Screen angle** lets you enter a different screen angle in the Image Control dialog box to override the printer default, which is typically 45 degrees.

◆ **Screen Frequency/lines per inch** (Windows only) overrides the printer default, which is usually 53 lines per inch (lpi) for 300-dpi LaserWriters, and either 90 or 150 lpi for Imagesetters (the default for an Imagesetter depends on the version of PostScript installed). Check with your service bureau if you're not sure whether to use this option.

To use Image Control:

1. Select the image you want to modify.

2. Choose Element > Image > Image Control. The Image Control dialog box appears (**Figures 9.17** and **9.18**).

3. Adjust the settings in the dialog box.

4. Click OK.
   The image changes to reflect the adjustments you made.

Placing Inline Graphics

Besides being able to place graphics anywhere in a document, PageMaker can place a graphic within a text block. This is called an inline graphic. The advantage of an inline graphic is that the graphic flows along with the text if you delete or resize a text block.

To create an inline graphic:

1. Click to place your cursor in a text block where you want the graphic to appear.

2. Choose File > Place or Ctrl+D/ Command+D.

   The Place document dialog box appears.

3. Locate and select the file you want to use as an inline graphic.

4. Select the Place as inline graphic option (**Figure 9.19**).

5. Click OK.

   The graphic appears in the text block (**Figure 9.20**).

✔ Tips

■ To delete an inline graphic, click to the right of it with the Text tool, then press the Backspace or Delete key.

■ If you accidentally place an image as an inline graphic when you meant it to be independent, the text block is often too small to show the image. This makes it difficult to select and delete. In this case, make sure the text block is selected, then choose Edit > Edit Story (or triple-click on a text block with the Pointer tool) to open the Story Editor. Inline graphics appear as small gray squares in the Story Editor, and are easy to select and delete.

■ The image appears as a small gray box in the Story Editor. (**Figure 9.21**) Type ^g in the Find or Replace dialog box to search a story for all inline graphics.

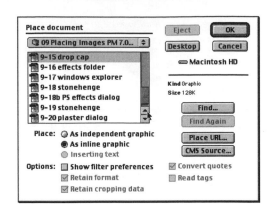

Figure 9.19 Make sure the Place document dialog box is set to import the graphic as an inline, then click OK.

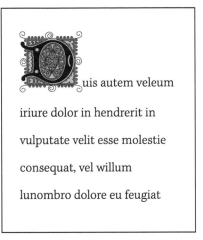

Figure 9.20 An inline graphic will reflow with the text.

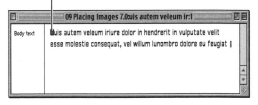

Figure 9.21 An inline graphic appears as a small gray box in the Story Editor.

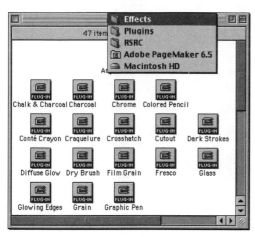

Figure 9.22 On the Mac, the Effects folder is where you store copies, or aliases, of Photoshop filters you want to use in PageMaker.

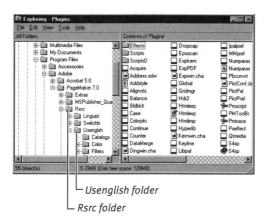

— *Usenglish folder*

— *Rsrc folder*

Figure 9.23 On Windows, the Plugins folder is where you store copies of Photoshop filters you want to use in PageMaker.

Adding Filters to PageMaker

PageMaker can apply Photoshop filters to black and white, grayscale and RGB TIFF images through its Photoshop Effects command. Third-party filters, like Kai's Power Tools, can also be used in PageMaker. To use these filters, you'll need to let PageMaker know where to find them.

To add Photoshop filters (Mac):

1. Quit PageMaker and Photoshop.

2. Find the Plug-ins folder inside the Photoshop folder and choose File > Make Alias.

3. Move the Filters' alias folder to PageMaker's Plug-ins folder and rename it 'Effects' (**Figure 9.22**).

4. Launch PageMaker.
   The new effects appear in the Element > Image > Photoshop Effects dialog box.

To add Photoshop filters (Windows):

1. Quit PageMaker and Photoshop .

2. Find the PageMaker folder and open it.

3. Open the folder called Rsrc.

4. Open the folder called Usenglish.
   If you have a non-US English version of PageMaker, open the folder that corresponds to your version.

5. Open the folder called Plugins (**Figure 9.23**).

6. Copy all the plug-ins you want to use in PageMaker to the Plugins folder.

7. Launch PageMaker.
   The new effects appear in the Element > Image > Photoshop Effects dialog box.

Applying Filters to Images

When you apply a filter to a placed image, PageMaker makes a copy of the source file, leaving your original file intact (**Figure 9.24**).

To apply a Photoshop filter to an image within PageMaker:

1. Select the image with the Pointer tool.

2. Choose Element > Image > Photoshop Effects.

   The Photoshop Effects dialog box appears (**Figure 9.25**).

3. In the Save new file as field, type a new name for the filtered image.

   To save the new image in a different location from the original image, click Save As. This calls up a standard Save As dialog box.

4. From the pop-up menu, choose the Photoshop effect you want to use.

5. Click OK.

   The filter dialog box (if there is one) for the effect you chose will appear (**Figure 9.26**).

6. Adjust the controls and values until the preview matches the effect you want, and click OK.

   The filter is applied to the image and PageMaker automatically links to the new image it just created.

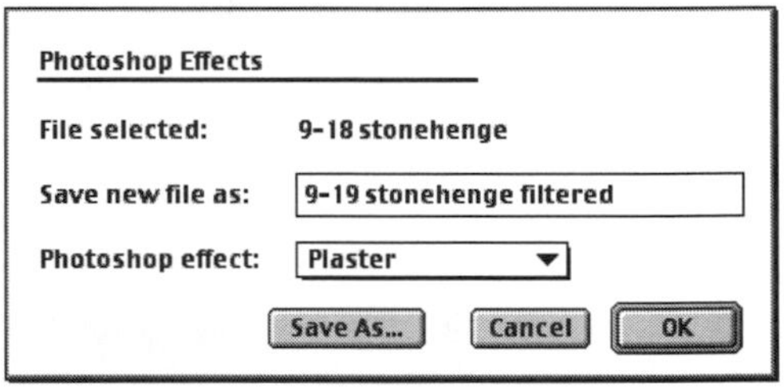

✔ Tips

- Some filters don't display previews. Each filter has different controls.

- Many filters are highly memory-intensive. In order to use some filters you may need to quit PageMaker and increase the memory allocated to it by your computer's operating system.

- Not all Photoshop-compatible filters work in PageMaker.

Figure 9.24 The image as it was placed in the document.

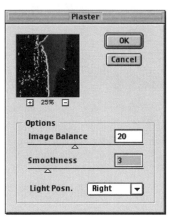

Figure 9.25 The Photoshop Effects dialog box.

Figure 9.26 The Plaster filter dialog box.

10

TRANSFERRING PAGEMAKER 7 FILES

Adobe's desktop publishing trio is one part Adobe PageMaker, one part Adobe Photoshop, and one part Adobe Illustrator. The interfaces of each program are similar, sharing many elements of their onscreen work environments. As part of its designers' efforts to weave the products together even more closely, PageMaker can now place native versions of Photoshop and Illustrator files, without the need to save a file in a specific file format.

PageMaker can also import PDF documents. The revised document converter in PageMaker 7.0 allows you to use files that were created in QuarkXPress (Mac and Windows) and Microsoft Publisher (Windows only).

PageMaker's publications travel seamlessly between different software platforms, but you may have to adjust fonts and graphics before they display and print properly on the new platform.

This chapter explores how PageMaker handles files created with other programs, other platforms, or previous versions of PageMaker.

Copy and Paste to PageMaker

At some point you may need to work in either Photoshop or Illustrator at the same time that you're working in PageMaker. You may need to edit a placed graphic quickly, or create a brand-new graphic on the fly. You don't have to use PageMaker's Place command to bring in an image from either Photoshop or Illustrator. And you don't even have to waste time saving the file in a special format, since PageMaker can import native Photoshop and Illustrator file formats.

To paste an image from Photoshop or Illustrator into PageMaker:

1. In Photoshop or Illustrator, select the image (or portion of an image) you want to copy (**Figure 10.1**).

   You can use any selection method and tool for your selection.

2. In Photoshop or Illustrator, choose Edit > Copy, or Ctrl+C/Command+C.

3. In PageMaker, place your cursor in the location you want the image to appear.

4. Choose Edit > Paste, or Ctrl+V/Command+V.

   The image appears in your PageMaker document.

✔ Tips

- Objects that are pasted into PageMaker are not linked to the document. If printing problems occur, delete the pasted image and use the File > Place command so that the file will be linked as it is placed in your document.

- Copying an object into PageMaker requires more memory than placing the same object. If you run into memory problems when copying and pasting, try using the Place command instead.

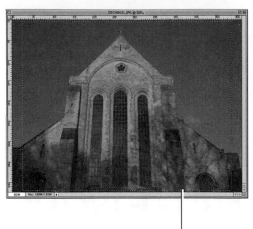

Photoshop's selection rectangle ⌐

Figure 10.1 In Photoshop, select the image, or part of an image, that you want to paste into PageMaker.

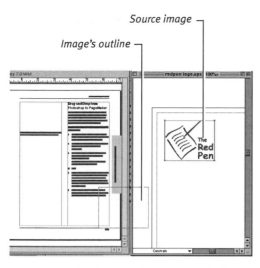

Source image ┐

Image's outline ┐

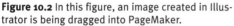

Figure 10.2 In this figure, an image created in Illustrator is being dragged into PageMaker.

Drag and Drop to PageMaker

When you're working at top speed, who has time for menu commands? With Photoshop or Illustrator and PageMaker open at the same time, you can simply select an image and drag it into your PageMaker document instantly.

To drag and drop an image to PageMaker:

1. Arrange the windows of the PageMaker and Photoshop or Illustrator documents so you can see at least part of each document (**Figure 10.2**).

2. In Photoshop or Illustrator, select the image, or the part of an image, you want to move into PageMaker.

3. Press the Ctrl/Command key (Photoshop only) and drag from the Photoshop window to the PageMaker window.

   If you're in Illustrator, you don't need to press any keys to drag an object.

   You'll see an outline of the image as you're dragging (**Figure 10.2**). When you release the mouse button, the image appears in your PageMaker document.

✔ Tips

- Objects that are dragged into PageMaker are not linked to the document. If printing problems occur, delete the pasted image and use the File > Place command so that the file will be linked as it is placed in your document.

- Use care when dragging and dropping. The image may not be the size you need it to be in PageMaker. Although you can resize the image by dragging its handles, it may be more efficient to resize the file in the source program first.

Importing PDF Files

You can place a PDF (Portable Document Format) file directly into a PageMaker document using either the Place command, or drag and drop. If the source image is changed, the changes will automatically appear in your PageMaker document.

PageMaker treats a PDF file the same way it treats an EPS graphic: You can't edit the image in PageMaker, instead you must return to the source document to make changes. The image will always print at its highest available resolution when sent to a PostScript printer, but will print at the document's specified resolution setting when sent to a non-PostScript printer.

The PDF Import dialog box lets you select a specific page from a multiple-page PDF file. You can also set the resolution of your preview (the image that will appear in the PageMaker document) and set Print options for the PDF image.

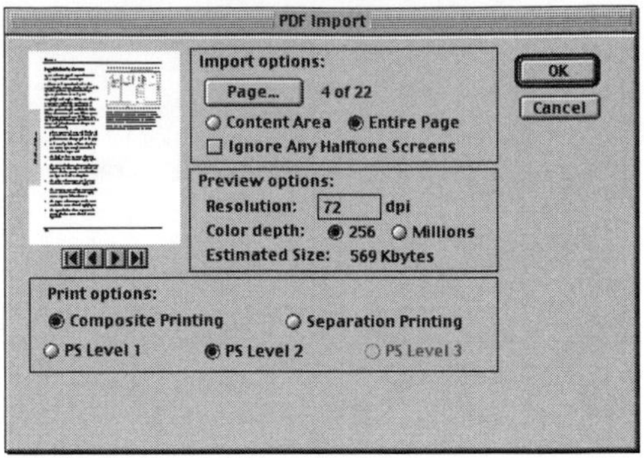

To import a PDF file:

1. Choose File > Place, or Ctrl+D/ Command+D.

2. Select the PDF file, then click OK.
    The PDF Import dialog box appears (**Figure 10.3**).

3. Choose the page you want to place in the document, if applicable, and set other appropriate options in the dialog box.

4. Click OK.
    The PS loaded image icon appears (**Figure 10.4**).

5. Click on your page to place the image.

Figure 10.3 The PDF Import dialog box lets you select a specific page from a multiple-page PDF file.

Figure 10.4 The PS loaded image icon.

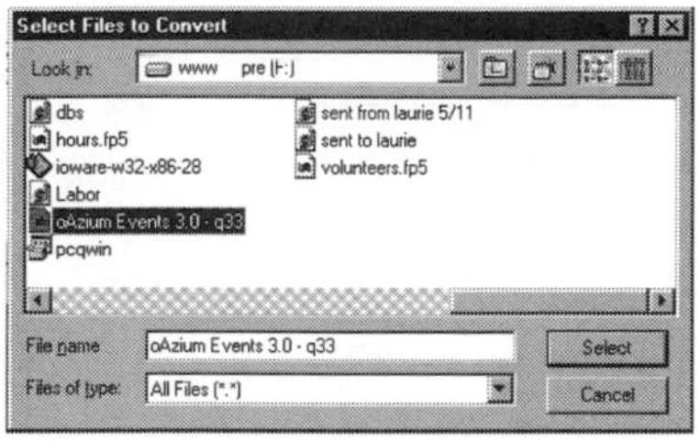

Figure 10.5 The Select Files to Convert dialog box lets you select one file or a set of files to be converted in a batch.

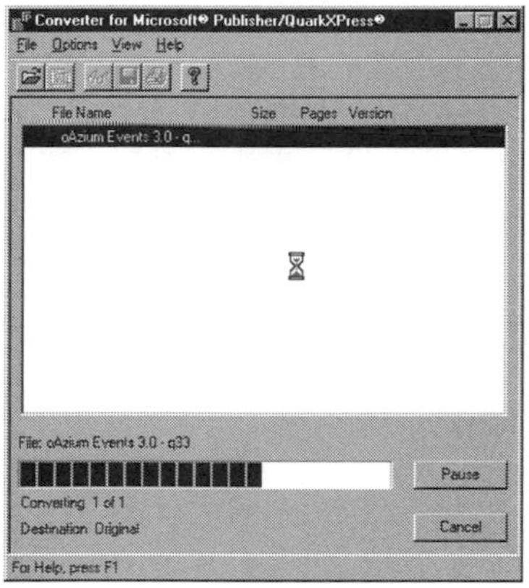

Figure 10.6 A progress bar shows the status of the conversion.

Converting QuarkXPress or Publisher Documents

A converter utility converts QuarkXPress 3.3–4.1 documents to PageMaker 7 format. On Windows, the converter also reformats Microsoft Publisher 97–2000 documents. You can convert a single file at the time, or select multiple files for batch conversions.

To convert QuarkXPress or Publisher documents to PageMaker 7 format:

1. Close the files you want to convert.

2. Find the MS Publisher Quark Converter program (Win) or the QuarkXPress Converter (Mac) program.

   The program is in a folder with PageMaker.

3. Launch the converter.

4. Choose File > Select Files.

   A dialog box appears, where you can select the files you want to convert (**Figure 10.5**).

5. Select the files you want to convert.

   If necessary, change the File of type option to see the files you need to convert.

6. If you're using Windows, repeat steps 4 and 5 as many times as necessary to select all the files you want to convert.

7. On the Mac, click Add for each document, or click Add All to add all the documents in a folder. Click Done when your list is complete.

8. Choose File > Save to Same Folder to call up the Choose Destination dialog box and save the files to a custom location.

9. Click Convert.

   The window shows a list of the files and a progress bar that indicates the status of the conversion (**Figure 10.6**).

Changing Conversion Settings

If the results of your file conversion aren't as good as you'd hoped, you can change the conversion settings to better match the content of the source document.

◆ **Convert White Boxes** retains a white background on frames, which is the QuarkXPress default. Deselect the option to convert the objects' backgrounds to a color of [None] in PageMaker.

◆ **Convert Runaround** retains runarounds, as PageMaker text wraps, on all objects.

◆ **Embed linked images** embeds, rather than links, objects in the converted document. Selecting this option increases the file size.

◆ **Convert text boxes to** lets you specify frames or text blocks for converted text.

◆ **Convert picture boxes to** lets you specify the conversion of graphics to include frames or not.

To change conversion settings:

1. Make sure the converter utility is the active application.

2. Choose Options > Conversion Settings . The Conversion Settings dialog box appears (**Figure 10.7**).

3. Set the appropriate options for your source documents.

4. Click OK.
   The settings will remain in place until you change them.

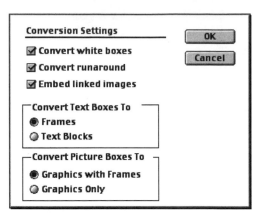

Figure 10.7 The Conversion Settings dialog box lets you specify how certain elements from your QuarkXPress document will convert to PageMaker.

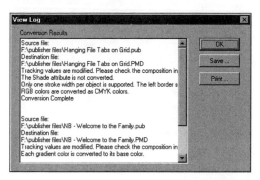

Figure 10.8 The conversion log lets you know which elements in your publication were not converted. You'll need to fix these items manually.

Viewing a Conversion Log

The Converter displays an icon to the left of each file once it's been converted. A checkmark means the publication was converted successfully. An 'x' means the publication was not converted at all, and an alert triangle means that the publication was converted, but there were problems that you will have to fix manually. You can view the conversion log to see what may have gone wrong.

Typical problems include drawn objects that do not have the same attributes when converted, or character-level styles (from QuarkXPress) that are not supported by PageMaker.

To view a conversion log in Windows:

1. Make sure the converter utility is the active application.

2. In the Converter utility, choose View > Log. The log appears (**Figure 10.8**).

To view a conversion log on Mac:

1. Make sure the converter utility is the active application.

2. In the Converter utility, choose Window > Log, or click the View Log button. The log appears.

Printing a Conversion Log

You may find it helpful to have a printout of the conversion log to refer to when you're looking at your converted documents. For publications that had problems during conversion, you can use the printed log as a checklist to find and fix all problems.

To print a conversion log:

1. Make sure the converter utility is the active application.
2. Choose File > Print Log.
   The log is printed (**Figure 10.9**).

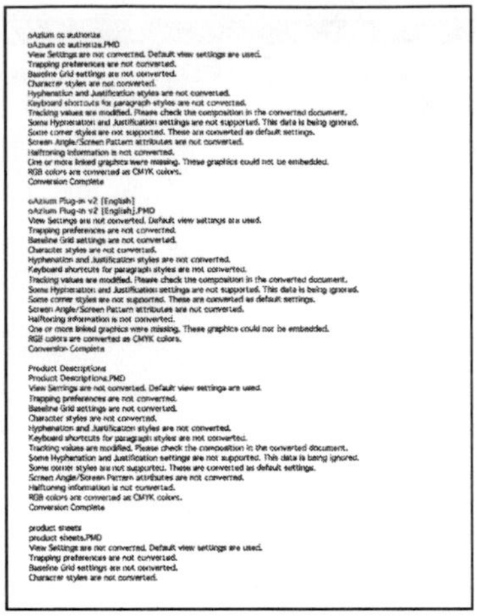
oAzium cc authorize
oAzium cc authorize.PMD
View Settings are not converted. Default view settings are used.
Trapping preferences are not converted.
Baseline Grid settings are not converted.
Character styles are not converted.
Hyphenation and Justification styles are not converted.
Keyboard shortcuts for paragraph styles are not converted.
Tracking values are modified. Please check the composition in the converted document.
Some Hyphenation and Justification settings are not supported. This data is being ignored.
Some corner styles are not supported. These are converted as default settings.
Screen Angle/Screen Pattern attributes are not converted.
Halftoning information is not converted.
One or more linked graphics were missing. These graphics could not be embedded.
RGB colors are converted as CMYK colors.
Conversion Complete

oAzium Plug-in v2 [English]
oAzium Plug-in v2 [English].PMD
View Settings are not converted. Default view settings are used.
Trapping preferences are not converted.
Baseline Grid settings are not converted.
Character styles are not converted.
Hyphenation and Justification styles are not converted.
Keyboard shortcuts for paragraph styles are not converted.
Tracking values are modified. Please check the composition in the converted document.
Some Hyphenation and Justification settings are not supported. This data is being ignored.
Some corner styles are not supported. These are converted as default settings.
Screen Angle/Screen Pattern attributes are not converted.
Halftoning information is not converted.
One or more linked graphics were missing. These graphics could not be embedded.
RGB colors are converted as CMYK colors.
Conversion Complete

Product Descriptions
Product Descriptions.PMD
View Settings are not converted. Default view settings are used.
Trapping preferences are not converted.
Baseline Grid settings are not converted.
Character styles are not converted.
Hyphenation and Justification styles are not converted.
Keyboard shortcuts for paragraph styles are not converted.
Tracking values are modified. Please check the composition in the converted document.
Some Hyphenation and Justification settings are not supported. This data is being ignored.
Some corner styles are not supported. These are converted as default settings.
Screen Angle/Screen Pattern attributes are not converted.
Halftoning information is not converted.
RGB colors are converted as CMYK colors.
Conversion Complete

product sheets
product sheets.PMD
View Settings are not converted. Default view settings are used.
Trapping preferences are not converted.
Baseline Grid settings are not converted.
Character styles are not converted.

Figure 10.9 The log is a list of items that weren't converted by the converter utility. Use the log as a checklist to find and fix all conversion problems.

Figure 10.10 The Search Volumes dialog box will find all files created with old versions of PageMaker.

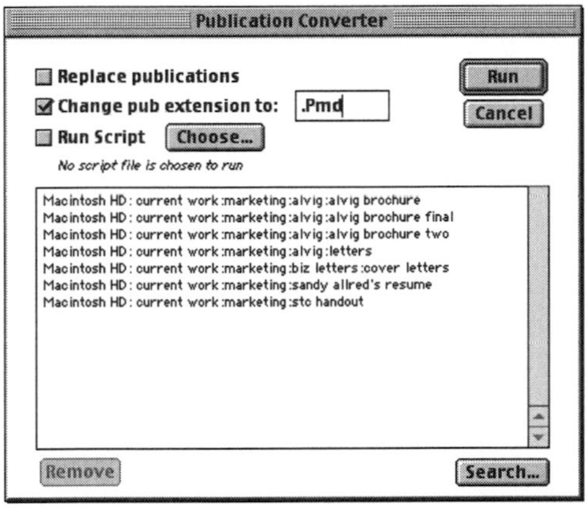

Figure 10.11 The Publication Converter dialog box.

Using the Publication Converter Plug-in

You can convert older PageMaker files by opening them in a newer version of the software. For example, you can open version 5 files using version 6, make a copy of the files, then open the files with PageMaker 7. But this method eats up disk space, not to mention your time. Instead, use the Publication Converter Plug-in. It can search your hard drive, or your network, for PageMaker 4, 5, and 6 files, then convert them all in one batch.

To use the Publication Converter plug-in:

1. Close all open PageMaker documents.

2. Choose Utilities > Plug-ins > Publication Converter.

   The Publication Converter dialog box appears.

3. Click Search, then set the options in the Publications Converter dialog box to search for the various versions of PageMaker publications on your hard drive or network (**Figure 10.10**).

   The Search Volumes dialog box appears.

4. Click Search.

   A list appears in the Publication Converter dialog box (**Figure 10.11**).

5. Set the appropriate options for your source publications.

6. Click Run.

   All publications are converted. The new files will be in the same locations as the old files.

✔ Tip

■ On Windows, you have to search for old PageMaker files by their root extensions. Old extensions are: pm4, pm5, pmd, p65, tmd, or t65.

Publication Converter Options

◆ **Replace Publications** replaces old publications with the new files.

◆ **Change publication extension to** lets you set a custom root extension or add a root extension to files that don't have one. If you're transferring files to Windows, the root extension should be .PMD. (Mac only)

◆ **Run Script** lets you choose a custom script to convert your documents.

◆ The **Remove** button lets you remove an item from the conversion list.

Transferring Files Across Platforms

PageMaker files can be used 'transparently' across the two major platforms. That is, so long as you name your files with the proper root extension for Windows (.pmd), the files can be moved from the Mac to Windows and back again, with no translation necessary. The fonts and graphics used in PageMaker publications are another story.

To solve font issues, you should use fonts that are available in both Mac and Windows versions. If you'll be moving the files across platforms many times during production, using paired sets of fonts is the only way to go. Make sure the fonts in your publication are installed on all computers that will be used to open the publication, so PageMaker can display a publication's text properly.

If cross-platform fonts are not available, you'll need to choose platform-specific fonts when the document is opened on its new platform. This solution works best when you intend to move the file only once. It isn't very practical to change fonts every time you have to proofread a publication across platforms. In this scenario, it makes sense to generate a PDF of the publication for transfer across platforms, instead of sending the source file.

Cross-platform graphics formats like EPS or TIFF will display and print perfectly on either platform. JPEG or GIF files may also work with your printer, but do a test print to ensure that the print resolution meets your standards.

If possible, make copies of the publications and copies of all linked graphics in the same folder. Then, move the folder across platforms as one unit. This will make it easier for you to relink the files the first time you launch the publications on their new platform, because you know the graphics are in the same folder as the PageMaker publications.

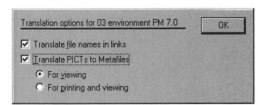

Figure 10.12 Make sure to select Translate file names in links in the Translation options dialog box to assist PageMaker in relinking the files. This dialog box will change options depending on which platform you open it on.

To Translate or Not to Translate?

◆ Don't bother translating graphics if you're moving the publication across platforms temporarily and don't need to see the graphics in the publication. In this case, make sure no translation option is selected.

◆ Perhaps you're moving the publication temporarily, but you still need to view the graphics. If so, select the For Viewing option. Metafile or PICT images will look fine onscreen, but will not print at high resolution.

◆ To move a publication to the other platform permanently or for final output, select the For Printing and Viewing option. PageMaker will convert all embedded Metafile and PICT graphics for viewing and printing at high resolution.

Translating Graphics Across Platforms

Whenever possible, use a cross-platform graphics format, like EPS or TIFF. But if you have to use Metafile or PICT graphics, PageMaker can translate these files for you.

PageMaker converts only graphics that are embedded in the publication. Graphics linked to the document are not translated. If linked graphics must be translated, use the application that created the graphic to translate it, and move the files to the new platform. Then relink or re-place them in your publication.

To translate embedded graphics across platforms:

1. Move the publication file to the new platform and launch PageMaker.

2. Choose File > Open.
   The Open dialog box appears.

3. Select the publication, then click OK.
   If the publication contains embedded PICTs or Metafiles, the Translation options dialog box appears.

4. Choose the appropriate translation option (**Figure 10.12**).
   If you'e moving a publication to the other platform permanently or for final output, make sure the Translate File names in Links option is selected. This option lets PageMaker link to cross-platform files that aren't embedded in the document.

5. Click OK.

✔ Tip

■ Despite your best efforts, PageMaker can somtimes lose track of its linked graphics. The first time you open the publication, PageMaker asks you to find your linked files. If they're all in the same folder, it'll just take a few seconds to relink them.

Matching Missing Fonts

PageMaker alerts you when a document contains fonts that aren't installed on your computer. If the fonts are of secondary importance, you can ignore this message. However, the text may not display properly; character shapes, and even line breaks may display very differently than they would with the correct fonts installed. Whenever possible, install the fonts on any computers you'll be using to work with PageMaker publications.

If this isn't possible—say when you've received a publication from an outside source and you don't intend to purchase the missing fonts—you can make font substitutions so that the text is easier to read.

Temporary substitutions last only as long as you have the document open. You'll have to match missing fonts again the next time you work with the document. Permanent substitutions will be stored in a substitution list along with the document.

To match missing fonts:

1. Choose File > Open and select the publication that contains missing fonts.

   The Font Matching Results dialog box appears (**Figure 10.13**).

2. Select a font from the missing font list, then choose a similar font from the Substituted font pop-up menu.

3. Select Temporary or Permanent from the substitute options.

4. Repeat steps 2 and 3 for each missing font.

5. Click OK.

✔ Tip

- Check your document carefully after making font substitutions. Line breaks, column breaks, and page breaks can all change with a new font.

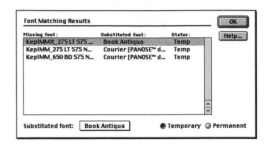

Figure 10.13 The Font Matching Results dialog box lets you choose how PageMaker will display text that uses fonts you don't have installed on your computer.

COLORS

PageMaker has some pretty incredible color controls and capabilities. Not only can you apply almost any color to any object, but you can also print color separations directly from PageMaker. PageMaker 7 supports CMYK, RGB, and spot colors.

This chapter shows you how to use the Colors palette, create new colors, and apply colors to objects.

Applying Color to Text

The Colors palette is PageMaker's color nerve center. Using it you can define, apply, and delete colors. You can even modify existing colors. It's the fastest way to handle your color-related tasks.

To apply a color to text:

1. Select the text you want to color.

   You must use the Type tool to select text.

2. Choose Window > Show Colors, or Ctrl+J/ Command+J.

   The Colors palette appears (**Figure 11.1**).

3. In the Colors palette, click on the color you want to use for the text.

   The text changes to the color you've chosen.

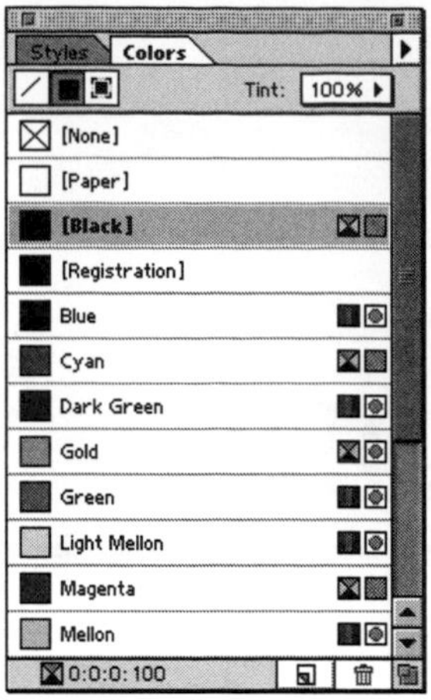

Figure 11.1 The Colors palette contains a list of all the colors used in your publication.

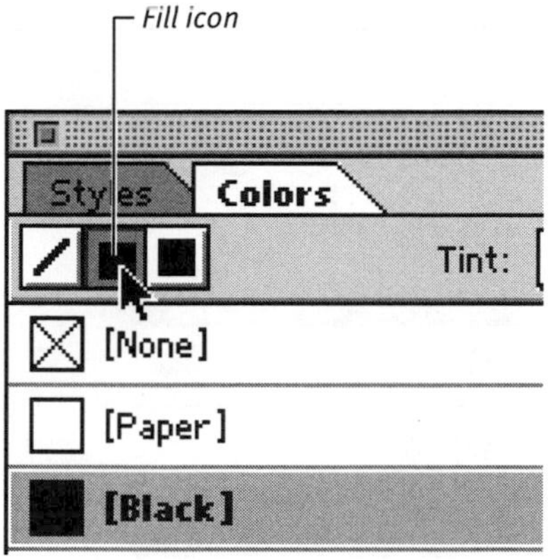

Fill icon

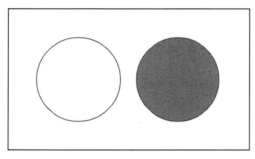

Figure 11.2 Change the color of an object's fill by clicking on the Fill icon, then selecting your new color in the Colors palette.

Figure 11.3 The object on the left has no fill. The object on the right has a color applied to its fill.

Applying a Fill Color

You can apply a color to the inside area (fill) of any object created with PageMaker's drawing tools.

To apply a fill color to a PageMaker object:

1. Select the object to be colored.

2. Display the Colors palette.

3. Click the Fill icon in the Colors palette (**Figure 11.2**).

4. Click on the color you want to use for the fill. The object's fill color will change to the color you selected (**Figure 11.3**).

✔ Tip

■ Remove a color from an object's fill by selecting the object, then clicking the Fill icon and clicking the color [None].

APPLYING A FILL COLOR

Applying a Stroke Color

You can apply a color to the line (stroke) around any object created with PageMaker's drawing tools.

To apply a color to the stroke of a PageMaker object:

1. Select the object to be colored.

2. Display the Colors palette, if necessary.

3. Click the Stroke icon in the Colors palette (**Figure 11.4**).

4. Click the color you want to use for the stroke.

   The object's stroke color will change to the color you selected (**Figure 11.5**).

✔ Tip

■ Remove a color from an object's stroke by selecting the object, then clicking the Stroke icon and clicking the color [None].

Stroke icon

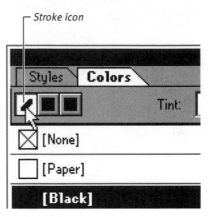

Figure 11.4 Change the color of an object's stroke by clicking on the Stroke icon, then selecting your new color in the Colors palette.

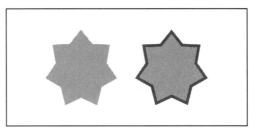

Figure 11.5 The object on the left has no stroke. The object on the right has a color applied to its stroke.

APPLYING A STROKE COLOR

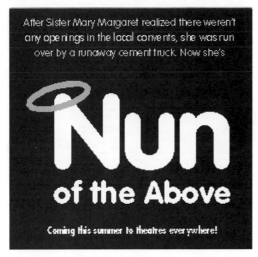

Figure 11.6 This "advertisement" was created entirely in PageMaker. The halo has a fill of [None], which lets the background show through.

Using [None] as a Color

In PageMaker, you can give an object a fill and stroke of [None]. This means that the object will be entirely transparent onscreen.

To apply [None] as the fill of an object:

1. Select the object you want to fill with [None].

2. Display the Colors palette, if necessary.

3. Click the Fill icon in the Colors palette.

4. Click the [None] option.

   The object has a fill of [None].

   For **Figure 11.6**, I used a fill of [None] on the ellipse to be used as a halo. This lets the background colors of white and black show through the middle of the halo.

Changing the [Paper] Color

One of the stranger entries in PageMaker's default color list is [Paper], which for the most part is white. The reason that PageMaker calls it [Paper] instead of White is as follows:

Generally, the paper you print your documents on isn't actually white. It's close, but it isn't the bright white you associate with the screen 'white.' If you regularly print on newsprint or colored paper, your paper is clearly something other than white. PageMaker's [Paper] 'color' is meant to be the same as whatever you're printing on.

In fact, you can even adjust PageMaker's [Paper] color to match colored paper if you're printing on a color other than white. This can help you judge how your images will appear once they're printed.

I also use the color [Paper] to cover portions of objects, or to crop objects that can't be cropped otherwise.

To change your [Paper] color:

1. Display the Colors palette.

2. Double-click the [Paper] color.
   The Color Options dialog box appears (**Figure 11.7**).

3. Move the Red, Green, and Blue sliders until the color matches the tint of the paper you'll be using.

   You probably won't get an exact color match, but don't worry. You're only trying to approximate the color so you can get an idea of what the images will look like when they've been printed on colored paper.

Figure 11.7 With these settings, the Color Options dialog box will tint the color [Paper] to a light tan.

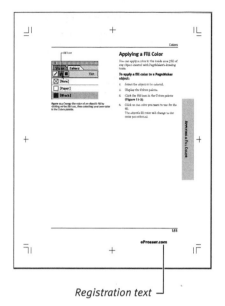

Registration text

Figure 11.8 This figure shows a printed page with its registration marks. The text "eProsser.com" will print on all printed plates because it's been colored with the color called [Registation].

Applying the [Registration] Color

[Registration] isn't really a color. Instead, it's something that appears on every printed plate of a document. Crop marks are [Registration] colored (**Figure 11.8**). Typically, [Registration] is used for marks and notes outside the borders of the printed page—objects that are used by your commercial printer to align colors and trim printed pages.

You can use [Registration] to make any object, or bit of text, appear on each plate printed from a PostScript printer. This can be helpful if you want to add your company's name or phone number to each plate printed from your publication.

To apply the [Registration] color:

1. Select the object you want to change to [Registration].

2. Click on the Fill or Stroke icon in the Colors palette.

3. Click [Registration] in the Colors palette. The object will be colored with the [Registration] color.

APPLYING THE [REGISTRATION] COLOR

Applying a Tint

A tint is a lighter version of a color, defined by a specific percentage that you set in the Colors palette. The lower the percentage, the lighter your tint. Tints are useful even if you're printing in black and white. You can make 100 different shades of gray (running from black to white) by using tints.

To apply tint:

1. Select the object that you want to apply a tinted color to.

2. Display the Colors palette.

3. Click the Fill or Stroke icon in the Colors palette.

4. Click on the color you want to use.
   By default, the tint value for each selected color is 100%.

5. Choose a different tint percentage from the Tint pop-up menu (**Figure 11.9**).
   The selected object is tinted.

✔ Tip

■ Use care when applying tints. Colors tend to wash out at low percentages, and text set in light tints can be difficult to read. Always do a test print before finalizing a tint used in text.

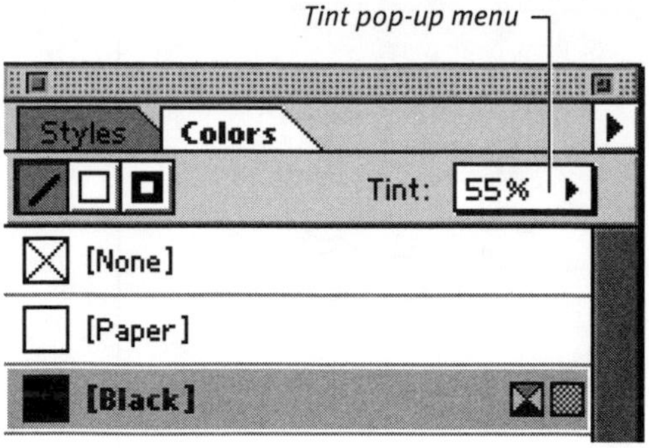

Tint pop-up menu

Figure 11.9 A tint of 55% black will be applied to the object selected in the publication.

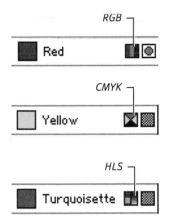

Figure 11.10 Color model icons from the Colors palette.

Understanding Color Models

When you use a color in PageMaker, you're picking it from a specific color model, whether you're consciously aware of the fact or not. PageMaker has three different color models to choose from.

◆ **CMYK** is the color model to use if you'll be printing your PageMaker document. Commercial printers use cyan (C), magenta (M), yellow (Y), and black (K) inks to create most printable colors. CMYK colors are indicated in the Colors palette by a square with four triangles in it (**Figure 11.10**).

◆ **RGB** is the color model to use when you're creating Web pages and onscreen documents (Acrobat documents, for example). Computer monitors use red, green, and blue light to simulate all the colors that appear on their screens, making RGB a perfect choice for documents viewed primarily onscreen. RGB colors are indicated in the Colors palette by a square with three vertical rectangles in it (**Figure 11.10**).

◆ **HLS**, or Hue, Lightness, and Saturation, is more of a way of working with colors than it is a color model of its own. I switch to HLS whenever I need to modify one of these specific components, especially saturation. HLS colors are indicated in the Colors palette by a square with two vertical rectangles: the left-hand rectangle displays hues, and the one on the right displays a grayscale gradient from white to black (**Figure 11.10**).

Making a Color into a Process Color

Process colors are colors that separate into CMYK color plates when printing.

For instance, if you have a color called 'Purple' that is 100 percent cyan, 80 percent magenta, and 20 percent yellow, those tints would appear on each separation, respectively. When all the plates are run, the inks mix to create your lovely purple.

If you plan to print your document using a four-color process (most commonly done at a full-service printer), all your colors will need to be process colors in order to print correctly. Some inkjet and color laser printers use a four-color process as well. Check your printer manual to see whether CMYK is the right color model for your publications.

To make a color a process color:

1. Double-click the color you want to change. The Color Options dialog box for that color will appear (**Figure 11.11**).

2. Choose Process from the Type pop-up menu.

3. Click OK. The color is changed to a process color.

✔ Tip

■ Always talk to the person doing your printing before finalizing your publication. He or she can help you set up your process colors so you'll get the best results.

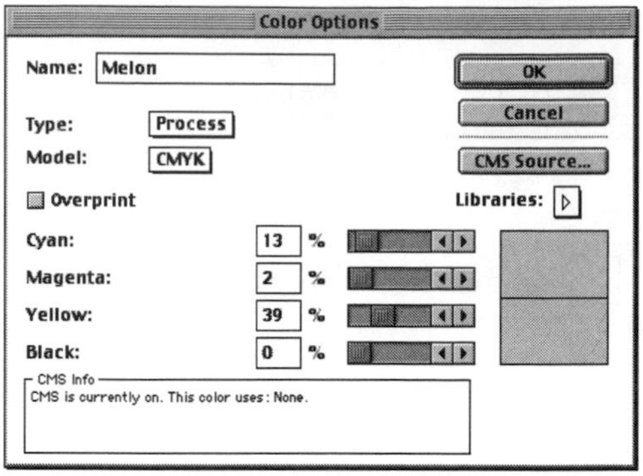

Figure 11.11 The Color Options dialog box lets you change an existing color to a process color.

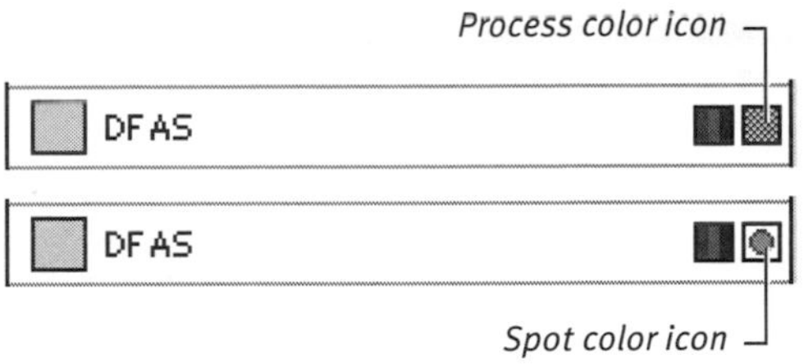

Process color icon ⌐

☐ DF AS ▮▮▓

☐ DF AS ▮◉

Spot color icon ⌐

Figure 11.12 The Spot and Process color icons.

Making a Color into a Spot Color

Spot colors print on their own exclusive plates. You can use spot colors when you're printing a two-color job (say, black ink and blue images). Some print jobs even use the four process colors with extra spot colors added. However you're using spot colors, the commercial printer will use a special ink to match your spot color when printing your publication.

To make a color a spot color:

1. Double-click the color you want to change. The Color Options dialog box for that color will appear.

2. Choose Spot from the Type pop-up menu.

3. Click OK.
   The color is changed to a spot color (**Figure 11.12**).

✔ Tip

- Using spot colors can save you money or add needless cost to a project, depending how they're used. Talk to the person doing your printing before finalizing your colors. He or she should be glad to help you get the best results for your budget.

Adding Pantone Colors

Pantone colors are special trademarked colors, usually used as spot colors, that are guaranteed to match a specified color when printed. PageMaker uses a library of colors that adds any Pantone color to the Colors palette.

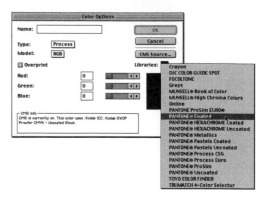

To add a Pantone color to the Colors palette:

1. Display the Colors palette.

2. Click the New Color icon.
   The Color Options dialog box appears.

3. Choose a Pantone library from the Libraries pop-up menu (**Figure 11.13**).
   The Color Picker dialog box appears (**Figure 11.14**).

Figure 11.13 Choose the proper Pantone series from the Libraries pop-up menu.

4. In the Color Picker, choose the Pantone color you want to use by clicking it.
   The list is very long and can take a long time to scroll through. You can type it in the Pantone CVC field to save time.

5. Click OK.
   The name of the color is automatically added to the Color Options dialog box.

6. Choose either Process or Spot from the Type pop-up menu.

7. Click OK.
   The Pantone color is added to the palette.

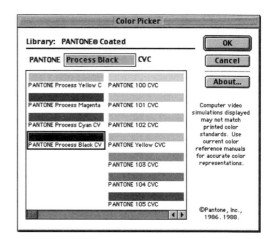

✔ Tip

- The Pantone company sells a Pantone color book that displays print samples of each spot color for reference. The color you choose on screen will be close to the printed Pantone color, but it won't be exact; such is the nature of colors viewed onscreen. If you plan to do a lot of printing with Pantone colors, you'll want to purchase a Pantone color swatch book because it gives you a better sample of the final printed color than your monitor can.

Figure 11.14 Select the Pantone color you need. If you know the Pantone number, you can type it in the Pantone CVC field.

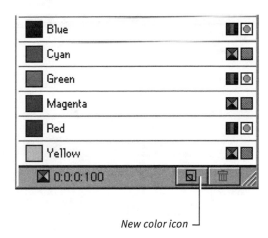

New color icon

Figure 11.15 The New Color icon lets you create and define new colors.

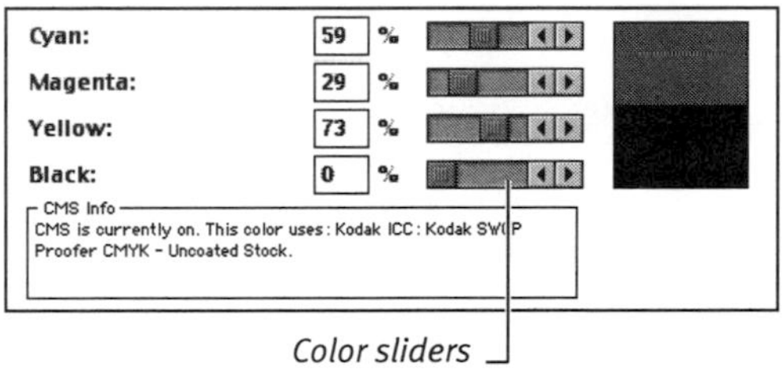

Figure 11.16 The color sliders in the Color Options dialog box.

Color sliders

Creating a New Color

Each PageMaker document comes with a predefined set of colors. These colors may not meet your needs. No problem: You can create as many customized colors as you need.

To create a new color:

1. Display the Colors palette.

2. Click the New Color icon (**Figure 11.15**). The Color Options dialog box appears.

3. Type the name of your new color.

   Try to give your color a name that accurately describes it. This will help later when you're trying to remember when to apply the color.

4. Choose a color type (Process or Spot) from the Type pop-up menu.

   The other option, Tint, is discussed later in this chapter.

5. Choose a color model from the Model pop-up menu.

   If the color you want already exists in a library, you can also choose a color from the Library by displaying the Libraries pop-up menu.

6. Move the color sliders until you have mixed the color you want (**Figure 11.16**).

   Or type numbers in the fields if you know the specific mix for your color.

   The color appears in the Colors palette.

7. Click OK.

CREATING A NEW COLOR

Creating a Color Tint

A few pages back, I explained how to make tints from existing colors. That method works fine for the occasional tinting needs you might have for a small document. But when you're working with a large document that uses several different tints of the same color, choosing the tint from the Tint pop-up menu gets tedious.

PageMaker allows you to create a tint color from any existing color, making it easier to apply a tinted color to objects. This way you can quickly apply a color directly from the Colors palette. This tinted color won't print on its own plate, but instead will appear on either its 'base' plate or on any CMYK plates its base color uses.

To create a color tint:

1. Display the Colors palette, then click the New Color icon at the bottom of the Colors palette.

   The Color Options dialog box appears (**Figure 11.17**).

2. Choose Tint from the Type pop-up menu.

   The Model pop-up menu changes to the Base Color pop-up menu.

3. Choose a base color from the Base Color pop-up menu.

4. Choose a Tint value and name the color tint.

5. Click OK.

   The color is added to the Colors palette.

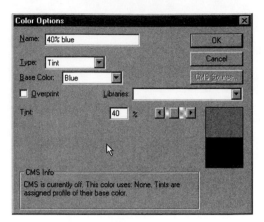

Figure 11.17 With the settings shown, the new tint will be a soothing light blue.

Figure 11.18 PageMaker will ask you to confirm that you want to delete a color before deleting it and changing all items with that color or tint to black.

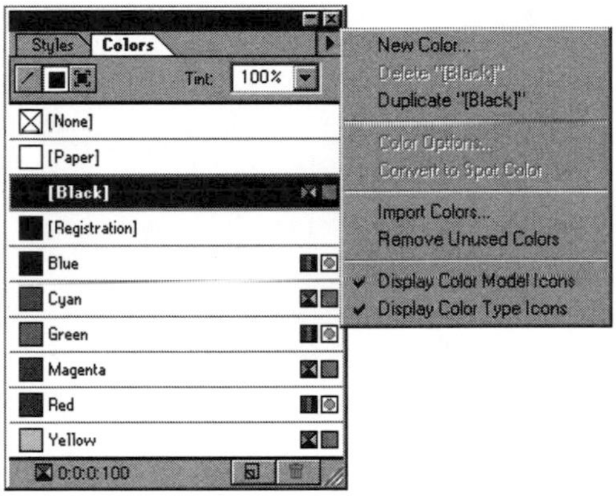

Figure 11.19 Remove Unused Colors can reduce file size instantly by deleting all the extra colors in one fell swoop.

Removing a Color

You can remove colors that aren't going to be used in your publication. This helps your service bureau understand which colors are in use. It can also slim down a large file. If you remove a color that's used in the publication, PageMaker changes all text and graphics that use the removed color to black. Any tints that used the color will be changed to a corresponding black tint.

To remove a color:

1. Click the color in the Colors palette.

2. Click the trash can icon in the Colors palette.

   A warning message asks if you're sure you want to get rid of the color (**Figure 11.18**). You can avoid this message by pressing Alt/Option as you click the Trash can.

✔ Tips

- You can't remove [None], [Paper], [Black], or [Registration].

- You can only remove colors imported with an EPS graphic after the graphic has been deleted from the publication.

- Choose Remove Unused Colors from the Colors palette's pop-up menu to remove all unused colors from your document at once (**Figure 11.19**).

Replacing a Color

Perhaps you've created two shades that are very close to one another, and you want to make all the items that use both colors the same. Or maybe you've decided not to use that deep amber color and would like to use light copper instead. Either way, PageMaker lets you replace one color with another.

To replace one color with another:

1. Choose Window > Show Colors.

   The Colors palette appears.

2. Double-click the color that you want to replace.

3. Change the name of the color you no longer want to exactly match the name of the color you want to replace it with. Remember that capitalization counts.

4. Click OK.

   A dialog box will ask you to confirm that you want to replace the colors (**Figure 11.20**).

5. Click OK.

   The original color is removed from your publication, and the replacement color is applied to all objects that formerly had the original color.

✔ Tip

- All tints based on the original color also change to the replacement color.

Figure 11.20 When you replace one color with another, PageMaker asks you to confirm that you want to change the color items formatted with the color you're replacing.

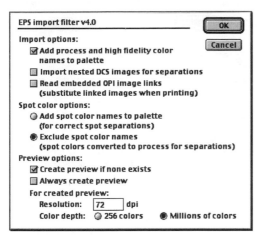

Figure 11.21 To see the EPS import filter dialog box, make sure the Show Filter Preferences option is selected when you place an EPS graphic.

EPS Import Filter Options

◆ **Add Process and High Fidelity Color Names to Palette** adds those colors to the Colors palette.

◆ **Import Nested DCS Images for Separations** includes data PageMaker needs to color-separate the graphic. If this option is not selected, PageMaker prints a low-resolution version of the DCS image to a single color plate.

◆ **Add Spot Color Names to Palette** ensures that PageMaker has accurate color data to spot-color-separate the EPS graphic.

◆ **Exclude Spot Color Names** converts the spot colors to their CMYK equivalents during printing. Use this option with care. The converted colors may not match your colors exactly.

◆ If you print to a non-PostScript device, experiment with values greater than the 72 dpi default setting, and select Millions of Colors for best results.

Limiting Colors Imported with EPS Graphics

When you import an EPS graphic, the colors used in the graphic are also imported into your PageMaker publication. They'll show up in your Colors palette and can be applied or edited just as if they'd been created in PageMaker. Sometimes, though, you won't want all those colors cluttering up your palette. That's okay: PageMaker lets you limit the number of colors that will be displayed in the Colors palette when you import an EPS image.

To limit colors imported with EPS graphics:

1. Choose File > Place.

2. Select the EPS file you want to import from the Place dialog box.

3. Select Show Filter Preferences, or press Shift as you double-click the filename.

4. In the EPS Import filter v4.0 dialog box, select options to specify the kinds of colors you want to include in the Colors palette (**Figure 11.21**).

✔ Tip

■ PageMaker will alert you if you import an EPS color that has the same name as a color already in your publication. Click Cancel to avoid importing the graphic, which would overwrite the color in your document.

Chapter 11

Overprinting

By default, colors in PageMaker knock out other colors underneath them. This works nicely when you have a blue oval on a yellow background, because if the yellow ink is printed under the blue ink, they'll combine to make the circle appear green (**Figure 11.22**).

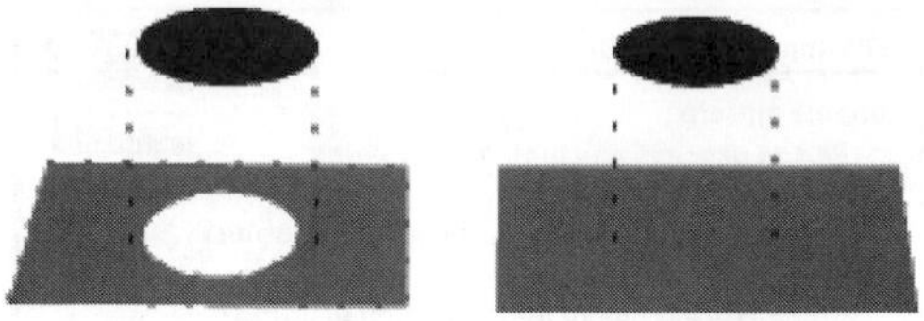

In certain circumstances, such as when black text is on top of a tinted background, it is a good idea to have the black text overprint the background. This way, the text will print slightly darker than it would if you knocked out the color. PageMaker lets you set colors to overprint using a checkbox in the Color Options dialog box.

To overprint:

1. Double-click the color that you want to set to overprint.

   The Color Options dialog box for that color appears.

2. Check the Overprint check box.

3. Click OK.

   The color is set to overprint throughout the publication.

Figure 11.22 The figure on the left shows a black circle printing as a knockout. A white area is "knocked out" for the black ink to print inside. On the left, the black circle will overprint the background color. Overprinting can make richer ink colors.

TEXT FLOW AND STORY EDITOR

Once you venture beyond a single-column Adobe PageMaker page, all sorts of things happen to your document. You can create column guides to help you lay out multi-column designs. You can link text from one page to another. Text can flow across multiple pages, in any order (it doesn't have to flow from the earlier pages to the later ones).

While this capability of PageMaker can create some intricate documents, editing can be a nightmare in page layout view. PageMaker provides the Story Editor for just this reason. The Story Editor provides a window similar to a word processor for editing the text within a story.

Other features let you add a Continued line to text blocks or balance text columns, which can help speed up your layout work.

Setting Column Guides

Say you want to create a three-column newsletter. You've set up your page size and margins, now you have to get out the calculator to find out how much column space you have left over when you've created two 1p6 gutters. Don't give yourself a headache—let PageMaker do the math with its automatic column guides.

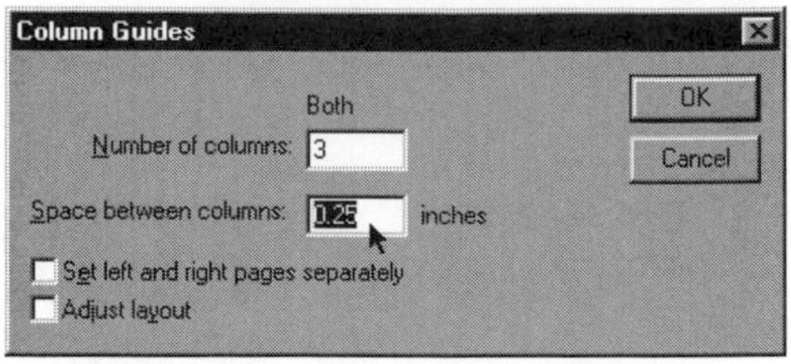

To create column guides:

1. Open the document in which you want to create column guides.

   With no documents open, changes you make to the column guides setting will affect all future documents you create.

2. Choose Layout > Column Guides.

   The Column Guides dialog box appears (**Figure 12.1**).

3. Enter the number of columns and space between columns in the text boxes.

   If you need to set the left pages differently from the right pages, select that option; two additional text boxes will appear (**Figure 12.2**).

4. Click OK.

   The columns are placed in the document (**Figure 12.3**).

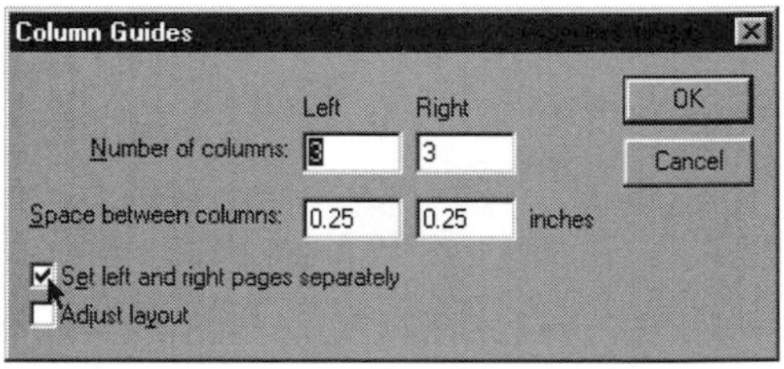

Figure 12.1 The Column Guides dialog box lets you set up the number of columns and the space between them, then PageMaker does the math and places guides on the page automatically.

Figure 12.2 Set left and right pages separately to make asymmetrical column guides.

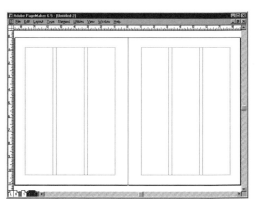

Figure 12.3 A publication with column guides.

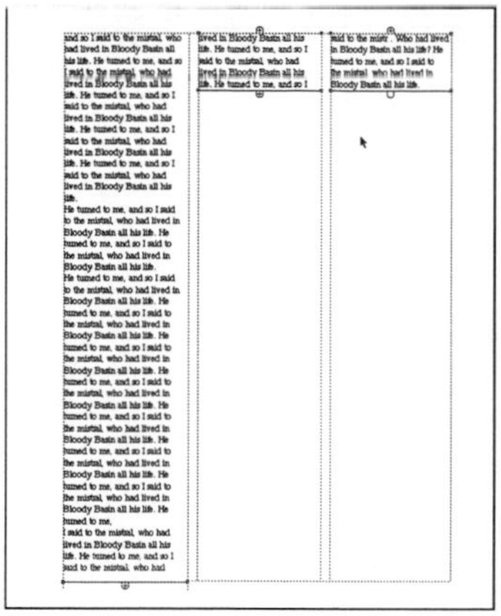

Figure 12.4 This page has three text columns of unequal length.

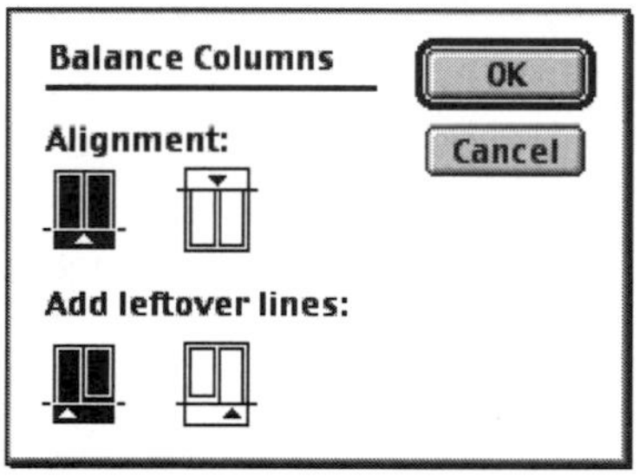

Figure 12.5 The Balance Columns dialog box.

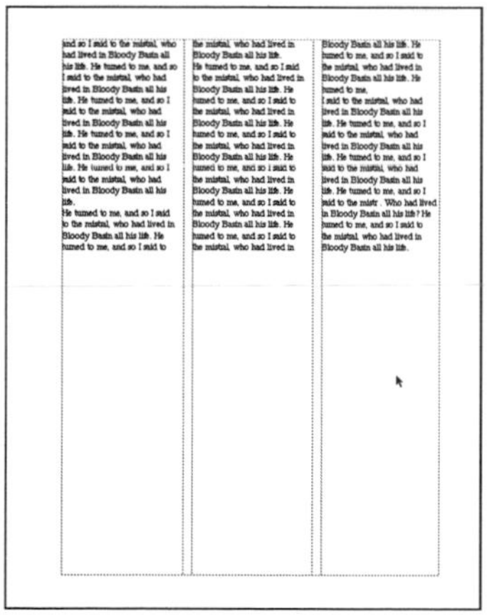

Figure 12.6 PageMaker's automatically balanced columns.

Balancing Columns

When a story doesn't fill a page that uses multiple columns, the result can be, well, ugly. You can take the time to shorten the first column and then any remaining columns, but since each change you make to one column may cause the later columns to reflow, manual column balancing can bring on nonstop cursing in even the holiest of men. PageMaker offers you an easier way.

To balance columns of text:

1. If necessary, flow additional text blocks so that there is a text block in each column you want to balance (**Figure 12.4**).

2. Using the Pointer tool, select all the columns you want to balance.

   The plug-in gives you an error message if you try to run it with no columns selected.

3. Choose Utilities > Plug-Ins > Balance Columns.

   The Balance columns dialog box appears (**Figure 12.5**).

4. Set the appropriate options for balancing.

   Select the left Alignment icon to make the columns balance along the bottom, and the right Alignment icon to have them balance along the top.

   Select the left Add leftover lines icon to put leftover lines in the leftmost column and the right icon to put them in the rightmost column.

5. Click OK.

   The columns are automatically balanced (**Figure 12.6**).

Autoflow

It would be nice if, when you imported a large text file into a PageMaker document, it just magically flowed throughout the document, filling column after column until the document filled with text. It would be even nicer if the program added additional pages if the current document didn't have enough.

Fortunately, PageMaker's Autoflow function does just that. Here's the brief how-to. For more details on Autoflow, see the section on Creating Linked Text Blocks Automatically in Chapter 4.

To turn on Autoflow:

◆ Choose Layout > Autoflow (**Figure 12.7**).

If a checkmark appears next to Autoflow, it is already turned on. When Autoflow is on, you can select Autoflow from the menu to turn it off.

To flow text into another column manually:

1. With the Pointer tool, click on the text block that currently contains text.

2. Click on the red triangle in the window-shade at the bottom of the text block.

   Your cursor changes shape, indicating that it is holding text.

   If there's no triangle, you'll need to shorten the text block a bit.

3. Click in another column to flow the text.

   The text flows into that column.

✔ Tip

■ You can click on a windowshade that displays a plus sign to reload text from that point in the story. This method can be helpful when you're adding pages in the middle of a story and need to create text blocks on the new pages.

Figure 12.7 A check appears to the left of Autoflow when it is turned on.

AUTOFLOW

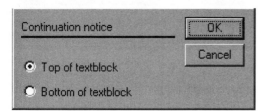

Figure 12.8 The Continuation notice dialog box.

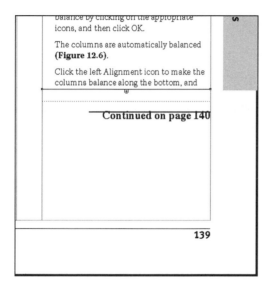

Continued on page 140

139

Figure 12.9 A column of text with a Continued on notice.

Adding Continued Lines

When you're designing a publication like a newspaper or a magazine, it's common for a story to 'jump' from one page to another. For instance, a front page newspaper article may be continued on page 6 of that section. PageMaker has a plug-in that will automatically place a Continued line at the bottom of a jumped story. You don't even have to remember what page the second portion of the story is on, because PageMaker remembers for you.

To add a 'continued on' line to the bottom of a text column:

1. With the Pointer tool, select the text block on which you want the 'continued on' notice added.

2. Choose Utilities > Plug-ins > Add Cont'd Line.

    The Continuation notice dialog box appears (**Figure 12.8**).

3. Choose the Bottom of text block option and click OK.

    A Continued on notice appears in a separate text block under the original text block (**Figure 12.9**). The page number that the text is continued on appears in the box. Be sure your page numbers are correct before you apply this function, as PageMaker does not automatically update page numbers in these boxes.

✔ Tips

- PageMaker will also place a Continued from notice at the top of the second text block, but you'll have to select that block and choose the Top of textblock option.

- A style called Cont. On is created when you use the Add Cont'd Line plug-in. Edit the style if you don't like the look of the text.

Viewing Stories in the Story Editor

With text strewn all over the document, it can be hard to edit; especially when you're moving paragraphs and words from one spot in the story to another. That's where PageMaker's Story Editor comes in handy.

Remember, a story is text that was created or placed as a unit. A story can be a single character or thousands of characters flowing through dozens of text blocks. PageMaker shows each story in its own Story Editor window, no matter how long or short it is.

To use the Story Editor with a single story:

1. Using the Text tool, click anywhere in a text block.

2. Choose Edit > Edit Story, or Ctrl+E/ Command+E.

   The Story Editor window for the story appears (**Figure 12.10**).

To use the Story Editor with several stories at once:

1. Using the Pointer tool, select the text blocks you want to view in the Story Editor.

2. Choose Edit > Edit Story, or Ctrl+E/ Command+E.

   A Story Editor window appears for each text block you've selected (**Figure 12.11**).

✔ Tips

- Choose Edit > Edit Layout to return to the layout without closing the Story Editor window.

- Choose Story > Close Story to close the Story Editor window and return to your previous position in the layout.

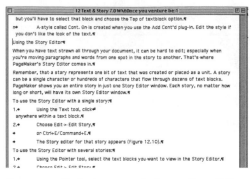

Figure 12.10 Each story opens in its own Story Editor window.

Figure 12.11 When you select multiple stories to open in Story Editor, you'll get multiple windows. The small story in the top window is for a caption used in this book.

Figure 12.12 PageMaker warns you if you try to close a Story Editor window for a story that has not been placed.

Creating a Story in the Story Editor

Sometimes you'll need to create a story that doesn't yet exist, either in PageMaker or in another word processing document. You can just click the Text tool and start typing away in Layout view. However, you may find it easier to type long bits of text in the Story Editor, since it looks a little more like a typical word-processing environment than PageMaker's Layout view does.

To create a story in Story Editor:

1. Make sure nothing in the publication is selected.

   Switch to the Pointer tool to deselect everything in the publication.

2. Choose Edit > Edit Story, or Ctrl+E/ Command+E.

   A blank Story Editor window appears.

3. Type your story.

4. Choose Edit > Edit Layout when you've finished typing.

   A dialog box will warn you that the story has not been placed (**Figure 12.12**).

5. Click Place.

   The loaded text icon appears, and you can then place the story in a text block.

   Clicking Discard will discard the story; clicking Cancel will return you to the Story Editor window.

6. Click in the text block to place the story.

Viewing Invisible Characters

The Story Editor can show you tabs, spaces, line breaks, and soft line breaks to help you while you're editing text.

To view invisible characters in the Story Editor:

◆ Choose Story > Display ¶ (**Figure 12.13**). All the invisible characters appear.

Figure 12.13 The Story menu, which only appears when you are in Story Editor mode.

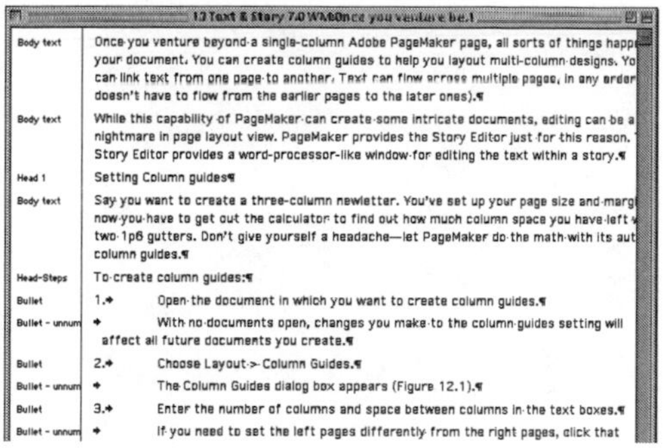

Figure 12.14 The Story Editor, with styles showing for each paragraph of text.

Viewing Paragraph Styles

It's useful to know which styles have been applied to paragraphs when you're in the Story Editor. Sometimes it's easier to apply paragraph styles in the Story Editor, undistracted by layout elements. And since the Story Editor displays text in a continuous word-processing environment, without the distraction of page breaks and graphics, it can be easier to select long bits of contiguous text in the Story Editor. This often makes working with paragraph styles easier, so long as you can tell which styles have been applied to the paragraphs you're working with. PageMaker lets you turn the display of paragraph styles off and on.

To view paragraph styles in the Story Editor:

◆ Choose Story > Display Style Names.
   Style names appear to the left of each paragraph of text (**Figure 12.14**).

Changing the Story Editor's Font Display

You may find certain fonts more legible on the smaller screen display of your laptop. Or maybe you just have those over-40 eyes that appreciate a large font, especially at the end of a long day of laying out pages. PageMaker lets you adjust the font and point size displayed by the Story Editor. This display doesn't affect the formatting you've chosen on the page—it just makes the Story Editor easier to use.

To change the Story Editor's font display:

1. Choose File > Preferences.

The Preferences dialog box appears.

2. Click the More button.

The More Preferences dialog box appears (**Figure 12.15**).

3. Change the font and size in the middle section, marked Story Editor.

4. Click OK.

The Preferences dialog box appears again.

5. Click OK.

The font in the Story Editor changes to your selection.

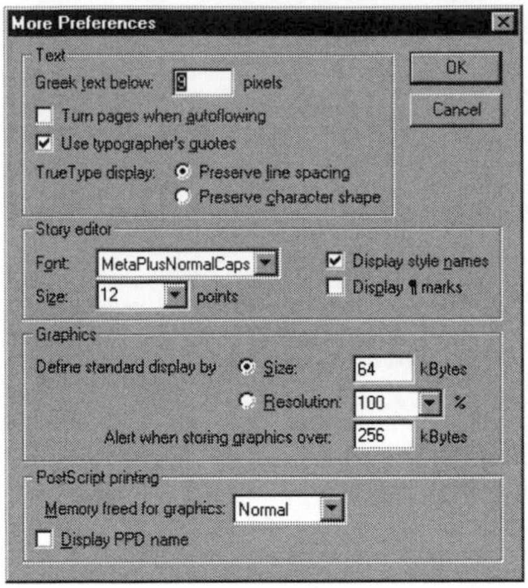

Figure 12.15 The More Preferences dialog box.

OBJECT MANAGEMENT

Organizing your artwork and text in Adobe PageMaker can be an all-consuming task. Fortunately, there are many tools and features that make this process much smoother.

The Control palette can help you precisely position, scale, and rotate objects. You can use PageMaker's grids and guides to keep objects orderly. Finally, you can use the built-in alignment and distribution tools to place your objects more consistently.

Using the Control Palette

In earlier chapters, we discussed two panels of the Control palette: one for editing character attributes, and another for editing paragraph attributes. There's also a third component called the Object panel. Depending on the type of work you do, you may find yourself using it even more than the other two panels.

The instructions in this chapter assume that you have the Control palette open on your screen all the time (which is a good idea). To see the Object panel of the Control palette, you must have one or more objects selected. The Selection Type Indicator tells you what type of object is selected **(Figure 13.1)**.

To show the Object palette:

1. Show the Control palette by choosing Window > Show Control Palette, or Ctrl+' (apostrophe)/Command+'.

2. Select any object with the Pointer tool.

   Even a text block selected with the Pointer tool obliges the Control palette to display the Object panel (**Figure 13.2**).

✔ Tip

■ The measurement system used in the Control palette is the one set in General Preferences.

T	Text Block
╲	Line
⊢	Constrained Line
▢	Rectangle
◯	Ellipse
⬡	Polygon/Star
⊠	Frame Rectangle
⊗	Frame Ellipse
⊗	Frame Polygon/Star
	More than one object
	Group

Figure 13.1 The Selection Type icon on the Control palette will change to indicate the type of object that is selected.

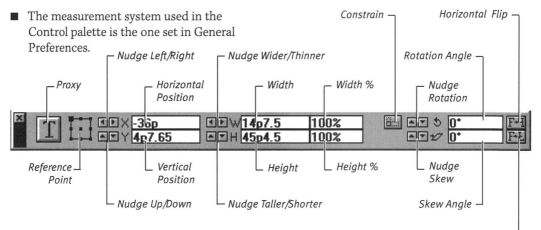

Figure 13.2 The Control palette as it appears when a text block is selected with the pointer tool.

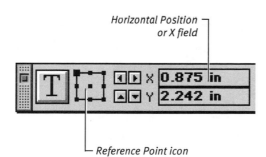

Horizontal Position
or X field

Reference Point icon

Figure 13.3 The Reference Point icon determines the starting point for the transformation of an object.

Moving Objects with the Control Palette

When precise positioning of layout objects is a concern, there's no more efficient way to move those objects than with the Control palette. You can manipulate objects much more precisely with the Control palette than you can by dragging them across the page.

To move an object with the Control palette:

1. Select an object using the Pointer tool.

2. In the Control palette, click the upper-left corner handle of the Reference Point icon (**Figure 13.3**).

   In some cases you'll choose another handle, but for these examples we'll use the upper-left corner.

3. Double-click in the X text field (**Figure 13.3**).

   The value in the X text field is highlighted.

4. Type the horizontal distance you want between the object and the zero point of the ruler, and press the Tab key.

   The Y text field is highlighted.

5. Type in the vertical distance you want between the object and the zero point of the ruler.

6. Click the Proxy button, or press the Enter key.

   The object is moved to the new location.

✔ Tip

■ You can move more than one object at a time using the Control palette. Select all the objects you want to move, then type in a location as in steps 3 through 5 above. PageMaker moves the objects as a group, using the Reference Point to determine their new location.

MOVING OBJECTS WITH THE CONTROL PALETTE

Scaling an Object to a Specific Size

When you import a graphic, you may need to scale it precisely to fit a column width. Or perhaps there's a space the graphic has to fit into. Maybe you've imported several graphics that are different sizes, and they should all be exactly the same size. In these instances you can use the Control palette's Height and Width fields to make objects exactly the size you need.

To scale an object to a specific size:

1. Select an object using the Pointer tool.

2. Click the Reference Point icon on the Control palette to resize from the proper handle, usually the upper left.

3. In the Control palette, change the W value to the width you want the object to be.

4. Press the Tab key.
   The H value is highlighted.

5. Change the H value to the height you want the object to be (**Figure 13.4**).

6. Click the Proxy button, or press the Enter key.
   The object is scaled to the size you've specified.

✔ Tips

■ Use the Width and Height nudge icons to incrementally resize an object. To use the nudge icons, select an object, then click the appropriate nudge icon until the object is the right size. This method is most useful when an object is close to the size you need, but you don't know the precise dimensions.

■ Change the amount that the nudge icons resize an object by choosing File > General Preferences.

Nudge icons

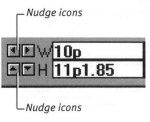

Nudge icons

Figure 13.4 The Width and Height fields in the Control palette let you resize any selected object to a specific size.

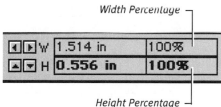

Width Percentage

Height Percentage

Figure 13.5 Use the Width and Height percentage fields to scale an object by a specific percentage.

Scaling an Object by Percentage

What if you have several images placed in your document and they don't seem to be the appropriate size relative to one another? Use the Control palette to set them all to the same reduction or enlargement percentage, so they'll look balanced together.

To scale an object by percentage:

1. Select an object using the Pointer tool.

2. Click the Reference Point icon on the Control palette to resize from the proper handle, usually the upper left.

3. In the Control palette, change the Width Percentage value (to the right of the W value) to the percentage you want to scale the width of the object, and press the Tab key (**Figure 13.5**).

4. Change the Height Percentage value (to the right of the H value) to the percentage you want to scale the height of the object.

5. Click the Proxy button, or press the Enter key.

   The object is scaled to the new percentage.

✔ Tip

■ If the Control palette won't let you type in a field, check your Reference point. PageMaker can't resize objects from the top-middle or bottom-middle handles of the icon.

Scaling an Object Proportionately

Often you'll know one measurement for an object, but you won't know the other. For instance, you may know that an object has to be three inches wide to fit in your column. But the height of the object also matters. You can't just scale them all to the same height and width, or some of the objects will be distorted. Instead, select the Constrain icon, then type in the measurement you know. The image will be scaled proportionately.

To scale an object proportionately:

1. Select an object using the Pointer tool.

2. Click the Constrain icon on the Control palette so it matches the Constrain icon as shown in **Figure 13.6**.

   If the icon already appears this way, clicking it will change it to the non-proportional constrain icon shown in **Figure 13.7**.

3. Double-click any value in the scaling area of the Control palette: W, H, or one of the percentage fields.

   Because you're scaling proportionately, changing any of these values will automatically change the others.

4. Enter a new value.

5. Click the Proxy button, or press the Enter key.

   The object is scaled proportionately to the value you entered.

✔ Tip

■ Make sure the Constrain icon matches the one in **Figure 13.7** if you want to be able to scale your objects without regard to proportion.

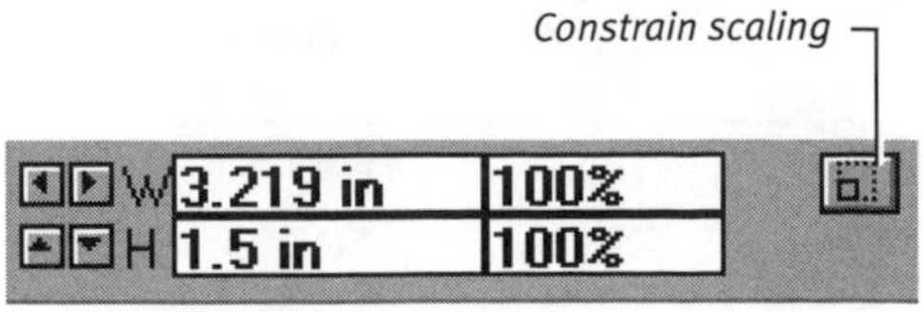

Constrain scaling ⌐

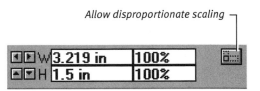

Figure 13.6 The Constrain scaling icon is selected in the Control palette.

Allow disproportionate scaling ⌐

Figure 13.7 The Allow disproportionate scaling icon is selected in the Control palette.

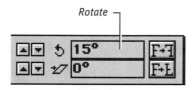

Figure 13.8 Rotating text makes it more eye-catching. This text block is rotated 15 degrees counterclockwise.

Figure 13.9 Type a number, then press the Enter key to rotate an object with the Control palette.

Rotating an Object

You can rotate any text or graphic object with the Control palette. Rotate text for a change of pace, but be careful not to place it at too steep an angle on the page, as that will make it hard to read (**Figure 13.8**).

Enter a positive number in the Rotate field to rotate an object counterclockwise by that number of degrees. Or use a negative number to rotate an object clockwise. It's usually easier to think of the value '-60' than it is to recall that +300 degrees will create the same rotation effect.

To rotate an object:

1. Select an object using the Pointer tool.

2. Click the Reference Point icon on the Control palette to rotate from the proper handle, usually the upper left.

3. Type the number of degrees you want to rotate the object in the rotate field of the Control palette (**Figure 13.9**).

4. Click the Proxy button, or press the Enter key.

   The object is rotated to the angle you entered.

ROTATING AN OBJECT

Skewing Objects

Skewing slides one edge of an image in one direction, while the opposite edge remains in place. Skewing typically involves sliding the top edge of an image to the left or right, while the bottom of the image stays put. This gives the image a slanted look (**Figure 13.10**).

To skew an object:

1. Select an object using the Pointer tool.

2. Click the Reference Point icon on the Control palette to skew from the proper handle, usually the upper left.

3. Type the number of degrees you want to skew the object in the Skew field of the Control palette (**Figure 13.11**).

4. Click the Proxy button, or press the Enter key.

   The object is skewed to the angle you specified.

✔ Tip

■ Skew large images, such as photographs, with care. Your print jobs may slow down radically if you're transforming a large object within PageMaker. For photographs and other high-megabyte images, it's usually best to transform the image in its native application, and then re-place the image in your PageMaker document.

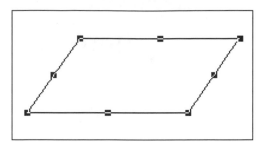

Figure 13.10 Skewing an image slides the top edge of an image to the left or right.

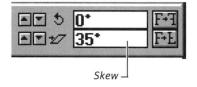

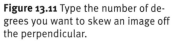

Figure 13.11 Type the number of degrees you want to skew an image off the perpendicular.

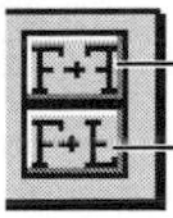

— Flip Horizontal

— Flip Vertical

Figure 13.12 Use the Flip icons to flip an object horizontally or vertically.

Flipping Objects

What if an object that you've created or imported needs to be flipped to work with your design? There are several examples of flipped objects on this very spread. Notice the lines we use for the callouts on our figures? They were all originally copied from the same object, then flipped around to meet the figure's needs.

To flip an object horizontally:

1. Select an object using the Pointer tool.

2. Click the Reference Point icon on the Control palette to flip from the proper handle, usually the upper left.

3. Click the Horizontal Flip button on the Control palette (**Figure 13.12**).
   The object is flipped horizontally.

To flip an object vertically:

1. Select an object using the Pointer tool.

2. Click the Reference Point icon on the Control palette to flip from the proper handle, usually the upper left.

3. Click the Vertical Flip button on the Control palette (**Figure 13.12**).
   The object is flipped vertically.

✔ Tips

■ Flip large images, such as photographs, with care. Your print jobs may slow down radically if you're transforming a large graphic object within PageMaker. For large photographs and other high-megabyte files, it's usually best to transform the image in its native application, then re-place the image in your PageMaker document.

■ Just as with other transformations, you can flip text blocks. Be careful of the effect, though. Obviously, flipped text won't be very legible.

Calculating with the Control Palette

The numeric fields in the Control palette can be modified using mathematical operations. For instance, if you wanted to move a text block, currently 1p8.3 from the left edge of the document, exactly 2.15 inches to the right, type +2.15 after the measurement in the X position field, then press the Enter key.

Of course, you can use this same technique for other transformations. Rotate an already rotated object five more degrees by typing +5 in the Rotate field, then press the Enter key.

To move an object using a calculation in the Control palette:

1. Select an object using the Pointer tool.

2. Click the Reference Point icon on the Control palette to move the image from the proper handle, usually the upper left.

3. In the Control palette, click to the right of the current X value.

   Instead of highlighting the X value, a blinking cursor appears to the right of it.

4. Type + and a number after the current value in the X field (**Figure 13.13**).

   If you enter a positive number (adding to the current position) the object will move to the right.

   If you enter a negative number (subtracting from the current position) the object will move to the left.

5. Press the Enter key.

   The object is moved the distance you specified.

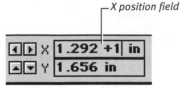

X position field

Figure 13.13 You can use the number fields in the Control palette as a type of mini calculator. Just type in an equation and PageMaker will do the math.

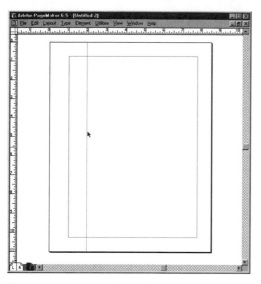

Figure 13.14 Drag a guide out from the ruler to use when placing objects on the page.

Creating Ruler Guides

Ruler guides are very helpful when you have lots of objects you need to line up on your page. Guides are 'pulled out' from the horizontal and vertical rulers. A single page can have up to 120 guides, in any combination of horizontal and vertical.

To create a ruler guide:

1. View rulers by choosing View > Show Rulers, or Ctrl+R/Command+R.

   Rulers appear along the top and left edges of your document window.

2. At the spot where you want a guide to appear, click and drag from the ruler onto the document page.

   As you drag, a dotted line accompanies your cursor, parallel to the ruler you dragged it from.

3. Release the mouse button.

   A ruler guide appears in your document (**Figure 13.14**).

✔ Tips

- Hide the guides temporarily by choosing View > Hide Guides.

- Remove a guide by dragging it back into the ruler or off the edge of the page.

- Choose View > Clear Ruler Guides to remove all guides on a page at once.

- Choose View > Snap to Guides to give objects a "magnetic" attraction to the guides. This is a big help when you're aligning several objects.

- Guides can be moved accidentally if they're too near an object you're trying to select. Choose View > Lock Guides to keep them from being moved. Or choose View > Send Guides to Back, which makes it a little harder to select them by accident.

Using the Grid Manager

If you have a complex layout that needs lots of ruler guides, you don't have to spend time dragging guide after guide onto the page. The Grid Manager is a plug-in that lets you set options for building a grid of ruler guides. The Grid Manager gives you complete control over columns, gutters, and other guides on your page.

To use the Grid Manager:

1. Choose Utilities > Plug-Ins > Grid Manager.
   The Grid Manager dialog box appears (**Figure 13.15**).

2. In the Define grid section of the dialog box, choose the guide type from the Guide type pop-up menu.
   You can define columns, ruler guides, and baseline guides.

3. For each guide type, adjust the attributes.
   For instance, for columns you might edit the number of columns on the left and right pages, and the gutter (or empty space) between those columns.

4. If you want to adjust an individual column, double-click the column.
   The Set Width or Height dialog box appears; enter new values to adjust the column size (**Figure 13.16**).

5. Click OK to exit the Set Width or Height dialog box.

6. Set the appropriate options in the Apply section of the Grid Manager dialog box.
   Select the pages that you want the new grid applied to.

7. Click Close.
   The Grid Manager dialog box is closed and the changes are applied.

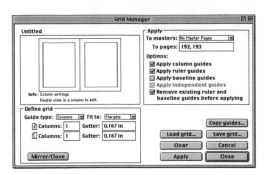

Figure 13.15 The Grid Manager plug-in lets you quckly set options that build a grid of ruler guides.

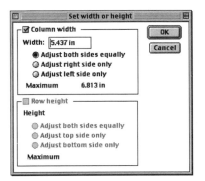

Figure 13.16 Adjust columns or rows in the Set Width or Height dialog box.

Figure 13.17 These two objects have a common face. The top edge of the rectangle matches the top point on the circle's arc. PageMaker uses these faces to create alignment.

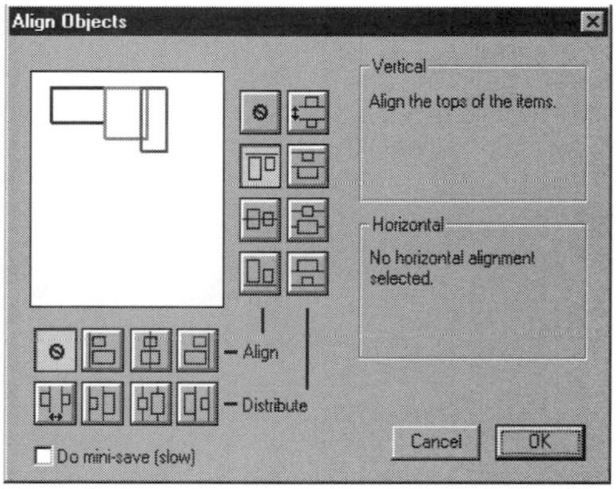

Figure 13.18 The Align Objects dialog box lets you line objects up along one of their faces. With these settings, objects will be lined up along their top face.

Aligning Objects

PageMaker lets you align objects in relationship to one another. Alignment is based on objects having a common edge, or face. In other words, you can line up a rectangle and a circle even though they aren't the same shape. Alignment occurs along the rectangle's straight edge and the furthest point of the circle's arc (**Figure 13.17**).

To align objects:

1. Select objects using the Pointer tool.
   Press Shift while clicking an object to add it to other selections.

2. Choose Element > Align Objects, or Ctrl+Shift+E/Command+Shift+E.
   The Align Objects dialog box appears (**Figure 13.18**).

3. In the Align Objects dialog box, choose the type of horizontal and vertical alignment you want to use.
   The preview area gives you visual feedback on the alignment you've selected. The Vertical and Horizontal areas give you text feedback about your settings.

4. Click OK.
   The objects are aligned according to your settings.

✔ Tip

■ Alignment can't be undone with the Edit > Undo command. If you aren't sure about your settings and think you might need to revert the document, select the Do mini-save option. The process takes a little more time, but it's better to be safe than sorry. If there is a problem with the alignment, File > Revert will take you back to the last saved version of the document.

ALIGNING OBJECTS

Distributing Objects

Use the Distribute icons in the Alignment dialog box to put an equal amount of space between a series of objects. PageMaker gives you two options for distribution. You can divide the total amount of space between the two most distant objects, and distribute the space equally among all the objects. Or you can set a fixed amount of space between each object and PageMaker will move the objects, if necessary, to insert the specified amount of space.

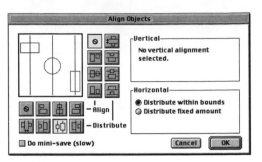

Figure 13.19 Click on the Align Objects' Distribute buttons to equally space a series of objects.

To distribute objects:

1. Select objects using the Pointer tool.

   Press Shift while clicking an object to add it to other selections.

2. Choose Element > Align Objects, or Ctrl+Shift+E/Command+Shift+E.

   The Align Objects dialog box appears (**Figure 13.19**).

3. In the Align Objects dialog box, click on the Distribute icons.

   The preview area gives you visual feedback on the alignment you've selected. The Vertical and Horizontal areas give you text feedback on the settings.

4. Click OK.

   The objects are distributed according to your settings.

✔ Tip

■ To get the best results from the Distribute feature, you may need to first align the objects along one face (top, bottom, left or right).

Figure 13.20 On the left, you can see the rectangle that covers the bottom of the circle. On the right, the rectangle has been filled and stroked with [Paper], so that it is invisible, but still will mask the shape.

Element	
Fill	▶
Stroke	▶
Fill and Stroke...	⌘U
Frame	▶
Arrange	▶
Align...	⇧⌘E
Text Wrap...	⌥⌘E
Group	⌘G
Ungroup	⇧⌘G
Lock Position	⌘L

Arrange submenu:
Bring to Front	⇧⌘]
Bring Forward	⌘]
Send Backward	⌘[
Send to Back	⇧⌘[

Figure 13.21 The Element > Arrange submenu.

Changing the Stacking Order

As you create or place objects on a page, PageMaker assigns a stacking order to the objects. That is, objects you placed more recently appear in front of older objects. This function can be quite useful: For example, it lets you use one object to cover part of another object, and thereby create a shape that PageMaker's tools couldn't draw using any other method.

In **Figure 13.20**, I drew a circle first, then drew a rectangle with a paper-colored fill and stroke to cover the bottom of the circle. This creates a shape that looks like circuit board wafers. This improvisation works because the stacking order makes the rectangle appear on top of the circle, cutting off a part of its shape.

However, a problem occurs when I try to place my caption under the circle. It is beneath the rectangle in the stacking order, so part of the text is covered. The solution is the same: I just change the stacking order.

To change the stacking order of objects:

1. Select an object using the Pointer tool.

2. Choose Element > Arrange > and choose a location for the object from the menu (**Figure 13.21**).

As the object moves through the stacking order, it retains its position and shape.

✔ Tip

■ The Arrange command lets you move items all the way to the front or back of the stacking order, or shuffle items through the stacking order with the Bring Forward and Send Backward commands (**Figure 13.21**).

Grouping Objects

It's useful to be able to work with several objects as a single unit. PageMaker's Group command lets you move, reshape, or transform multiple objects together.

To group objects:

1. Select objects using the Pointer tool.

   Press Shift while clicking an object to add it to other selections.

2. Choose Element > Group, or Ctrl+G/ Command+G.

   The elements are now grouped together and share a single set of handles, indicating that they will be transformed as a unit (**Figure 13.22**).

✔ Tip

■ Ungroup objects by choosing Element > Ungroup. Objects retain all changes made to them while they were grouped together.

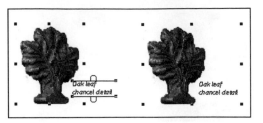

Figure 13.22 The objects on the left are separate, as indicated by the separate selection handles. On the right, the same objects have been grouped. Now they share a set of selection handles and can be moved as one unit.

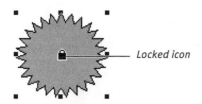

Figure 13.23 If you try to move a locked object, the pointer turns into a lock icon to indicate that the object's position is locked.

Locking an Object's Position

Once you've done all the work to position, scale, and transform an object, it would be nice to be able to protect it so the object isn't moved accidentally.

Or, you may have several people working on a publication, and you want to lock all objects that people shouldn't be moving, resizing, skewing, or rotating . In both cases just apply the Lock command: PageMaker won't let these objects be moved or resized until they've been unlocked. The pointer changes to a locked shape if you try to drag a locked object. The Control palette's fields won't accept text entries when a locked object is selected.

The good news is that you can continue to make certain changes to locked items. You can change a locked object's fill or stroke color, and you can edit text in a locked text block.

To lock an object's position:

1. Select objects using the Pointer tool.

Press Shift while clicking on an object to add it to other selections.

2. Choose Element > Position, or Ctrl+L/ Command+L.

The object's position is locked (**Figure 13.23**).

✔ Tip

■ Choose Element > Unlock to unlock an object.

Masking Objects

Earlier in this chapter, we talked about using a shape designed with PageMaker's drawing tools to mask part of an object, in order to create a shape the tools themselves couldn't draw. PageMaker has a more powerful Mask command that will allow a shape drawn in PageMaker to mask an imported graphic. Masking covers part of an object so that a portion of it appears through a shape drawn with the Rectangle, Ellipse, or Polygon tools.

To mask objects:

1. Draw or select the object you want to use as a masking object.

   The drawn object should have no fill, if you want the masked object to show through.

2. Move the masking object over the object you want to mask (**Figure 13.24**).

3. Select the mask and the object you want to be masked.

4. Choose Element > Mask.

   The drawn object masks the imported object.

✔ Tips

- You can't use a frame as a mask.

- Drag the imported image to change what portion of the image shows through the mask.

- Hold down the Shift key as you choose Element > Mask to group the objects as they're masked. Grouping locks the position of the image under the mask.

- The masking object can be behind the object being masked. In that case, the masking object's fill will show through the transparent areas of the object being masked.

- Choose Element > Unmask to remove a mask.

Figure 13.24 On the left is an imported TIFF graphic and a shape drawn in PageMaker. The mask has a heavy stroke for illustration purposes, which will be removed later. On the right, the objects have been masked and grouped.

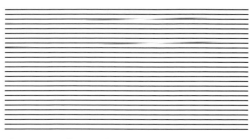

Figure 13.25 These 25 lines were drawn and aligned in one step using the Paste Multiple command.

Paste Multiple	
Paste [25] copies	OK
Horizontal offset: [0] inches	Cancel
Vertical offset: [0.05] inches	

Figure 13.26 The Paste Multiple dialog box. These settings created the lines in the figure above.

Using Paste Multiple

If you need multiple copies of an object, use the powerful Paste Multiple command to paste and align the objects at the same time (**Figure 13.25**).

To paste multiple objects:

1. Select objects using the Pointer tool.

2. Choose Edit > Copy.

3. Choose Edit > Paste Multiple.
The Paste Multiple dialog box appears (**Figure 13.26**).

4. Set options to specify the number of copies to be pasted and the offset distance between each.

✔ Tips

■ Positive horizontal and vertical offset values move the copies to the right and down, respectively. Negative offset values move copies to the left and up.

■ Save your work before choosing Paste Multiple, because you can't choose Edit > Undo to delete a Multiple Paste. If things go wrong, you can choose File > Revert to revert to the last saved version of the publication.

USING PASTE MULTIPLE

Using Power Paste

Many publications have elements that need to appear in the same spot of every page in the document. If you're familiar with Master Pages, you can use that technique to place the element. However, you can't customize Master Page elements on the individual pages in which they appear.

By using Power Paste, you can place customizable objects at the same location on a series of pages. For example, I used a template for all the chapters in this book, but the template only had a few pages. When I add pages, some repeating elements, like the text in the thumb tabs, aren't automatically created for me (**Figure 13.27**).

So I just copy a pair of existing thumb tab text blocks, turn the page, then use Power Paste. Voila! I've got customizable duplicates (**Figure 13.28**). This is a huge time-saver because I don't have to measure anything: I can trust PageMaker to place the objects in precisely the right spot.

The key to using Power Paste is understanding how it differs from PageMaker's normal Paste function. Ordinarily when you paste an object, it is offset slightly from the original. Power Paste creates the new copy in the exact location of the original. If you turn pages between the copying and the pasting, you've got matching elements on your pages. You can even apply a Power Paste from document to another.

To use Power Paste:

1. Select objects using the Pointer tool.

2. Choose Edit > Copy.

3. Click in the new location for the selected objects.

4. Press Ctrl+Alt+V/Command+Option+V.

   The item appears in the same relative location as the original.

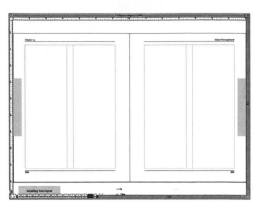

Figure 13.27 When I create a new spread in this book, some repeating elements are not created for me.

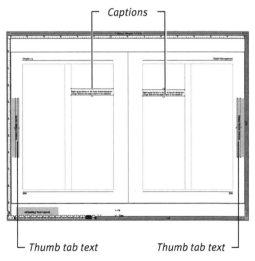

Figure 13.28 With Power Paste, I copy elements from other pages and paste them in the same location as the originals on the new page.

Figure 13.29 Options in the Paste Special dialog box will change based on the object in the clipboard.

Using Paste Special

You can use Paste Special to change the format of an object. This command is useful when you want to select an area of a spreadsheet or a table in a word processor file, and paste it into PageMaker. This control is similar to the Place dialog box's Filter command.

To use Paste Special:

1. Select objects using the Pointer tool.

2. Choose Edit > Copy.

3. Click in the new location for the selected objects.

4. Choose Edit > Paste Special.

   The Paste Special dialog box appears (**Figure 13.29**).

5. Set options to change the format of the object in the clipboard.

   Available options change based on the type of object in the clipboard.

✔ Tip

■ You can scale a bit of text as if it were a graphic object, if you change a text block into a image. Select a text block, choose Edit > Cut to put the text on the clipboard, then use Paste Special to convert the text block to a PICT object (Mac only).

Making Objects Non-Printing

It's often useful to be able to leave notes in a publication for other people who'll be working on the file, whether they are your co-workers or the service bureau technician who'll be printing your color plates. Just type up your notes in a normal text block, then set the block to be non-printing. You'll never have to worry that your notes may end up included in the finished publication.

To make objects non-printing:

1. Select object(s) using the Pointer tool.

2. Choose Element > Non-Printing.

   The object(s) remain visible in the document, but will not print (**Figure 13.30**).

✔ Tips

- Non-printing objects do not appear in PDFs.

- Choose View > Display Non-Printing Items to toggle the display of non-printing items off and on.

- Make a non-printing object printable again by selecting it and choosing Element > Non-Printing.

Figure 13.30 The large gray note on this page has been set to non-printing as a message to the service bureau.

LAYERS

The more complex your documents are, the more you'll appreciate Adobe PageMaker's layering capabilities. Layers let you link objects together without actually grouping them, which makes them easier to select and manipulate.

Think of layers as somewhat like those cool cutaway sections of a frog's anatomy in a Biology textbook. The skin and its callouts are on the first layer of film. When you turn the page, you see the musculature on the next layer. Then, as you peel back more layers, you get to the organs, then the skeleton. Layers in a PageMaker document are like that—similar objects linked together so that they can be worked with as one unit.

One very cool use of layers is to have them incorporate different translations of a document. For example, you could create four layers for your publication: English text, French text, Spanish text, and an image layer. By printing each text layer with the image layer, you can create three versions of your publication, but only have to place the graphics once.

Showing the Layers Palette

Once you know how to find and work with the commands, you can add, duplicate, remove, and lock layers. Like most major features in PageMaker, layers have their own work palette. The Layers palette is the nerve center for organizing your publications.

To show the Layers palette:

◆ Choose Window > Show Layers, or Ctrl+8/Command+8.

The Layers palette appears (**Figure 14.1**).

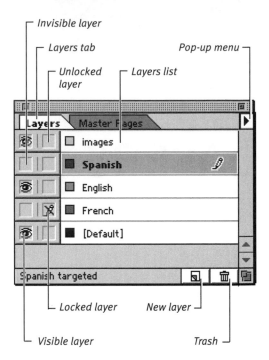

Figure 14.1 The Layers palette has many icons that indicate the status and formatting of each layer. In this palette, the Spanish layer is active, or targeted.

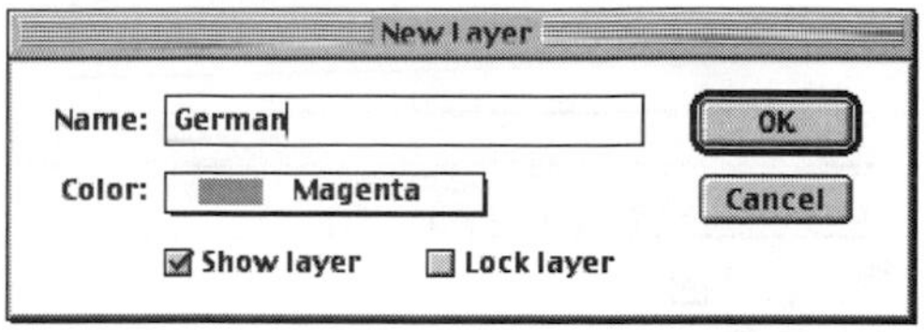

Figure 14.2 Type a descriptive name for your new layer in the New Layer dialog box. This will help you remember which items belong on the layer.

Creating a New Layer

By default, all PageMaker documents start with only one layer. Add new layers to documents with the New Layer icon in the Layers palette, or use the New Layer command in the Layers palette's pop-up menu.

To create a new layer:

1. Click the New Layer icon in the Layers palette.

   The New Layer dialog box appears (**Figure 14.2**).

2. Type in a name for the layer.

   Use a descriptive name to help you remember which items go on your new layer.

3. Pick a color for the layer.

   PageMaker assigns a different color to each layer as it's created. The color corresponds to the color of the selection handles for each object in that layer, so that you can tell at a glance which layer an object belongs to.

4. Click OK.

   The new layer is added to the top of the layer list in the Layers palette.

✔ Tip

■ If you create new layers with no documents open, all new documents you create will have multiple layers.

Moving an Object to a Layer

Sometimes you'll create objects before realizing that you want to use a layering system to organize the publication. Or perhaps you just placed an object on the wrong layer by mistake. It's easy to fix: Just move the object to the right layer.

To move an object to a layer:

1. Select the object you want to place on another layer.

   When an object is selected in PageMaker, a small square appears in the Layers palette next to the name of the layer that currently contains the selected object (**Figure 14.3**).

2. In the Layers palette, click and drag the square to the target layer, then release the mouse.

   The object is moved to the new layer, and the square now appears on its new layer.

✔ Tips

- If you try to move an object to a layer that is locked or hidden, PageMaker will warn you and ask whether you want to unlock and show the appropriate layers (**Figure 14.4**).

- Use cut and paste to move an object to another layer. Just cut the object, select the target layer, and paste.

- You can move objects from different layers to the same target layer with a single cut and paste sequence.

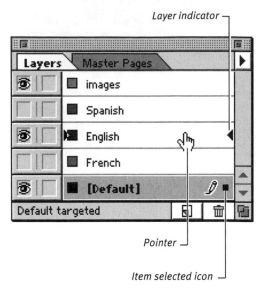

Layer indicator

Pointer

Item selected icon

Figure 14.3 In this figure, an item's icon is being draged to another layer. The pointer changes shape as you drag. Notice the triangle, which indicates that the English layer will receive the item.

> ⚠ **You are attempting to place, paste or drag into one or more layers that are locked or hidden. Do you want to unlock and show all appropriate layers?**
>
> [OK]　[Cancel]

Figure 14.4 You'll see this dialog box when you try to move an object to a locked or hidden layer.

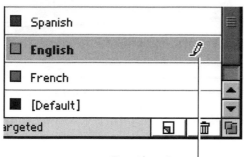

Target layer icon

Figure 14.5 The English layer is the target layer. All new objects will be "written" on this layer.

Creating an Object on a Layer

Once you've created a layer, it becomes the target layer. All new objects you create will be on that layer, until you select a new target layer. If you want to select another target layer, click on the name of the layer in the Layers palette.

To create an object on a specific layer:

1. Click on the layer in which you want to create an object.

   The layer you click on is highlighted. It displays a pencil icon, indicating that it is the target layer and all new objects will be written on this layer (**Figure 14.5**).

2. Create your object.

   If you create the object with a tool other than the Text tool, you'll see a little square to the right of the layer name, indicating that there is an object selected on that layer.

✔ Tip

- You can't create an object on a layer that's locked or hidden. If you try to, the pointer turns to a pencil with a slash through it to indicate that it can't make changes to that layer. Unlock or show the layer to create your object.

Removing a Layer

Removing layers that have objects on them can be tricky because all items on the layer can either be deleted or moved to another layer. Fortunately, the Edit > Undo command will restore deleted layers.

To remove a layer:

1. Select the layer you want to remove.

2. Click the trash can icon.

   Or drag the layer to the trash can.

   If there are objects on the layer you're removing, a dialog box will ask whether you want to delete those objects or move them to another layer (**Figure 14.6**).

✔ Tip

- Choose Delete Unused Layers from the Layers palette's pop-up menu to remove all layers that currently have no objects on them. PageMaker generates a dialog box for each of these layers (**Figure 14.7**). If you want, you can click the Yes to All button to delete all the "empty" layers at once.

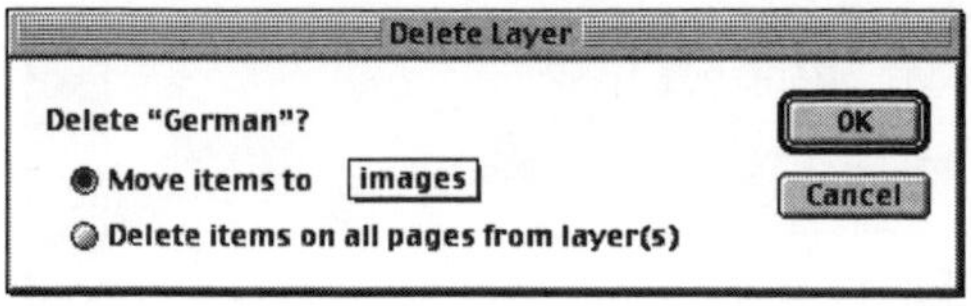

Figure 14.6 If you try to remove a layer that contains objects, you'll be asked to decide whether all objects should be deleted or moved to another layer.

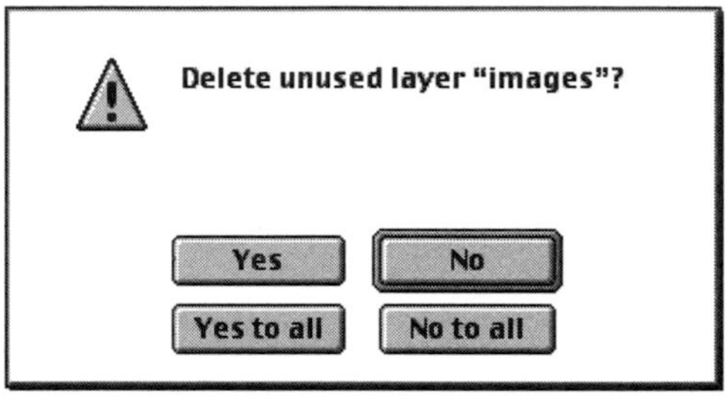

Figure 14.7 PageMaker asks you to confirm that you really want to delete all unused layers when you choose Delete Unused Layers.

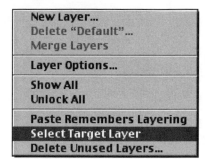

Figure 14.8 The Select Target Layer command selects all objects on the target layer.

Selecting All Objects on a Layer

PageMaker lets you quickly select all items from the same layer on a page or a two-page spread. Both permutations of this technique are described below.

To select all objects on a particular layer:

◆ Press Ctrl+Alt/Command+Option and click the name of the layer on which you want to select objects. Also press Shift if you want objects currently selected on other layers to remain selected.

All objects on the layer you clicked on are selected.

To select all objects on the target layer:

1. Click a layer in the Layers palette to make it the target layer.

2. Choose Select Target Layer from the Layers palette's pop-up menu (**Figure 14.8**).

All objects on the target layer are selected.

✔ Tip

■ This command will be unavailable unless you have the Pointer tool selected.

Locking Layers

Once you have the objects on a layer just the way you want them, you can lock the layer to prohibit their selection, so that they can't be mistakenly altered.

Locked layers have a lock icon in the box immediately to the left of their names (**Figure 14.9**).

To lock or unlock one layer at a time:

◆ Click the box immediately to the left of the layer name.

The lock icon (a pencil with a slash through it) appears.

✔ Tips

■ Click a second time to unlock the layer.

■ Drag up or down through the list to quickly lock or unlock other layers.

To lock all but the target layer:

1. With no layers locked, click a layer name to make it the target layer.

2. Choose Lock Others from the Layers palette's pop-up menu.

Or press Alt/Option while you click the box immediately to the left of the target layer's name.

The lock icon appears on all locked layers.

To unlock all layers:

◆ Choose Unlock All from the Layers palette's pop-up menu.

Or press Alt/Option while you click any lock icon.

All lock icons disappear.

✔ Tip

■ If you're clicking away madly on a page but find you can't highlight anything, check your Layers palette. You may have locked all your layers.

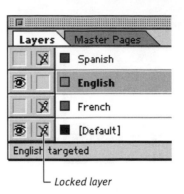

Locked layer

Figure 14.9 A pencil with a slash through it indicates a locked layer. Click on this icon to unlock a layer.

Visible layer

Figure 14.10 The eye icon indicates that the layer is visible. Click on this icon to hide a layer.

Hiding Layers

Obviously, hidden layers don't show in the document. What's not immediately obvious is that they don't print as part of the document or image if you generate a PDF.

An eye icon appears in the box furthest to the left of each visible layer's name (**Figure 14.10**).

To show one layer at a time:

◆ Click the box furthest to the left of the layer name.

The eye icon appears, indicating that the layer is visible.

✔ Tips

■ Click a second time to hide the layer.

■ Drag up or down through the list to quickly show or hide other layers.

To hide all layers but those selected in the palette:

1. Select the layer(s) you want to be visible.
   Shift-click to add a layer to the current selection.

2. Choose Hide Others from the Layers palette's pop-up menu.
   Or press Alt/Option while you click the eye icon for the selected layers.

To make all layers visible:

◆ Choose Show All from the Layers palette's pop-up menu.
   Or press Alt/Option while you click the box furthest to the left of any hidden layer.
   The eye icon appears beside each layer, indicating that they are all visible.

HIDING LAYERS

Layer Shuffling

Not only are layers good for organizing artwork, but they're also good for making sure certain objects stay in front of (or behind) other objects. The layers at the top of the list are placed on top of the layers below them.

Moving a layer up and down through the list lets you quickly place all text in front of all images (if you have text on one layer and images on another), or vice versa.

Layer shuffling functions like the stacking order (discussed in Chapter 13) on steroids. When you move layers backwards and forwards, whole groups of items move as one unit.

Keep in mind that layers work document-wide, so adjusting layer positions for specific pages only works if you've been very careful about placing items on the appropriate layers.

To shuffle a layer:

◆ Click and drag the layer you want to move up or down in the list.

When the indicator line is where you want the layer to be, release the mouse button (**Figure 14.10**).

The layer moves to the new location in the layer list.

✔ Tip

■ Stacking order for objects within a layer remains unchanged when you move layers.

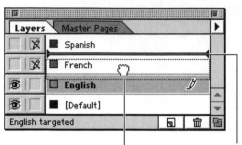

Layer is being dragged ⎯ *Layer will land here*

Figure 14.11 The English layer is being dragged between the Spanish and French layers. The thin gray bar with triangles on either end indicates where the layer will land.

LAYER SHUFFLING

WORKING WITH PAGES

While most of Adobe PageMaker's tools deal with composing pages, this chapter focuses on working with the pages themselves. In it, you'll learn how to insert new pages into a document, remove existing pages, move between pages, and sort pages in a large document.

Going to a Specific Page

PageMaker provides several methods for navigating the pages in your publication. You can move from one page or spread to another by using the Page Up and Page Down keys on your keyboard. This is probably the navigation method you'll use most often.

You can also click one of the page icons at the bottom left of the screen to go to a specific page. Or you can use the Go to Page dialog box. Though it may seem slower to use a dialog box, it can actually be faster in a long publication because the page icons may need to be scrolled so you can see the page icon you need (**Figure 15.1**).

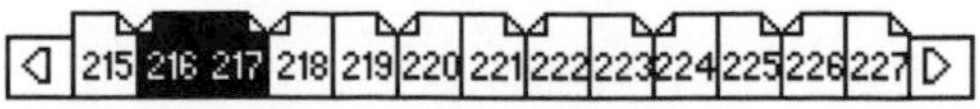

To go to a specific page in a document:

◆ Click the page number icon along the bottom left of your document window that corresponds to the page you want to view (**Figure 15.1**).

The page is displayed.

To go to a specific page in a document with the dialog box:

1. Choose Layout > Go to Page, or Ctrl+Alt+G/Command+Option+G.

    The Go to Page dialog box appears (**Figure 15.2**).

2. Type in the number of the page you want to view.

3. Click OK.

    The page is displayed.

✔ Tip

■ Use Layout > Go to Page as a slide show, by pressing Shift while you choose the command. Stop the slide show by clicking the mouse or pressing any key.

Figure 15.1 PageMaker's page icons have arrows at either end so you can scroll through the icons in a large document.

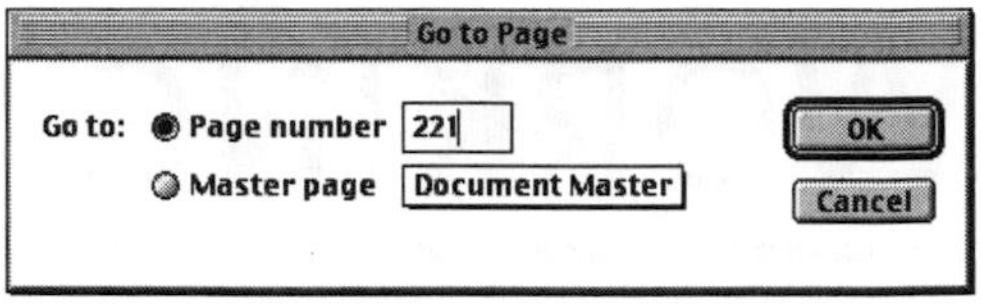

Figure 15.2 Type the number of the page you want to view in the Go to Page dialog box.

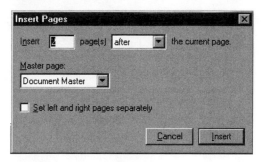

Figure 15.3 The Insert Pages dialog box lets you specify how many new pages to create and where to put them in the publication.

Inserting Pages

You'll often need to add pages to a document. PageMaker gives you lots of flexibility in creating new pages. You can insert pages before, after, or between the pages (spread only) you're currently viewing.

When you insert pages, PageMaker automatically renumbers the pages in your publication.

To insert pages:

1. Go to the page immediately before the pages you want to insert.

2. Choose Layout > Insert Pages.
   The Insert Pages dialog box appears (**Figure 15.3**).

3. Type the number of pages you want to insert.

4. To insert pages before the current page, choose 'before' from the pop-up menu to the right of the Insert page field.
   If you're working in a document with left/right page spreads, you can also choose 'between,' which puts the new pages between the current pages of the spread.

5. Click OK.
   The new pages are inserted in your publication.

✔ Tip

■ Use the Document Setup dialog box to change the Number of Pages option. For instance, add four pages by changing an eight-page document's Number of Pages to 12. When you add pages this way, PageMaker always puts the pages at the end of the document.

Removing Pages

Unused pages in a publication can easily be removed with a dialog box. The trick is remembering that all text and graphic objects on the pages you remove will be deleted along with the pages themselves. This can be disastrous if you remove pages that contain text blocks in a threaded story. To keep the story intact while deleting pages, just drag the bottom windowshade up to close each threaded text block on the page you're planning to delete. To preserve unthreaded text blocks or graphics, drag them to the pasteboard before removing pages.

To remove one or more pages:

1. Choose Layout > Remove Pages.
   The Remove Pages dialog box appears (**Figure 15.4**).

2. Type the page range you want to remove.
   To remove a single page, enter the same page number in the Remove page(s) and Through fields in the dialog box.

3. Click OK.

✔ Tips

- Use care when removing an odd number of pages from a double-sided publication. These pages are usually mirrored; that is, they have different inside and outside page margins. When you remove a single page or any odd number of pages, you'll find that your left-hand-page objects end up on a right-hand page, and vice versa.

- Use the Document Setup dialog box to change the Number of Pages option. For instance, remove two pages by changing an eight-page document's Number of Pages to six. When you remove pages this way, PageMaker always removes the pages from the end of the document.

Figure 15.4 Type the page range to remove pages using the Remove Pages dialog box.

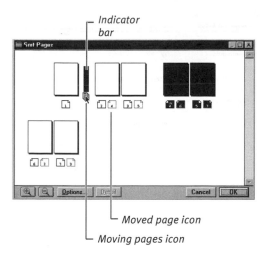

Indicator bar

Moved page icon

Moving pages icon

Figure 15.5 The Sort Pages dialog box lets you rearrange the order of the pages in your publication. In this figure, the page 2–3 spread is being moved to the end of the publication.

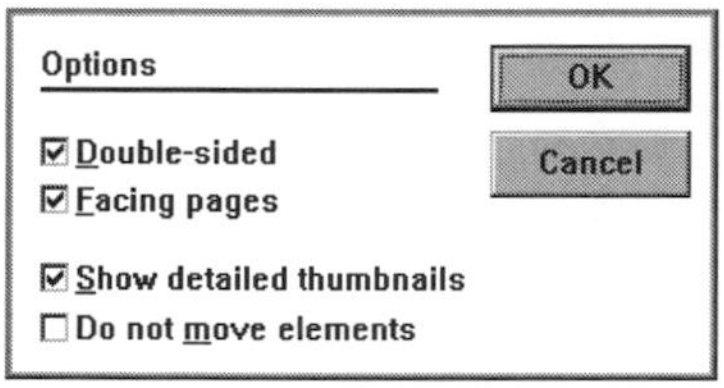

Figure 15.6 Use the Options dialog box to change the display of page icons in the Sort Pages dialog box.

Sorting Pages

PageMaker has a handy method for sorting pages in a document. For instance, you can quickly move your current page 3 between pages 4 and 5. If you're working with spreads, you can move pages 8–9 between the page 4–5 spread and the page 6–7 spread. This is all done with the Sort Pages dialog box.

Click the Options button in the Sort Pages dialog box to specify page display:

◆ Double-sided makes the first page of your publication a left-hand page.

◆ Facing pages shows thumbnails as spreads, and moves spread pages together.

◆ Show detailed thumbnails makes the icons display the elements on the page.

◆ Do not move elements will make all objects fit within the new page margins if you sort an even page to an odd position, or vice versa.

To sort pages:

1. Choose Layout > Sort Pages.

   The Sort Pages dialog box appears, showing all the pages in the current document **(Figure 15.5)**. Drag the lower-right corner of the dialog box to expand it.

2. Click the Options button to display the Options dialog box **(Figure 15.6)**.

3. Set the display options, then click OK.

4. Click the page (or spread) you want to move, and drag it to its new location.

   The page moves between those pages, as indicated by an icon **(Figure 15.5)**.

   Select more than one page (or spread) at a time by Shift-clicking additional pages.

5. Click the OK button.

   The pages are rearranged. This may take a few seconds. Scan your pages to make sure everything is in order.

SORTING PAGES

Changing the Start Page of a Publication

When you're creating a lengthy publication, like a book, you may want to break the book up into chapters to make it easier to work with. To do this, however, you need to be able to start Chapter Two's page numbering at the proper page. Use the Document Setup dialog box to change a publication's page numbering.

To change the starting page number in a document:

1. Choose File > Document Setup, or Ctrl+Shift+P/Command+Shift+P.

   The Document Setup dialog box appears (**Figure 15.7**).

2. Enter a different Start page number.

3. Click OK.

   The document's page numbers change to reflect the new start page.

✔ Tips

■ If you're working on a document that uses spreads (mirror pages), make sure your first page is an odd number. It's customary to use even numbers on the left page and odd numbers on the right page of most printed documents.

■ Use the technique of dividing parts of a book into separate PageMaker documents to number those parts of your publication (Table of Contents, Index, Appendix) separately from the main body of text. The Numbers button (in the Document Setup dialog box) gives you options for numbering systems in a publication (**Figure 15.8**).

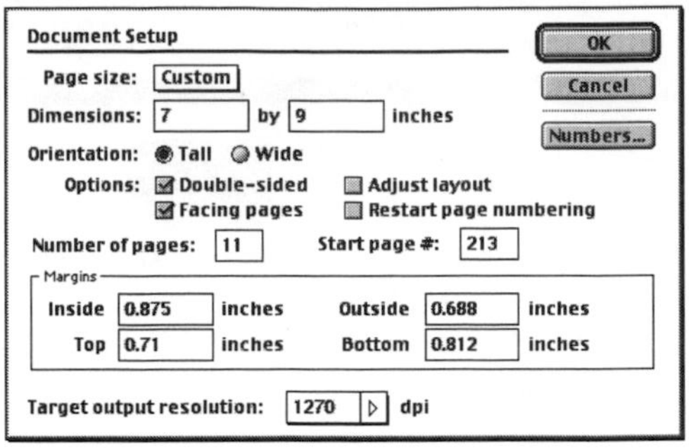

Figure 15.7 Use the Start Page # option in the Document Setup dialog box to renumber the pages in a publication.

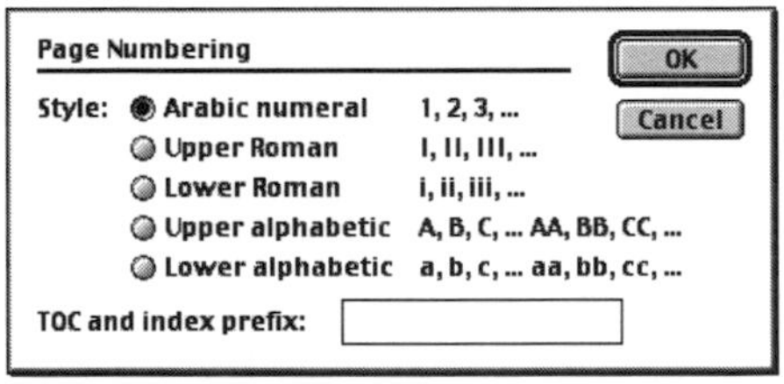

Figure 15.8 The Page Numbering dialog box lets you number different parts of your publication using different numbering systems.

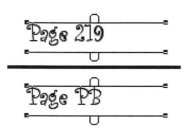

Figure 15.9 Automatic page numbering behaves differently depending on where it's placed in the publication. Above, the same text block is copied at the bottom of the page and on the pasteboard. On the page, the proper page number is displayed. On the pasteboard, the abbreviation "PB" is displayed.

Automatic Page Numbering

You don't have to 'hard code' a page number on every page in your document. Use a special keyboard command to let PageMaker automatically renumber your pages if you insert, remove, or sort them in your publication.

To place a page number on a page:

1. Using the Text tool, click where you want the page number to be.

   Type 'Page' if you want your page number to start with that word.

2. Press Ctrl+Alt+P/Command+Option+P.

   The current page number appears (**Figure 15.8**).

   If you change the Start page number, or sort your pages, or insert or remove pages, the page number is adjusted to reflect the correct number.

✔ Tips

- Format the page number text block just as you would any other text block in the publication.

- You can place a page number text block on any page in a publication. However, this feature is best used on a Master Page in a document. See Chapter 16 for more details on using Master Pages.

MASTER PAGES

Master pages in Adobe PageMaker contain objects that appear on each page in the document. In this book, we use many Master Page elements: the thumbtab backgrounds, chapter titles, page numbers, and headers.

Using Master Pages does three great things for your publications. It shortens the amount of time you have to spend doing tedious tasks, because you don't have to create the same objects repeatedly on subsequent pages.

Using Master Pages unifies each publication because you can't accidentally forget an element or make it slightly different on a individual page. All pages that share the same Master Page will show all the elements, so there won't be any deviation from form.

Finally, if you want to tweak your design, you can change all the pages in the document just by changing what is on the Master Page.

PageMaker even allows you to create multiple Master Pages, so that you can have several independently consistent styles within a single document.

Chapter 16

Understanding Master Pages

PageMaker uses Master Pages to create an uneditable background for each document page. When you put an element on a Master Page, it will appear on any page to which that Master is applied. Elements that will change on a given page must be created on the page, not on a Master.

By default, each new page you create has a Master called [Document Master] applied to it. You can change the Master that is to be applied to any new page or spread, or you can apply [None], which means that no Master will be applied.

When producing this book, I used two Master Pages: one for each chapter's opening page, and one for all other spreads. The Spread Master, an edited version of [Document Master], contains the shaded boxes for thumbtabs, along with the running heads, running head rules, and folios (page numbers) for each page (**Figure 16.1**).

The Chapter Opener Master contains the chapter title and number, a thumbtab, and a page number on the right page of the spread (**Figure 16.2**). Notice that the left page is blank. Our chapters always begin on right-hand pages, so we never need to apply the left page of the Chapter Opener Master.

✔ Tip

- Use Power Paste (Ctrl+Alt+V/Command+ Option+V) to paste an object at the same location on a series of pages. I used Power Paste to create the text for my thumbtabs throughout my documents. See Chapter 13 for more details on Power Paste.

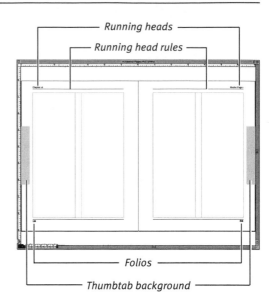

Figure 16.1 The [Document Master] from this book.

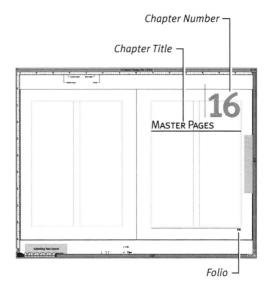

Figure 16.2 The Chapter Opener Master from this book.

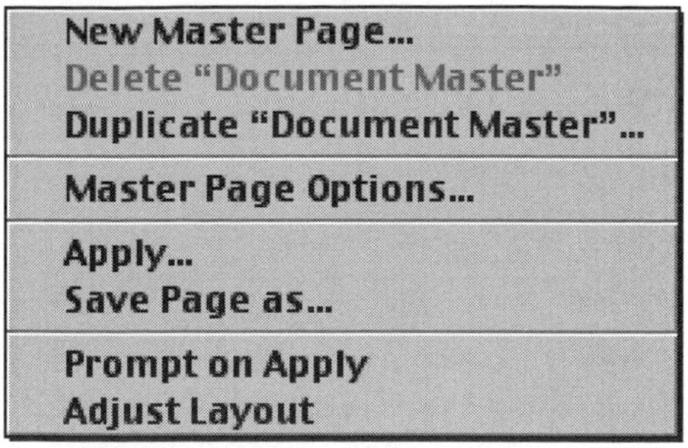

New Master Page...
Delete "Document Master"
Duplicate "Document Master"...

Master Page Options...

Apply...
Save Page as...

Prompt on Apply
Adjust Layout

Figure 16.3 The Master Pages palette contains a pop-up menu that centralizes the commands you'll need to work with Master Pages.

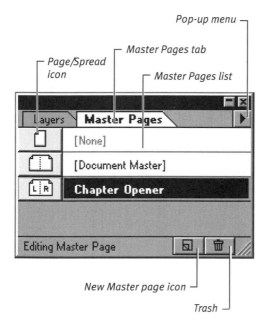

Pop-up menu

Master Pages tab

Page/Spread icon

Master Pages list

Layers | **Master Pages**

☐ [None]

☐ [Document Master]

L R **Chapter Opener**

Editing Master Page

New Master page icon

Trash

Figure 16.4 The Master Pages palette organizes all the commands you'll need to work with Master Pages.

Showing the Master Pages Palette

The Master Pages palette organizes all the commands you'll need to work with Master Pages. You can create, edit, and apply Master Pages to document pages using icons and commands found in the palette.

Like the other palettes in PageMaker, the Master Pages palette has a pop-up menu that centralizes the commands you'll need to work with Master Pages. This menu lets you create a new Master Page, duplicate an existing Master Page, set options for the Master Pages, apply Master Pages to a range of pages, and other features (**Figure 16.3**).

To display the Master Pages palette:

◆ Choose Window > Show Master Pages, or Ctrl+Alt+8/Command+Option+8.

The Master Pages palette appears (**Figure 16.4**).

Creating Master Pages

By default, all PageMaker documents have a Master Page already created, called [Document Master]. Most documents, particularly those with special opening pages, like newspapers or books, will require more than one Master Page.

When you create a new Master Page, you'll be asked to name the new Master and set its margins and column guides. You can also create the new Master as a single page or as a spread.

To create a new Master Page:

1. Click the New Master Page button in the Master Pages palette.

   The New Master Page dialog box appears (**Figure 16.5**).

2. Enter the name of the new Master Page in the Name field.

3. Make the appropriate changes in the Margins and Column Guides fields.

4. Click OK.

   A new Master Page appears in the Master Pages palette, and the view switches to the new Master Page you've just created.

5. Make the appropriate additions and edits to the Master Page.

✔ Tip

■ Being whisked away to the new Master Page can be disorienting if you aren't expecting the switch. It may seem as if all the elements on the page you were working on have disappeared. Remember, the page you were working on is still there, you just have to click its page icon to see it.

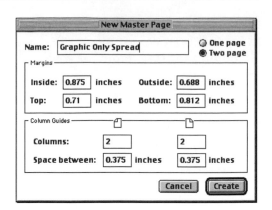

Figure 16.5 The New Master Page dialog box lets you name the new Master and set its margins, column guides and whether or not it's a spread.

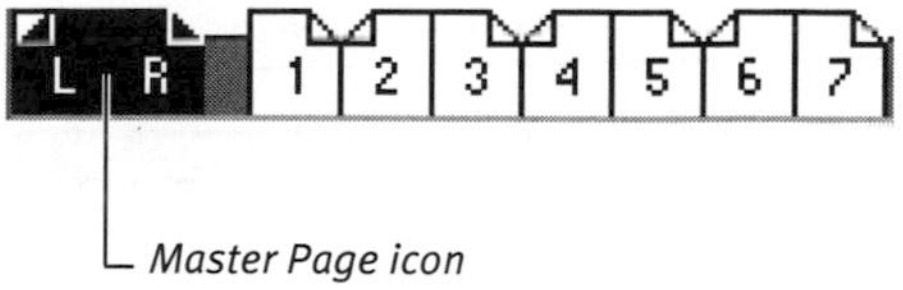

— *Master Page icon*

Figure 16.6 The Master Page icon appears to the left of the regular page icons. Click the Master Page icon to view a Master Page.

Adding Objects to a Master Page

In a brand new document, the [Document Master] is blank. You have to create all the elements you need for each Master. Create and format objects on a Master Page just as you would on a normal page. You can apply all formatting commands that are normally available to objects on Master Pages.

Just make sure you're working on the appropriate Master Page. Check the Master Pages palette to see which Master is active. If the one you want to work on isn't active, just click the proper one in the list of Master Pages.

To add an item to a Master Page:

1. Click the Master Page icons (the pages with an L or R in them) at the bottom left of the document window (**Figure 16.6**).

   The document window displays the Master Pages for that document. In a new document, the Master Page, called [Document Master], is blank.

2. Click a Master Page in the Master Pages palette to work on a different Master.

3. Using any of PageMaker's tools, add text, create an object, or place an image.

4. Return to the document by clicking any page icon along the bottom left of the document window.

✔ Tips

■ The Page Down key on your keyboard takes you from a Master Page back to the page you were viewing, if you haven't switched Masters. If you have switched Masters, you'll go to the first page that has the new Master applied.

■ When Double-sided pages (see File > Document Setup) is turned on there are two Master Page icons. If Double-sided is off, you'll only have one Master Page icon.

Applying a Master Page

It's a good idea to use [Document Master] as your main Master, since all new pages or spreads you create will have [Document Master] applied automatically. You can specify a different Master when you create new pages or spreads with the Insert Pages dialog box. If you forget to set this option, or if you just want to change the Master you've applied to a page or spread, click the proper Master in the Master Pages palette.

To apply a Master Page:

◆ Click the Master Page (in the Master Pages palette) that you want to apply (**Figure 16.7**).

The Master you clicked is applied to the current page or spread.

✔ Tip

■ Click [None] if you want a page or spread to have no Master applied to it.

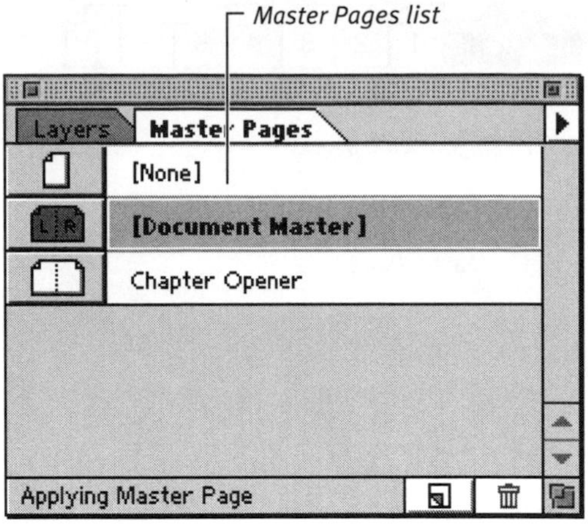

Master Pages list

Figure 16.7 Apply a Master by clicking on an item in the Master Pages palette list.

APPLYING A MASTER PAGE

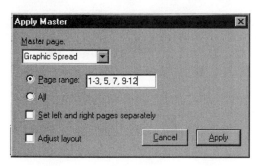

Figure 16.8 The Apply Master dialog box lets you apply a single Master Page to many pages or spreads at once.

Applying a Master Page to Multiple Pages

When you create a new Master Page, you may need to apply it to many pages in your document at one time. It would be tedious to page through a long document and click an item in the Master Pages list once for every page or spread that needs the Master applied to it. There is a shorter way to apply a single Master Page to many pages or spreads at once.

To apply a Master Page to multiple pages:

1. Choose Apply from the Master Pages palette menu.

   The Apply Master dialog box appears (**Figure 16.8**).

2. Type the range of pages that you want to apply Master Pages to.

3. Set the Master Page option to the Master you want to apply.

   To apply a single Master, select its name from the Master Pages pop-up menu.

   If the publication is double-sided, and you want to apply one Master to all left-hand pages in the range and another Master to all right-hand pages, check the Set Left and Right Pages Separately check box, then select the Masters you want to apply.

4. Check the Adjust Layout check box if you want objects and guides on the specified pages to be repositioned or resized, as appropriate, for the margins and columns of the Master you are about to apply.

5. Click Apply.

✔ Tip

■ You can get creative with page ranges, so long as you follow a couple of rules of thumb: Separate page ranges with a hyphen, and separate noncontiguous pages with a comma (**Figure 16.8**).

Duplicating a Master Page

Since you can't customize Master Page items on individual pages, it's sometimes efficient to duplicate an existing Master and edit an item for a small number of pages or spreads. You don't want to overdo this technique, however. It defeats the purpose of a Master Page if you end up creating a new Master for every page in the document.

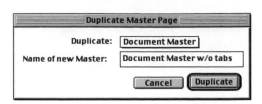

Figure 16.9 The Duplicate Master Page dialog box lets you rename the new Master as it's created.

To duplicate a Master Page:

1. In the Master Pages palette, drag the name of the Master Page you want to duplicate to the New Master Page icon.

   The Duplicate Master Page dialog box appears (**Figure 16.9**).

2. Name the new Master Page.

3. Click the Duplicate button.

   The duplicate of the Master Page appears in the palette.

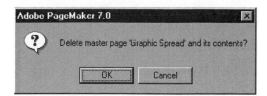

Figure 16.10 PageMaker asks you to confirm that you want to delete a Master Page when you drag it to the Trash icon.

Deleting a Master Page

Deleting a Master Page is just as easy as creating one. Just drag it to the Trash icon.

To delete a Master Page:

1. In the Master Pages palette, choose the Master Page you want to delete and drag it to the trash can icon in the palette.

   A warning dialog box appears, asking if you're sure you want to delete the Master Page (**Figure 16.10**).

2. Click OK.

   The Master Page is deleted.

   Any document pages that used that Master Page will have all Master Page items removed from those pages, but will otherwise remain the same.

✔ Tip

- You can't delete the item [None] or the [Document Master].

Displaying Master Page Items

Sometimes you want to apply a Master Page to a page in your document, but you don't want those items to display onscreen, to print, or to image when you generate a PDF file. For instance, if there is no text on the last page of the Visual QuickStart Guide's chapters, we don't put the Master Page items on the page either. In other words, we don't print the folios or thumbtab backgrounds. I could set the Master to [None], but then I'd have to reapply a Master if I add a page to the spread later. It's easier just to turn off the display of the Master Page items.

To turn off Master Page items on a document page:

1. Make sure the page on which you want to suppress the Master Page items is the current page.

Use the page icons near the bottom left of the screen.

2. Choose View > Display Master Items.

The Master Page items are hidden.

Figure 16.11 shows this page without the Master Page items displayed.

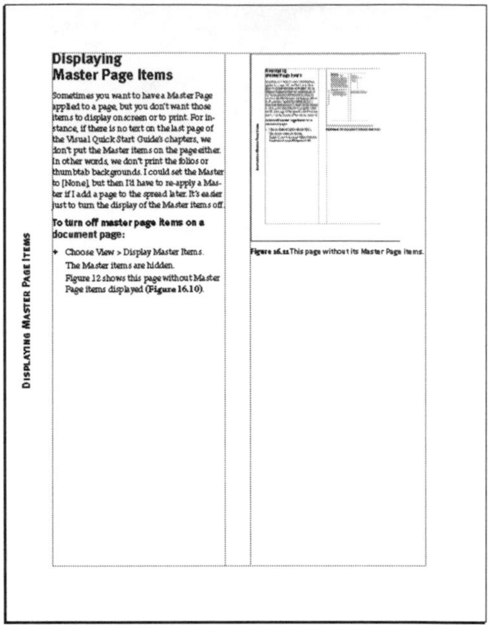

Figure 16.11 This page without its Master Page items.

MERGING DATA

At first glance, data merges may not seem like appropriate tasks for a page layout program. After all, word processing programs have long been used for merging data with text to produce mailing lists and form letters. But when you use a word processor to do a data merge, you're limited by its capabilities. Adobe PageMaker allows you to combine its sophisticated design tools with the brute force of a data merge, giving you a publishing powerhouse that can automate the creation of sophisticated documents.

In this chapter, we'll discuss general information about data merges, then look at how PageMaker handles the task. To make the most of this chapter, you'll want to read it sequentially. Follow the steps from page to page, and the learning process will go more smoothly.

Understanding Data Merges

Data merges may sound complicated, but they aren't tough once a few terms are defined.

First, a database is just a place to store specific information, like a contacts list or an inventory. Data is usually stored in a database file, but can also be stored in a spreadsheet or even a word-processing file that's been formatted with tabs or tables. For this chapter, we'll work on a form letter that needs to be sent to each customer in our database. The file that contains our customer contact information will be called the "data source file."

The data in our file is broken up into manageable bits, called fields and records. Fields are designated categories of information: for instance, First Name, Last Name, Street Address, City, State, and Zip. The combined information from each field, i.e., one person's full name and complete address, is called a record.

PageMaker doesn't work directly with database or spreadsheet files themselves, but it can extract data from a file that's been exported from the database or spreadsheet. When you export this file, you'll need to format it properly (**Figure 17.1**).

PageMaker uses comma-delimited data, meaning that the information fields in each record are separated by commas and enclosed within double quotes. The records are separated by line breaks (¶). This delimited file will become your data source file. Check your database program's manual for more information on exporting a comma-delimited file.

Figure 17.1 The upper image is a database file. The text file in the lower image shows comma-delimited data that's been exported from the database.

Figure 17.2 The target publication contains all the material that's common to each of the letters we'll create in our form letter.

Next, we'll need to define the term "target publication." This is the PageMaker document containing all the elements that are common to each of our letters: the date, the return address at the top of the letter, the "Dear" part of the salutation, the body of the letter, and any other boilerplate information (**Figure 17.2**). You can use any of PageMaker's design features to create your target publication.

In your target publication, you'll insert fields that act as placeholders for the information taken from the data source file.

When we're ready to create our form letter, we'll merge the data source file with the target publication. The data merge will create a third file, which we'll call the "merged publication." If our example form letter was a single page, merged with 150 customers, we'd end up with a 150-page merged publication—that is, one page for each letter.

Once you have created your merged document, you can print any or all of the pages, just as you would with any other publication.

Creating Data Source Files

Most often, you'll use an existing database or spreadsheet file to create your data source file. But it is also possible to create the file from scratch. Type your data in a word-processor file, separating the fields with commas and enclosing the data in double quotes. Each record must be separated by a paragraph return (**Figure 17.3**). When you save the file, make sure to save it in .txt format.

In other cases, your database file may export properly formatted comma-delimited data, but will not include field names in the first line of the file. In these instances you'll need to type in the field names, followed by a paragraph return—this will become the first "record." Field names are not enclosed in double quotes (**Figure 17.3**).

The basic details to watch for in your data source file are:

◆ Comma-delimited data

◆ Unique, easy-to-understand field names

◆ File exported or saved in .txt format

To create a data source file:

1. Using the original application, open the spreadsheet or database file that contains the data you want to use.

2. Check to make sure the file is properly organized for the data merge.

   In spreadsheet files, the names in the top row become the data field names. In database files, the table field names become the data field names.

3. Use the program's Save As feature to save the file as a comma-delimited file.

   Some programs also use the term "Merge" to designate the proper format. Check the program's user guide or do test exports before running your data merge.

Figure 17.3 The first line of the data source file must contain the field names, which are delimited like the data that follows. Field names are not enclosed in double quotes, however.

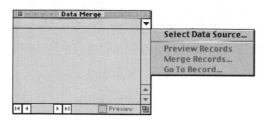

Figure 17.4 Use the Data Merge palette's pop-up menu to select a data source file.

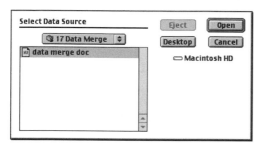

Figure 17.5 The Select Data Source dialog box lets you find and select the data source file.

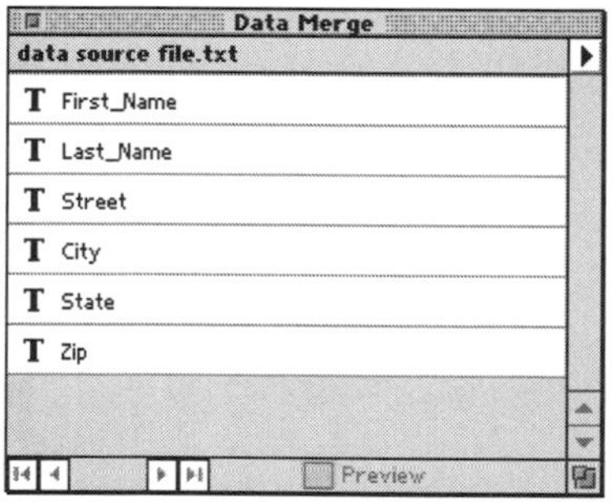

Figure 17.6 The data source file's fields appear in the Data Merge palette.

Selecting a Data Source

Once you've created your data source file, you can begin designing your target publication. Use any of PageMaker's design tools to create your document. In the example below we'll use a simple, single-page form letter. But you can also use data merges to create complex documents like product catalogs or pictorial directories.

When you've finished creating your target publication, use the Data Merge palette to select a data source. There can be only one data source file per target publication.

Your data source file can be stored anywhere on your computer system, but it's often easier to find if you move it into the same folder with your target publication.

To select a data source:

1. Create or open the target publication.

2. Choose Window > Plug-in Palettes > Show Data Merge Palette.

   The Data Merge palette appears, with no information.

3. Choose Select Data Source from the Data Merge palette menu (**Figure 17.4**).

   The Select Data Source dialog box appears (**Figure 17.5**).

4. Navigate to the data source file and click Open.

   The field names appear in the Data Merge palette (**Figure 17.6**).

   If an alert message appears or if incorrect fields appear in the Data Merge palette, open the data source file and check the data to make sure it's properly formatted. See the previous page for more details.

Inserting Field Placeholders

Your target publication will contain field placeholders that change for each merged document. For instance, in our form letter example we would type the word "Dear" followed by a space and a field placeholder for each person's first name.

Insert a field placeholder in each location within the target publication where you want data from a field to appear.

To insert a field placeholder:

1. Working in the target publication, click in a text block where you want the field placeholder to appear, or select text you want to replace.

2. Click the text field name in the Data Merge palette.

    The field placeholder appears within double angle brackets (<<First_Name>>) formatted with the attributes of the surrounding text (**Figure 17.7**).

✔ Tips

■ You can change data source files after you've inserted field placeholders, but if you do, PageMaker may not recognize the fields. It's usually best to delete and re-insert placeholders in this case.

■ It may seem like you could save time by manually typing the brackets and field names. Unfortunately, this won't work. You must use the Data Merge palette to insert field placeholders.

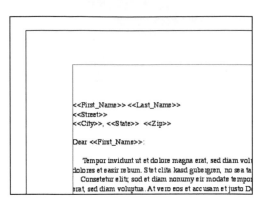

Figure 17.7 Field placeholders in a target publication.

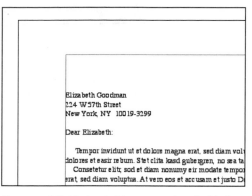

Figure 17.8 Field placeholders are replaced with data from the first record in your data source file when you preview the data.

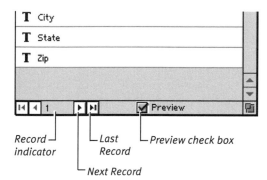

Record indicator — Last Record — Preview check box

— Next Record

Figure 17.9 Use the Next Record and Last Record navigation buttons to scan through all the records in your merged document.

Previewing the Data

It's a good idea to check your data before performing the merge. You want to make sure all the elements will appear properly. When you preview the data, the field placeholders are replaced by data from the first record in the data source file. For instance, you might see "Elizabeth" in place of the <<First_Name>> field placeholder.

To preview records:

1. Choose Preview Records from the Data Merge palette pop-up menu.

   Data from the first record in the data source file appears in your target ublication (**Figure 17.8**).

2. Click the navigation buttons to cycle through data from different records (**Figure 17.9**).

✔ Tips

- If the preview is incomplete or data is missing, there is a problem in the data source file. Check the file names first, as these are the source of most previewing errors.

- Go to the data source file to correct any mistakes you find in the records.

- You can also preview your records by clicking the Preview check box at the bottom of the Data Merge palette (**Figure 17.9**).

Viewing a Specific Record

Often you may have a question about a specific record, and want to check it without scrolling through hundreds of other records. Or you might want to spot-check information in a data source file that contains thousands of records. In such cases it's helpful to be able to call up specific records.

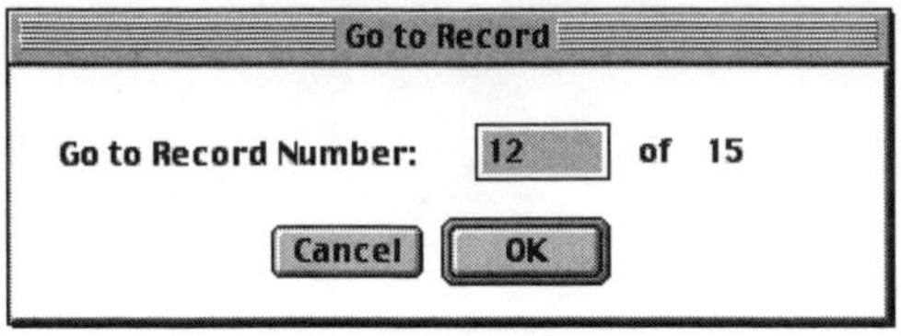

Figure 17.10 The Go to Record dialog box.

To go to a specific record:

1. Choose Go to Record from the Data Merge palette pop-up menu.

   The Go to Record dialog box appears (**Figure 17.10**).

2. Type the number of the record you want to preview.

3. Click OK.

✔ Tips

■ Any errors in the list of fields, such as typos, empty fields, and unintended field types, should be corrected in the source application.

■ You can also preview a specific record by clicking the record number between the navigation buttons at the bottom of the palette. When the current number highlights, type the record number you want to preview, then press Enter.

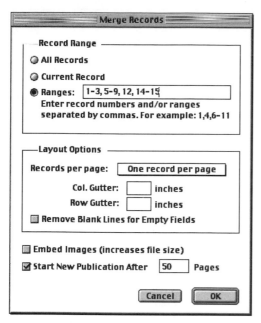

Figure 17.11 The Merge Records dialog box.

Merging Records

Once you've previewed the data and corrected any problems you noted, you're ready to create your merged document. When you merge the data source and the target publication, PageMaker creates a third document that contains one iteration of the target material for each record in the data source file.

These options are available in the Merge Records dialog box (**Figure 17.11**):

◆ **All Records** creates one iteration of the target material for each record in the data source file.

◆ **Current Record** creates a single iteration of the target material for the record that's being previewed in the target publication.

◆ **Ranges** allows you to specify a range of records to merge. As with other page range fields in PageMaker, you can specify non-contiguous record ranges.

◆ **Records per page** lets you determine whether each iteration begins at the top of a new page, or whether the merged document will follow the manual layout in the target publication.

◆ **Column Gutter** and **Row Gutter** let you specify a width for gutters if you're merging several records onto a single page.

◆ **Remove Blank Lines for Empty Fields** closes up horizontal space if a field is empty. This is especially useful for optional fields, like Company Name or the second line of a street address.

◆ **Embed Images** will embed images in the publication instead of linking to them. As indicated, the file's size will increase if images are embedded.

◆ **Start New Publication After** lets you set the maximum page length for your resulting documents.

(continued on next page)

To merge records:

1. Working in the target publication, choose Merge Records from the Data Merge palette menu, or choose Utilities > Plug-ins > Merge Records.

   The Merge Records dialog box appears

2. Set the proper options in the Record Range area.

3. Set the proper options in the Layout Options area. Enter gutter measurements, if applicable.

4. Check Remove Blank Lines for Empty Fields, if applicable.

5. Set the proper option for Embed Images.

6. Enter the proper page number for Start New Publication After.

7. Click OK.

   PageMaker will create the merged publication, using the records from the data source file, the text in the target publication, and your specifications from the Merge Records dialog box.

✔ Tips

- Save time by reusing the target publication. You can edit it, including field placeholders, and perform another merge without starting the process from scratch.

- Sometimes it makes sense to merge all the records in your source file rather than select a range of records to merge. That way the work is already done, should you need those records merged later. Remember, you don't have print every page in the merged publication.

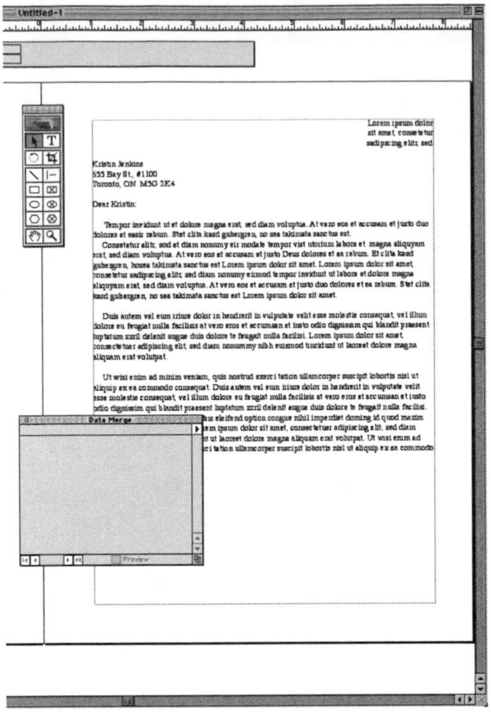

Figure 17.12 The merged publication contains one page for every record specified in the merge. Notice that the Data Merge palette is empty in the new pubication. This is normal.

MERGING RECORDS

BOOK FUNCTIONS

Adobe PageMaker has extraordinary capabilities for handling long documents. You can link documents together to form a book, allowing page numbers to be automatically updated when pages in individual documents are added or removed. PageMaker's book application also keeps track of items in a table of contents, and can automatically index words for you.

Creating a Book Publication List

Theoretically, PageMaker can manage documents that are several hundred pages long, but this isn't practical. For a start, opening, saving, and navigating through a giant document can make some of PageMaker's functions grind to a halt. Second, PageMaker documents that are too large may become unstable or corrupted.

Instead of working with a single massive file, I created a separate PageMaker document for each chapter in this book. At the end of this process I'll create a book list, then generate a table of contents and an index, each of which will be created as separate publications.

To set a Book publication list:

1. Choose Utilities > Book.

   The Book publication list dialog box appears.

   You can make a Book publication list in any chapter of your publication, but it's usually best to put it in the first chapter of the book.

2. Find each chapter file that you want to add to the book, and click the Insert button.

   The document will be added to the list on the right side of the dialog box (**Figure 18.1**).

   This list should match the intended order of the book, e.g., Chapter 1, Chapter 2, Chapter 3, and so on.

3. Click OK.

✔ Tip

■ If a publication's contents aren't in correct order, click the chapter that's out of order, then use the Move up or Move down buttons to rearrange the items in the list.

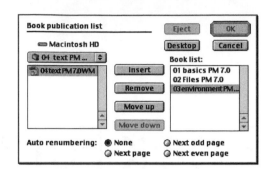

Figure 18.1 The Book publication list dialog box.

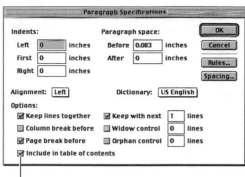

TOC option

Figure 18.2 Make sure the Include in table of contents option is chosen for the paragraph style you want to use to generate your table of contents.

Creating a Table of Contents Style

PageMaker's Table of Contents feature works with Styles. When you generate a table of contents (TOC), PageMaker searches the entire publication (or Book publication list) for all paragraphs formatted with a style option that includes the paragraph in the TOC. If you create this style before you begin designing or laying out your publication, the TOC will essentially be generated at the same time you are compiling the document. Once it's done, you simply instruct PageMaker to gather the paragraphs that will make up the TOC.

In this book, the style used at the top of this column is formatted for inclusion in the book's TOC. We knew at the start that a TOC would be needed, so all of the chapters were created from the same template with identical styles. If you aren't able to plan ahead, you can still add the "Include in table of contents" option to a style at any time. You may have to repeat the process in several publications, if you're using a Book publication list.

To create a table of contents style:

1. In the Styles palette, double-click the style you want to use for your table of contents paragraphs.

   The Style Options dialog box appears.

2. Click the Para button.

   The Paragraph Specifications dialog box appears (**Figure 18.2**).

3. Check the "Include in table of contents" check box, and click OK to exit the Paragraph Specifications dialog box, then click OK to exit the Style Options dialog box.

   Or hold down the Alt/Option key while you click the first OK to exit all dialog boxes at once.

   All text formatted with this style will be included in the table of contents.

Creating a Table of Contents

Whether you're generating a table of contents from a single publication or from many files linked by a Book publication list, the process is the same. When you generate the TOC, PageMaker searches the publication (or publications) for all paragraphs formatted for inclusion in the table of contents. Each paragraph, and the page number the paragraph appears on, are pulled out and compiled into a story, which you can place in your publication just like any other story.

When creating a TOC from multiple publications using a book list, make sure the first publication in the series is active when you begin the process. If you issue the command from a later publication, earlier TOC entries may be skipped.

Once you've created the TOC, it'll have to be placed. It's often placed in the document in which it was created. In this case, you'll usually insert new pages at the beginning of the document. Or see the following section ("Creating a New Publication for the Table of Contents") for details on putting the TOC in a separate publication.

◆ **Replace Existing Table of Contents** replaces an existing table of contents with the table of contents you are generating. This item is grayed out when there is no existing TOC.

◆ **Include Book Publications** creates one table of contents for all publications in the book list, and renumbers the book's pages.

◆ **Include Text on Hidden Layers** includes paragraphs on hidden layers in your TOC.

◆ **Format** lets you decide whether to include a page number with each paragraph in the TOC, and if so, whether the page number appears before or after the entry.

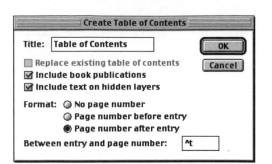

Figure 18.3 The Create Table of Contents dialog box.

Figure 18.4 The loaded text icon.

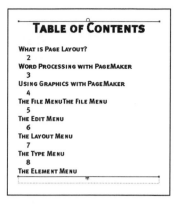

Figure 18.5 The Table of Contents story, as it is flowed onto the PageMaker publication.

TOC title	⌐Table of Contents
TOC Head 1	⌐What is Page Layout? ↑2
TOC Head 1	⌐Word Processing with PageMaker ↑3
TOC Head 1	⌐Using Graphics with PageMaker ↑4
TOC Head 1	⌐The File MenuThe File Menu ↑5
TOC Head 1	⌐The Edit Menu ↑6
TOC Head 1	⌐The Layout Menu ↑7
TOC Head 1	⌐The Type Menu ↑8
TOC Head 1	⌐The Element Menu ↑9
TOC Head 1	⌐The Utilities Menu ↑10
TOC Head 1	⌐The View Menu ↑11
TOC Head 1	⌐The Window Menu ↑12
TOC Head 1	⌐The Help Menu ↑13
TOC Head 1	⌐Launching PageMaker ↑16

Window title: 18 Book Functions PM 7 WM:Table of Contents:1

Figure 18.6 The TOC story as it appears in the Story Editor. Notice the new styles that are created along with the TOC story.

◆ **Between entry and page number** lets you put virtually any character you like in this space. The most frequently used is a tab, the symbol for which is seen in **Figure 18.3**.

To create a table of contents:

1. Choose Utilities > Create TOC.

   The Create Table of Contents dialog box appears (**Figure 18.3**).

2. Set options as desired and click OK.

   In a publication that uses a Book publication list, PageMaker repaginates all the publications in the book list, gathering TOC entries from each one.

   Your cursor changes into the loaded text icon (**Figure 18.4**).

3. Click the column where you want to place your TOC.

   A table of contents story is flowed onto the page (**Figure 18.5**).

✔ Tips

- The TOC story uses two new styles that were created as the TOC was generated (**Figure 18.6**). The first, for the heading of the TOC, is called TOC title. The second new style is based on the paragraph that was formatted to be included in the TOC. Its name will be TOC, plus the name of the style it is based on, for example, TOC Head. You will almost always want to edit this new style. Use the techniques described in the Style chapter to edit the new TOC style.

- TOC page number references are not dynamic. That is, if you edit text after you've created a Table of Contents story, the TOC will not be updated to reflect any page number changes. You'll need to generate another TOC to ensure the page number references are correct.

Creating a New Publication for the Table of Contents

In a Book publication project, where you have many files linked together to make up a book, you'll want to create a separate publication for your newly created table of contents. First you'll follow the normal process for creating a TOC, then you'll create a new publication and move the TOC story into it. You could just copy and paste, but as usual PageMaker provides a better way. You can actually place any PageMaker story from another PageMaker publication.

To create a new publication for the table of contents:

1. Follow Steps 1–2 under "To create a table of contents."

2. Click the pasteboard of your document to place the TOC story.

   Don't worry about displaying the whole story, or even making it look good. Just make sure that it is properly placed as a story in the publication.

3. Create or open a new publication for your TOC.

4. Choose File > Place.

   The Place Document dialog box appears.

5. Select the publication that contains your TOC story.

   The PageMaker Story Importer dialog box appears (**Figure 18.7**).

   The dialog box lists all the stories in the PageMaker publication you've selected. It may be helpful to change the "List only stories over" option and then click Relist, so that the list only shows the longest stories in the publication.

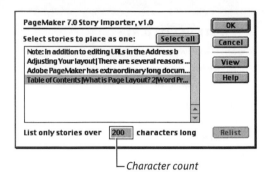

— *Character count*

Figure 18.7 The PageMaker Story Importer filter dialog box. Change the character count field to display fewer stories and make it easier to find the story you need to place.

Figure 18.8 The loaded text icon.

6. Select the Table of Contents story from the list.

7. Click OK.

The pointer changes into the loaded text icon (**Figure 18.8**).

8. Click in the new publication to place the TOC story.

The TOC and its new styles are imported into the new publication.

9. Edit the styles, if appropriate.

10. In the original publication (the one from which you generated the TOC), delete the TOC story.

✔ Tips

■ Follow Steps 3–8 any time you want to place a story from one PageMaker publication into another. This process can serve as a last-ditch resort if a publication file gets corrupted and can't be opened. You can often place stories from a corrupted publication even if it won't open.

■ To re-create an entire publication quickly, use the Select All button in the Story Importer dialog box. All the stories will be combined into a single story, which you can flow into a new document. The results aren't pretty, but in an emergency it may still beat re-creating a document from scratch.

CREATING A NEW PUBLICATION FOR THE TOC

Creating an Index Entry

When your document is finished, or close enough to being finished that you don't expect any more major editing, select words or phrases throughout the publication(s) to mark them as index entries.

An index entry can refer to a single page or to a range of pages:

◆ **Current Page** is the most common option for simple indexes. This page reference will always be for the specific page where the index entry occurs.

◆ **To Next Style Change** marks a page range that includes all subsequent paragraphs with the same paragraph style. The page range ends at the first instance of a different style.

◆ **To Next Use of Style** page range ends at the next occurrence of a given paragraph style, selected by you from the pop-up menu.

◆ **For the Next __ Paragraphs** is useful when you know exactly how many paragraphs to mark for the entry.

◆ **Suppress Page Range** can be used to temporarily leave out the page range for an entry. Most commonly, you'll change this to another option before creating your final index.

◆ **Page # override** changes the style of the page number in the story.

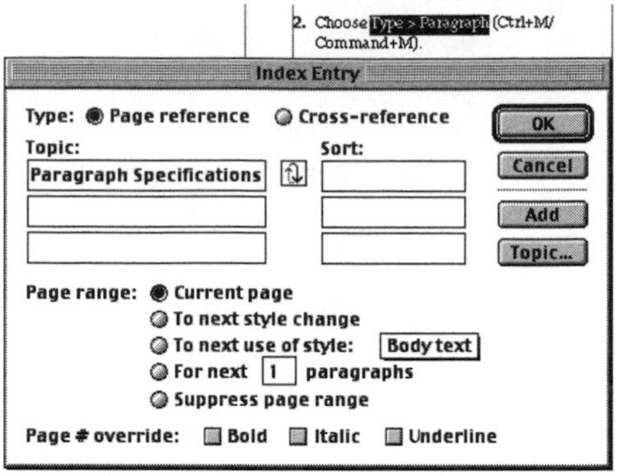

Figure 18.9 The Index Entry dialog box. Notice that the actual text that was selected appears above the dialog box. You can edit the entry to make it more clear when it appears in the Index.

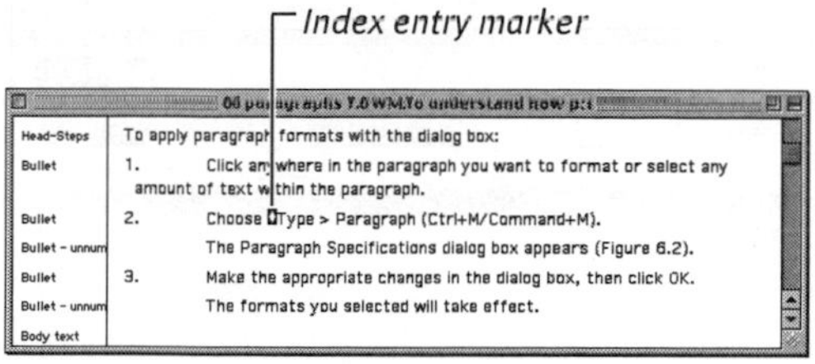

Index entry marker

Figure 18.10 In the Story Editor, an Index entry is indicated by a small diamond before the word or phrase that's been marked.

To create an index entry:

1. Select the word or phrase you want to use as an index entry.

2. Choose Utilities > Index Entry, or Ctrl+Y/ Command+ Y.

 The Index Entry dialog box appears.

 The selected text appears in the Topic field. Edit the text in the topic field if it will make the index entry easier to understand (**Figure 18.9**).

3. Click OK.

 The entry is added to your index.

 There is no indication of the index entry in the layout view of your publication. But in the Story Editor, you'll see a small diamond before each index entry (**Figure 18.10**).

✔ Tips

■ You don't have to select a specific bit of text for an index entry, but doing so en-sures that the spelling will match and that the word you're entering actually occurs in your document. If you don't select a word or phrase, you'll have to enter the word in the Index Entry dialog box by typing it in the Topic field.

■ The index entry marker itself is indepen-dent of the text you selected. Remove an index entry by deleting the diamond marker in Story Editor. Do not try to delete and retype your text. This almost never works unless you select a lot of text before and after the marker.

CREATING AN INDEX ENTRY

Showing an Index

Before you generate an Index story, it is help-ful to view the entries. It's possible to make the edits directly in the Index story, but this manual process will waste time if you make changes to the document such that page num-bers change. The index is not dynamic, so the page numbers in the Index story won't change, even if the markers move due to text editing.

To view an index:

1. Open the publications that contains the index entries you want to view or edit.

2. Choose Utilities > Show Index.

   The Show Index dialog box appears (**Figure 18.11**).

   In a publication that uses a Book publica-tion list, PageMaker repaginates all the publications in the book list, gathering index information from each one.

3. Use the Index section pop-up menu to view the sections of the index.

   The pop-up contains the word 'symbol' (for digits and other non-alphabetical charac-ters) and all the letters of the alphabet, so that you can view the index by section alphabetically.

4. Double-click an Index entry to edit it.

   The Edit Index Entry dialog box appears (**Figure 18.12**).

5. Make your changes, then click OK in the Edit Index Entry dialog box.

   The Show Index dialog box remains.

6. Repeat steps 3–5 to edit other entries.

7. Click OK to close the Show Index dialog box.

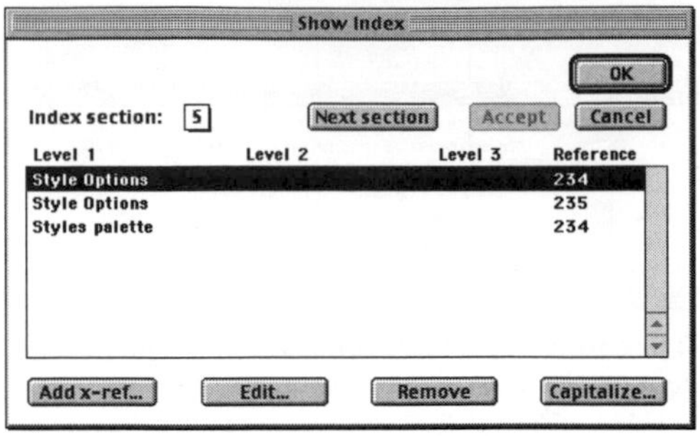

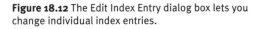

Figure 18.11 Use the Index section pop-up menu to view all the sections of an index. Double-click an entry to edit it.

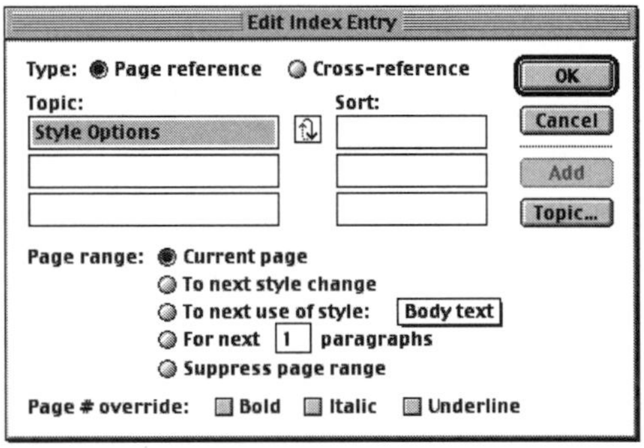

Figure 18.12 The Edit Index Entry dialog box lets you change individual index entries.

✔ Tip

- To view only the index entries from the current publication, hold down Ctrl (Windows) or Command (Mac) while you choose Utilities > Show Index.

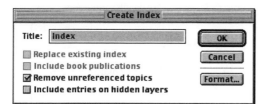

Figure 18.13 The Create Index dialog box.

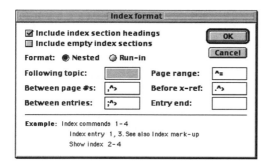

Figure 18.14 The Index Format dialog box controls the appearance of all entries in an index.

Creating an Index

Once you've marked your entire publication for index entries, PageMaker can create index entries for an entire publication in just a few minutes. Just remember that PageMaker repaginates all publications in a book list before it generates the index, so it may be a little while before you see the loaded text icon and can place your Index story. Options in the Index Format dialog box allow you to define certain parameters for your index.

◆ **Include Index Section Headings** breaks the story up with subheadings (Symbol, A, B, C, and so on) at the beginning of each letter's listings.

◆ **Include Empty Index Sections** includes a subheading even if there are no entries for that section.

◆ **Nested indents** format makes each sub-entry (Level 2 or 3) a separate paragraph.

◆ **Run-in** format includes all levels of the entry in one paragraph.

For the six fields that allow you to type delimiter characters (Following topic, Page range, Between page #s, Before x-ref, Between entries, and Entry end), watch the example at the bottom of the dialog box to see the effect on your final index entries. The dialog box's defaults are set for a standard index.

To create an index:

1. Choose Utilities > Create Index.

   The Create Index dialog box appears (**Figure 18.13**).

2. Edit the Index name, if necessary.

3. Click the Format button.

   The Index Format dialog box appears (**Figure 18.14**).

(continued on next page)

CREATING AN INDEX

4. Edit the format of the index as you like.

5. Click OK.

The Index Format dialog box closes, and the Create Index dialog box remains.

6. Click OK again.

PageMaker repaginates the publication(s). The cursor changes to the text placeholder.

7. Click the column where you want your index to begin.

The Index story flows into the publication (**Figure 18.15**).

✔ Tips

■ To create a separate publication for the index, see the section called "Creating a New Publication for the Table of Contents" earlier in this chapter.

■ Index page number references are not dynamic. If you edit text after you've created an Index story, the Index story will not be updated to reflect any page number changes. You'll need to generate another index to ensure the page number references are correct.

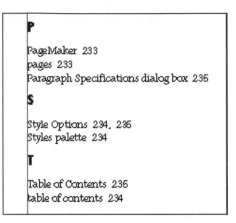

Figure 18.15 A few sections of an index, showing its default styles. Notice that the index is case sensitive. This index should be corrected so that the two entries under "Table of Contents" are combined into a single entry with two page number references, as in the Style Options entry.

WEB PAGES

One of PageMaker's most useful functions lets you repurpose your PageMaker documents as World Wide Web pages. PageMaker 7 can take advantage of HTML and Web capabilities. Once you've finished creating a document for print publication, you can have PageMaker convert the publication to HTML files for distribution on the Web.

Understanding the HTML Export Options

Compared to the myriad of options PageMaker provides for formatting text, the options available when you convert to HTML coding are pretty dismal. Although HTML is still evolving, it will still be quite some time before you see HTML Web pages that look as refined as PageMaker pages.

Because of the inherent limitations of HTML, the options PageMaker can give you will be limited. But with a little planning, you can use PageMaker to obtain good results relatively quickly.

First you'll need to decide whether you want to approximate the look of your PageMaker document by using HTML tables, or just translate the page to a single-column format, with graphics occupying their own paragraph within the text. Because every document is different, you'll want to try both options to see which gives you the best results.

Then you'll also need to decide whether you want to run all the pages in your publication together, or create a separate HTML file for each page in the publication. Again, you may want to make a few trial runs to gauge your results before making the final Web pages.

Finally, the HTML export command will translate the imported graphics used in your publication. PageMaker will make copies of your graphics in either GIF or JPEG format. Objects drawn with PageMaker's drawing tools are not translated or exported, except when horizontal lines can be translated to horizontal rules.

When you're ready to start generating HTML, you'll need to know how to set the series of export options that you'll find under Options in the Export dialog box (**Figure 19.1**):

Figure 19.1 The Options dialog box for HTML export.

- **Approximate layout using HTML tables when exporting pages** attempts to recreate the layout in the PageMaker publication. Graphics, columns, and other page elements will be scaled to try to preserve your layout.

- **Exported Page Width** controls the width (in pixels) of the HTML document. The default value is always the page width of the current publication.

- **Style Assignments** lets you match the PageMaker styles in your publication to HTML styles. Use the pop-up menu beside each style name to match styles as appropriate for your publication.

- **Preserve Character Attributes** lets you add the color and type style of your paragraph style definitions to the styles you've chosen with the Style Assignments option. Note that HTML colors may not exactly match the colors in your publication. Use the Online Colors library, available from the Libraries menu in the Color Options dialog box, to limit color shifting when you repurpose a document for the Web.

- **Export as** lets you select whether you want images converted to GIF or JPEG. PageMaker Chooses instructs the program to match the file format to the content of the graphic; GIF format is generally used for line art, and JPEG format for continuous color tones like those in photographs. Leave this default intact unless you're sure that all your graphics are suitable for either GIF or JPEG.

- **File Names** controls whether the existing file name is used, or adapted to the 8.3 naming convention.

- **Downsample** converts documents to 72 dpi, which is most suitable for the Web. As with other options, test this option first to see whether it yields suitable results.

Exporting to HTML

After you've run a couple of tests and know how you want to set your export options, you can export the publication to HTML.

To export HTML from a PageMaker publication:

1. Open the PageMaker document you want to repurpose into HTML code for the Web.

2. Choose File > Export > HTML.

   The Export HTML dialog box appears (**Figure 19.2**).

3. Click Edit.

   The Export HTML: New Contents dialog box appears (**Figure 19.3**).

4. Type the name of the HTML file in the Document Title field.

   The dialog box is set to create a single HTML document from your publication. Click Done if this is appropriate for your publication.

5. If you want to change the content of the new file, click Rem All.

   All pages in the publication are removed from the Assigned to Document list. Double-click each page that you want added to the Assigned to Document list, then click Done.

   The New Content dialog box closes and the Export HTML dialog box remains.

6. Click Document in the Export HTML dialog box.

   The Document location dialog box appears (**Figure 19.4**).

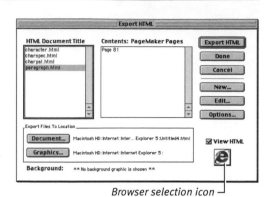

Browser selection icon

Figure 19.2 The Export HTML dialog box.

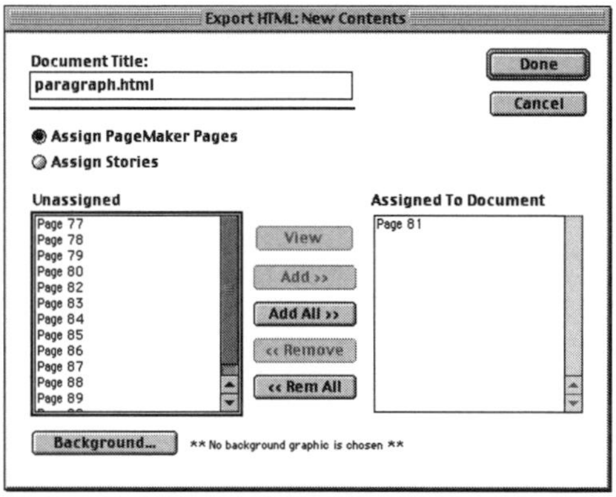

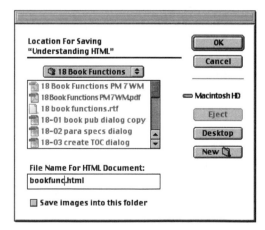

Figure 19.3 The Export HTML: New Contents dialog box. Use this dialog box to set the contents of each HTML file that is exported.

Figure 19.4 The Export Document location dialog box.

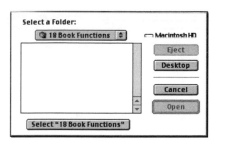

Figure 19.5 The Export Graphic location dialog box.

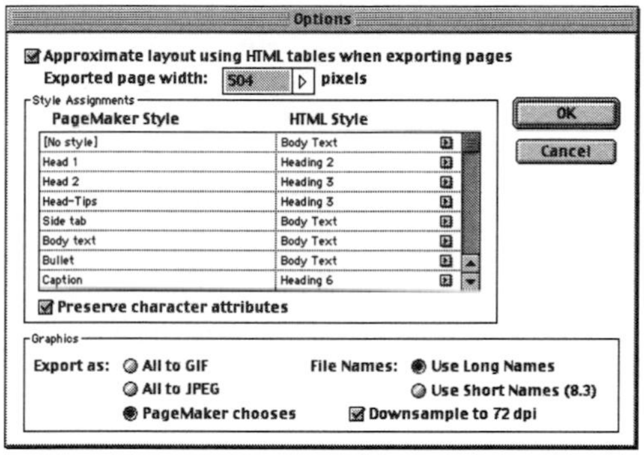

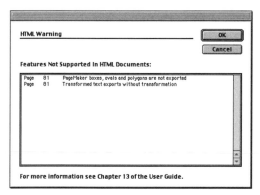

Figure 19.6 The Options dialog box for HTML export.

Figure 19.7 The HTML Warning dialog box gives you feedback about problems encountered during the export process.

7. Set the options to save the HTML files in the location of your choice, name the file, then click OK.

8. Click Graphics in the Export HTML dialog box. The Graphics location dialog box appears (**Figure 19.5**).

   Set the options to save the HTML files in the location of your choice, then click OK.

9. Click Options in the Export HTML dialog box. The Options dialog box appears (**Figure 19.6**).

10. Set options as appropriate.

    Use the list in the previous section to help you decide how to set the options.

11. Click OK. The Options dialog box closes and the Export HTML dialog box remains.

12. Click the Export HTML button.

    The HTML file and graphics for the selected document are exported. PageMaker displays a warning dialog box to let you know if any elements could not be translated (**Figure 19.7**). Click OK when you've finished reading the warnings.

13. Click New to create a new HTML file.

14. Repeat steps 3–13 for each HTML file you want to create from the publication.

✔ Tips

- If you're familiar with HTML programming, you can open the HTML files in an HTML-editing program, and refine or add to the code that PageMaker created.

- Select the View HTML option in the Export HTML dialog box to have PageMaker automatically show you the newly created HTML file in a browser. The first time you export HTML, you may need to specify which browser you want to use to view HTML files. Click the Browser selection icon to select a browser (**Figure 19.2**).

EXPORTING TO HTML

Viewing an HTML Page

Once the HTML and graphics files have been exported, you'll want to view them in a Web browser.

To view your new Web page:

◆ From the desktop, drag the HTML file on top of the icon for your Web browser.

Or choose File > Open from your Web browser and select the file from the Open dialog box.

Your HTML file appears in your browser (**Figure 19.8**).

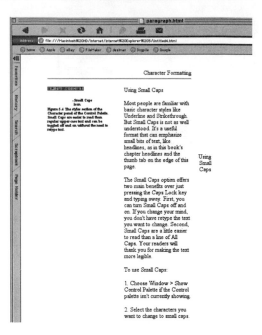

Figure 19.8 An HTML file that was created from a chapter in this book.

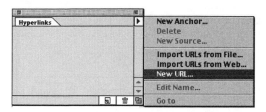

Figure 19.9 The Hyperlinks palette with no links created, and its pop-up menu.

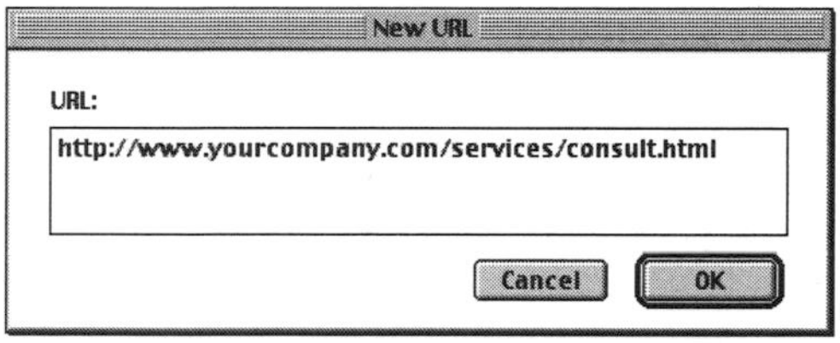

Figure 19.10 The New URL dialog box.

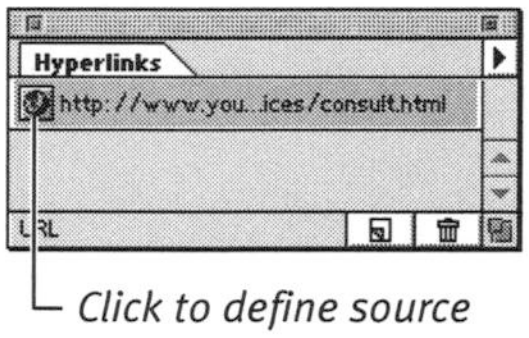

Figure 19.11 Hyperlinks palette with a link created.

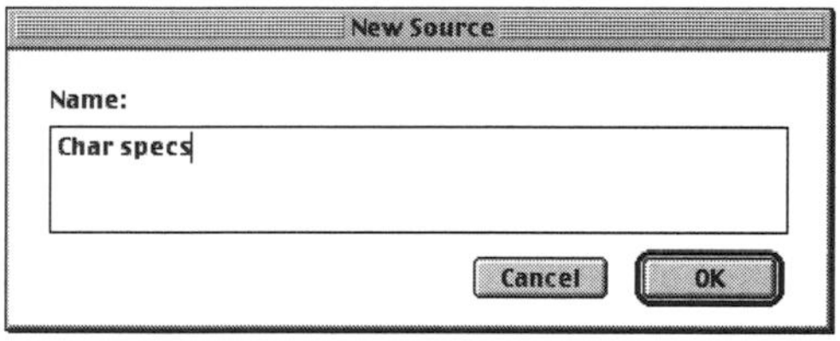

Click to define source

Figure 19.12 The New Source dialog box.

Figure 19.13 Hyperlinks palette, with a link and a source created.

Adding a Link to a Page

To manage the links that are created in your HTML files, you can create hyperlinks to help your viewers navigate through your Web site. These hyperlinks can be used to navigate to another Web page on your site, an external Web page, or to resources like movie or audio files. Hyperlinks can also let your Web audience send an email back to you, or to anywhere else you specify.

You need to define two elements for each hyperlink: a source (the text or graphic that is clickable), and a destination (the 'place' the click navigates to).

The Hyperlinks palette lets you create, import, edit, and manage hyperlinks.

To add a link to a page:

1. Select the object or text you want to use as a link.

   If you want to select text within a text block, be sure to use the Text tool.

2. Choose Window > Show Hyperlinks to display the Hyperlinks palette (**Figure 19.9**).

3. Choose New URL from the pop-up menu on the Hyperlinks palette.

   The New URL dialog box appears (**Figure 19.10**).

4. Type a URL in the URL field and click OK.

   The URL appears in the Hyperlinks palette (**Figure 19.11**).

5. Click the icon to the left of the URL.

   The New Source dialog box appears (**Figure 19.12**).

   Type a name for the source. You can also leave the name as Source1.

6. Click OK.

   The URL and source appear in the Hyperlinks palette.

Editing a Link

Once you've created a link you may need to edit it, either because the link doesn't work or because your Web site has changed.

To edit a hyperlink:

1. Double-click the link you want to edit in the Hyperlinks palette.

   The Edit URL dialog box appears (**Figure 19.14**).

2. Type the new URL or edit the existing one.

3. Click OK.

   The edited URL appears in the Hyperlinks palette.

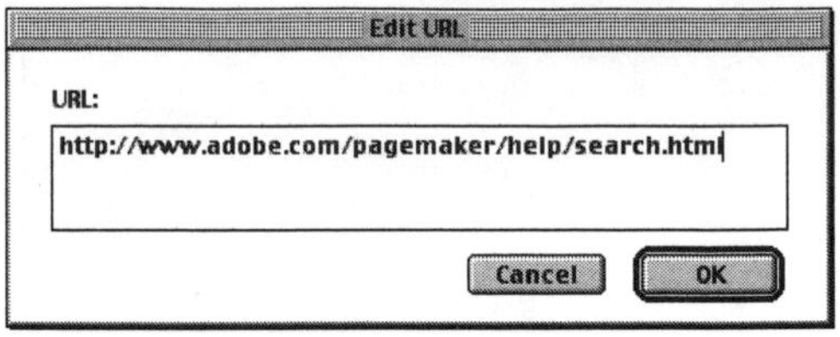

Figure 19.14 The edit URL dialog box.

Figure 19.15 The Delete Hyperlink warning dialog box asks you to confirm that you want to delete a URL.

Removing a Hyperlink

You'll want to remove any unused links, or links that don't work in your PageMaker publication. Nothing will annoy your Web audience as much as clicking a defective link.

To remove a hyperlink:

1. Choose Window > Show Hyperlinks, if the Hyperlink palette is not visible.

2. Click the item you want to remove.

3. Click the trash button at the bottom of the palette, or choose Delete from the pop-up menu to remove your item name from the Hyperlinks palette menu.

   A warning dialog box appears (**Figure 19.16**).

4. Click OK (Windows) or Delete (Mac).

   The hyperlink is removed from the palette.

Formatting Hyperlinks

The style conventions of the Web have taught readers to expect to see hyperlinks highlighted in blue and underlined. To highlight all your links, you need to select each bit of text and then make your format changes manually. This process can be tedious, so PageMaker has provided a helpful shortcut.

A script that lets you format hyperlinked text has been provided. Note: you don't have to use this script to ensure that the links export to HTML correctly. Hyperlinks are formatted as part of the HTML export process.

But you may want your publication to mirror the live links on the HTML pages created from that publication. And if you'll be exporting to PDF, this can be especially useful, since hyperlinks work like a charm in a PDF document, but their text doesn't get formatted automatically when you export to PDF. It's a good idea to help your readers out by formatting all hyperlinks so it's clear where you want them to click.

To format hyperlinks:

1. Define all the hyperlinks and source text in your publication.

2. Choose Window > Plug-in Palettes > Show Scripts.

   The Scripts palette appears.

3. Click the triangle to the left of the Online folder icon in the Scripts palette.

   The Online scripts folder opens and the online scripts appear (**Figure 19.16**).

4. Double-click the Apply Hyperlink Style script.

   The script begins to run and the Define Hyperlink Text Style dialog box appears (**Figure 19.17**).

5. Set the style options as appropriate.

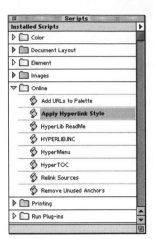

Figure 19.16 The Scripts palette with the Online folder open and its scripts displayed.

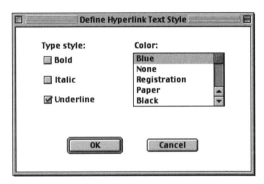

Figure 19.17 The Define Hyperlink Text Style dialog box. The default settings are for text to be blue and underlined.

Figure 19.18 An "X" and "Running" appear at the bottom of the Scripts palette while scripts run.

Scripts

Scripts are mini-programs that perform lengthy and/or tedious routines for you. More than 50 scripts have been provided in PageMaker 7. These predefined scripts run the gamut from color controls to layout to trapping. You'll learn a lot about Page-Maker's high-end features by testing these scripts, because you actually see much of the work performed as the script runs.

Scripting is generally considered a fairly advanced concept, but given a command of PageMaker's basic features, just about anybody can tackle scripting. If you're willing to learn a relatively simple programming language, called PageMaker Script Language, you can write custom scripts that automate many of your most common production processes. Also, check the Internet for free or shareware scripts that are written by third parties. They can save you hours of production time.

Check the ScriptGuide.pdf for details about creating custom scripts. You'll find it in the Tech Info folder in the PageMaker 7 folder on your hard drive.

6. Click OK.

You'll see the script begin to work. An "X" and the word "Running" will appear at the bottom of the Scripts palette (**Figure 19.18**) while the script is running.

In the publication, you'll see text being highlighted and hyperlinks being formatted according to your settings.

Wait until the script stops running to resume work.

✔ Tips

■ You don't have to format hyperlink text to be the standard blue underlined text. But if you depart from convention, make sure you've given your readers some clue about identifying hyperlinks. You might want to use a note in a PDF file, or you may prefer to create a legend that explains what your links look like.

■ Don't worry if the script seems to be taking awhile to run, especially in a large document. The script isn't meant to be faster than you are, but it probably will be more thorough at finding all your links and applying consistent formatting.

FORMATTING HYPERLINKS

Setting Online Preferences

PageMaker has a special dialog box for setting your preferences for online behaviors. One of the choices you'll use most frequently is the option on how to display hyperlinks and sources (anchors).

◆ **Outline link sources when hand tool is selected** lets you preview hyperlinks by clicking on the Hand tool.

◆ **Center upper-left of anchor when testing hyperlinks** can realign the view of a publication page when you're viewing it at sizes larger than Fit in Window. PageMaker will use the upper-left corner of the source or anchor as the centerpoint of the enlarged view.

◆ **Proxies** and **No proxies** let you specify the names or IP addresses of any proxy servers you use. Talk to your network administrator for details on these settings.

◆ **Port** lets you specify a port for your Internet server.

◆ **Download to folder** lets you specify the location of files downloaded from the Web that are to be imported into PageMaker.

◆ **Web browser** lets you specify the Web browser you want to use to preview your HTML files.

To set online preferences:

1. Choose File > Preferences > Online.

   The Online Preferences dialog box appears (**Figure 19.19**).

2. Set options as appropriate.

3. Click OK.

   Your settings will take effect.

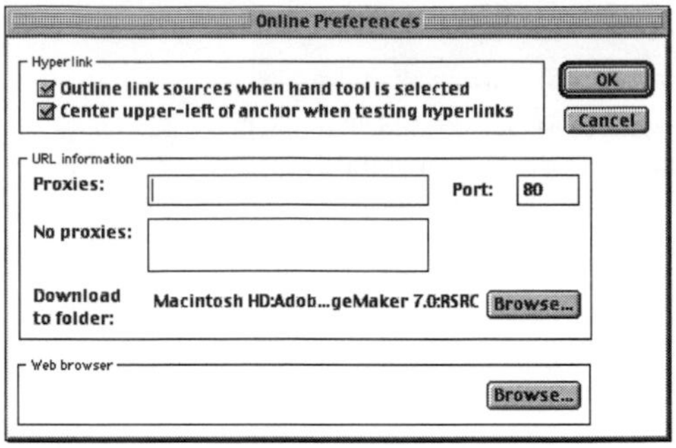

Figure 19.19 The Online Preferences dialog box with its default settings.

Hyperlink   Hyperlink

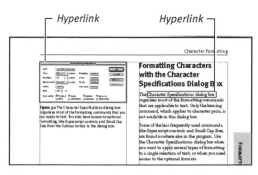

Figure 19.20 A PageMaker publication with a graphic and a bit of text used as links.

Viewing Links

Look at your document to check how the links appear.

To view your links in PageMaker:

◆ Click the Hand tool in the toolbox.

All links in your document will be surrounded by a blue frame (**Figure 19.20**).

PDF Files

I'm not sure who's luckier: PageMaker users who benefit from having Adobe Acrobat work so seamlessly with PageMaker, or Acrobat users who can use PageMaker as an authoring tool for PDF documents. It's a match made in desktop publishing heaven (where the dpi is infinite, everybody meets their deadlines, and everything is 100 percent compatible).

PDF (Portable Document Format) files are cross-platform document standards. Anyone with a copy of the free Acrobat Reader for Mac, Windows, or even UNIX can view an Acrobat PDF document. PDFs look exactly like the original document, copying everything from fonts to photos and preserving all styles and formatting. It's the perfect format for giving your PageMaker files to people who don't have PageMaker. PageMaker includes Acrobat Distiller, which is the software that transforms your PageMaker publications into PDFs.

Although the coverage that follows is sufficient to get you started, it's not an in-depth guide. For more information on creating and working with Acrobat documents, Peachpit Press's *PDF with Acrobat 5: Visual QuickStart Guide*, by Jennifer Alspach is an excellent general reference.

Understanding Portable Document Format

Portable Document Format (PDF) is the standard format for transferring files when you aren't sure what kind of computer programs, or skill level, the recipient possesses. Files are translated into a format that's read by Adobe Acrobat Reader, a common, freely distributed program. PDF documents are often posted on the Web, both for download and for printing information directly from the Web.

When you create PDF documents, you can control how your document appears when it reaches your audience, regardless of the operating system, computer programs, or fonts they are using.

Everything you need to create, view, and print PDF documents is included on the PageMaker installation disk. Before reading further in this chapter, make sure that you've installed the following items: Adobe Acrobat Distiller, the Acrobat Distiller PPD file, the Adobe PostScript printer driver, and Acrobat Reader. Check the ReadMe file on the installation CD for details on installing these components:

♦ The **Adobe PostScript printer driver** converts the PageMaker publication to PostScript.

♦ **Acrobat Distiller** converts the PostScript file to a PDF.

♦ A **PostScript Printer Description (PPD)** must be installed and selected in the Print Document dialog box in order for PageMaker to create a PostScript file.

♦ **Acrobat Reader** lets you view and print PDF files. You probably already have a copy of Reader on your computer. The version included with PageMaker 7 is an upgrade from the previous version, so you'll want to install it in order to use its new features.

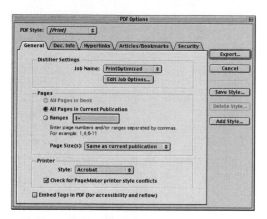

Figure 20.1 The PDF Options dialog box lets you specify document settings, page ranges, and printer style settings for the new document.

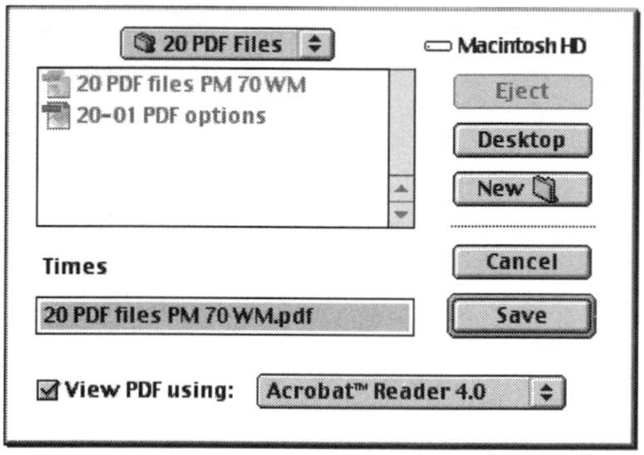

Figure 20.2 The Save As dialog box lets you give the PDF a name and decide where it will be saved.

Exporting to PDF

Exporting a publication to a PDF is a two-step process. First, PageMaker creates a PostScript file from the publication. Next, Acrobat Distiller converts the PostScript file to a PDF. Fortunately, you don't have to issue two commands: PageMaker automatically passes the job on to Distiller, which can even open the new PDF in Acrobat Reader when it's finished with the conversion.

To export to PDF:

1. Choose File > Export > Adobe PDF.

   The PDF Options dialog box appears (**Figure 20.1**).

2. Select one of the predefined Distiller Settings options.

   Make your choice based on the medium in which the PDF is likely to be viewed. For example, choose Print Optimized if your viewers will be printing the document and you want the graphics to be high quality.

3. Select a page range and page size.

4. Select a Printer Style.

5. Click Export.

   A dialog box appears, asking you to name your PDF file and choose a location to store it in (**Figure 20.2**).

   The View PDF option is selected by default. Your document will be opened in whichever version of Acrobat Reader is specified in this dialog box.

6. Click the Save button.

   Several things will happen on your screen. First, PageMaker translates the file into PostScript. You'll see a progress bar for this step. Next, Distiller launches automatically and processes the PostScript files. A dialog box appears that includes a progress bar and Distiller's preferences. Finally, the new PDF will open in Acrobat.

Distilling PostScript Files Manually

When you have many PDF files to export, you may save time by dividing up the two-step process and distilling the files manually. Or you may prefer to use Distiller's more robust features to set specific options for a PDF file.

To distill PostScript files manually:

1. Choose File > Print.

   The Print dialog box appears.

2. Select a PostScript Printer Description (PPD) from the PPD pop-up menu.

3. Click Options in the Print dialog box.
   The Print Options dialog box appears (**Figure 20.3**).

4. Check the Write PostScript to file check box, and type the name of the PostScript file.

   Note that the root extension .ps is automatically appended to the file name. It is important to retain this extension for all operating systems.

5. Click Save As if you want to save the file in a folder other than the one in which the current file resides.

   Use the Save As dialog box to save the PostScript file in a location of your choice.

6. Click Save.
   A progress bar appears (**Figure 20.4**).
   The Postscript file is created and saved in the location you specified.

7. Open the resulting PostScript (.ps) file in Distiller. See your Acrobat Distiller documentation for details on using Distiller's features.

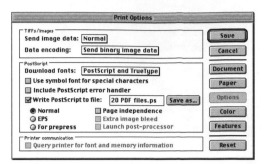

Figure 20.3 The Print Options dialog box.

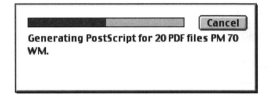

Figure 20.4 The Generating PostScript progress bar.

DISTILLING POSTSCRIPT FILES MANUALLY

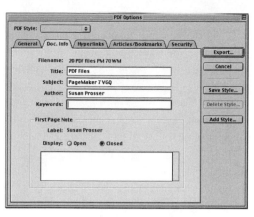

Figure 20.5 The PDF Options dialog box lets you add information to the document, including author, title, subject, and keywords.

Adding Document Information

You can send background information along with your PDF document, including author, title, subject, and keywords. This data appears in Document Properties for the PDF.

In the PDF Options dialog box, select the First Page Note option to create an Acrobat note that will appear on the first page of the PDF. The Open option makes the note appear in an open note window, while Closed displays an icon for the note. Either option provides your readers with useful introductory material.

To add document information:

1. Choose File > Export > Adobe PDF.
   The PDF Options dialog box appears.
2. Click the Doc. Info tab.
   The Doc. Info fields appear
   (**Figure 20.5**).
3. Add the appropriate information.
4. Type a note in the First Page Note text box, if applicable.
5. Click Export in the PDF Options dialog box.
   The publication is exported to a PDF file.

Changing Distiller Options

Although Distiller works in the background while you're generating PDFs from PageMaker, you can still open the program independently. There are a couple of reasons you might want to do this. First, you might want to manually distill PostScript files as described earlier in this chapter. Second, you might open the program so you can change its preferences.

But you don't even have to go to this trouble. PageMaker lets you set local preferences that will override those set in Distiller.

Among the basic preferences you can set are compatibility with earlier versions of Distiller and Acrobat, text and graphics compression, and how to handle the publication's fonts.

♦ **Compatibility** (**Figure 20.6**) lets you select which versions of Acrobat the PDFs will be compatible with. PDFs created for Acrobat 4.0 or above may not be readable using older versions of Acrobat.

♦ **Optimize for Fast Web View** reduces file size. The resulting file can be downloaded one page at a time from a Web server. Text and line art are compressed no matter what settings you've selected under the Compression options.

♦ **Embed Thumbnails** creates a thumbnail view of each page in the PDF file.

♦ **Auto-Rotate Pages** rotates pages automatically, based on the orientation of the text. Select Individually to rotate each page, based on its text orientation. Collectively by File rotates all pages in the document, according to the text orientation of the majority of pages.

♦ **Page Range** lets you specify which pages in the document will be converted to PDF.

♦ **Binding** lets you choose how the PDF file might be prepared for binding after printing—either right or left.

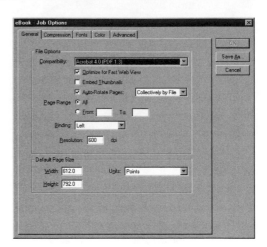

Figure 20.6 The General tab of the Job Options dialog box.

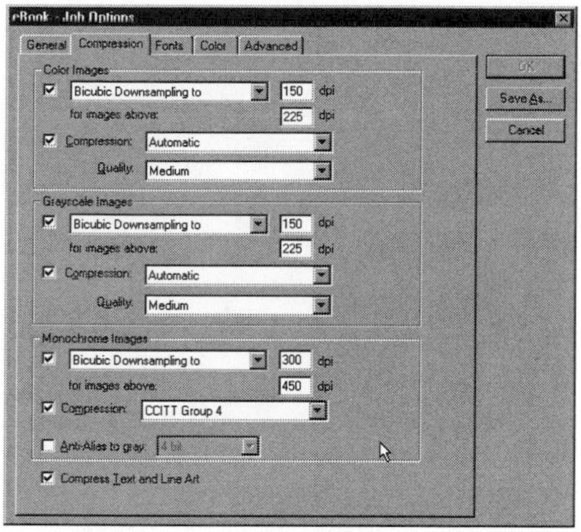

Figure 20.7 The Compression tab of the Job Options dialog box.

Figure 20.8 The Fonts tab of the Job Options dialog box.

◆ **Resolution** lets you specify the resolution of vector objects and type in EPS files. Enter any value from 72 dpi to 4000 dpi.

◆ **Default Page Size** overrides the publication's dimensions.

◆ **Downsampling** (**Figure 20.7**) reduces the resolution of all images by averaging the color of a sampled area.

◆ **Subsampling** is a faster method of compressing images, but the trade-off is in the quality of the color that's produced.

◆ **Embed All Fonts** (**Figure 20.8**) loads each character of all fonts used in the document in the PDF.

◆ **Always Embed** is where you can specify the fonts you want embedded.

◆ **Never Embed** lists specific fonts you want to prevent embedding in a PDF.

To change Distiller options:

1. Choose File > Export > Adobe PDF.
The PDF Options dialog box appears.

2. Select the setting you want to edit from the Job Name pop-up menu.

3. Click Edit Job Options.
The Job Options dialog box appears (**Figure 20.6**).

4. Set your new General options.

5. Click the Compression tab.
The Compression panel appears (**Figure 20.7**).

6. Set your new Compression options.

7. Click the Fonts tab.
The Fonts panel appears (**Figure 20.8**).

8. Set your new Fonts options.

9. Click OK.
The publication is exported to a PDF file.

CHANGING DISTILLER OPTIONS

279

Setting Security Options

You can assign passwords to your PDF files to restrict users from printing and editing them. Passwords can restrict access to the files themselves, or they can restrict other people's ability to change the security settings you have set.

Encryption levels and their options are tied to the compatibility levels you set on the General tab in the Job Options dialog box. Acrobat 5 provides the highest level of security, but it is only compatible with Acrobat Reader 5.

To set security options:

1. Choose File > Export > Adobe PDF.
   The PDF Options dialog box appears.

2. Set all options as appropriate.

3. Click the Security tab in the PDF Options dialog box.
   The Security options panel appears (**Figure 20.9**).

4. Check the Required to Open Document check box, and type the password you've chosen for opening the file.

5. Check the Required to Change Permissions and Password check box, and type the password for setting or changing security options.

6. Choose options for user access.

7. Click Export in the PDF Options dialog box.
   The publication is exported to a PDF file.

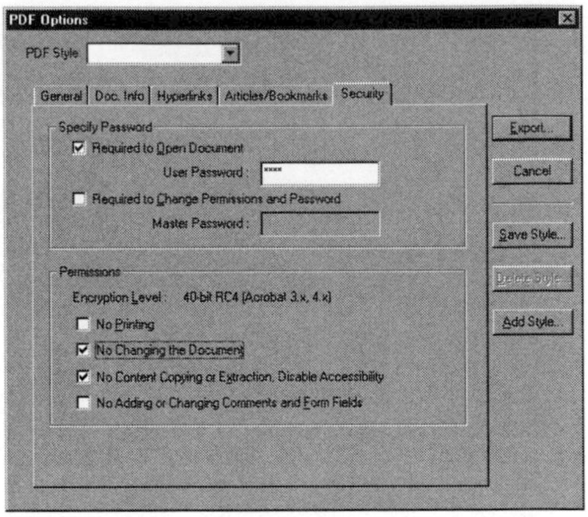

Figure 20.9 The Security panel of the PDF Options dialog box.

SETTING SECURITY OPTIONS

PRINTING

It's fitting that this chapter is the last in the book, since printing is typically the last thing you do with a Adobe PageMaker document. The "last but not least" rule applies, though, because printing is one of the most critical operations in a PageMaker publication.

PageMaker's printing features give you several methods of controlling how your document appears on the printed page, from specifying pages to be printed to choosing which color plates should print.

Checking the Links Manager

PageMaker keeps track of the locations of all files (text or graphic) that have been placed in a publication. If a file is moved or its name is changed, PageMaker can lose its link to the file. Files with altered links may not print properly. To ensure the least amount of trouble when printing, you should check the links to all items placed in the publication.

To check the Links Manager:

1. Choose File > Links Manager, or Ctrl+Shift+D (Windows)/Command+Shift+D (Mac).

   The Links Manager dialog box appears (**Figure 21.1**).

2. Select any item with a question mark to the left of its name.

   The question mark indicates that PageMaker has lost track of the file.

3. Click the Info button.

   The Links Info dialog box appears (**Figure 21.2**).

4. Locate the missing file and select it.

5. Click Link.

   A dialog box asks you to confirm that you want to change the link to the new file (**Figure 21.3**).

   The item is now linked to the correct file.

✔ Tips

■ It's helpful to keep all your placed files in the same folder with your PageMaker publication. That way you won't have to search all over your hard drive if any files need to be relinked.

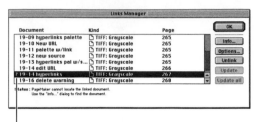

Lost link indicator

Figure 21.1 The Links Manager dialog box lists all text and graphics that have been placed in your publication. A question mark appears beside any file that PageMaker has lost track of.

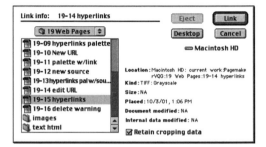

Figure 21.2 Use the Links Info dialog box to link a missing graphic back to the publication.

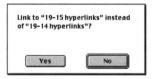

Figure 21.3 The Links to warning dialog box lets you confirm that you want to change the link to an image or text file.

Figure 21.4 The Print Document dialog box, with its default settings.

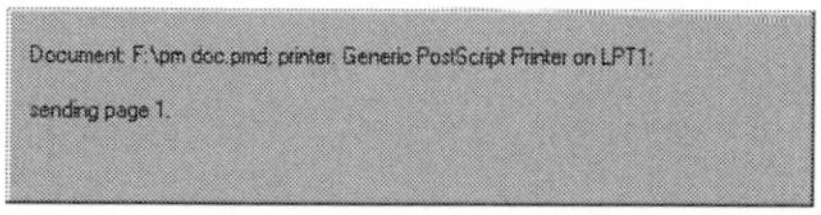

Figure 21.5 The Sending pages dialog box.

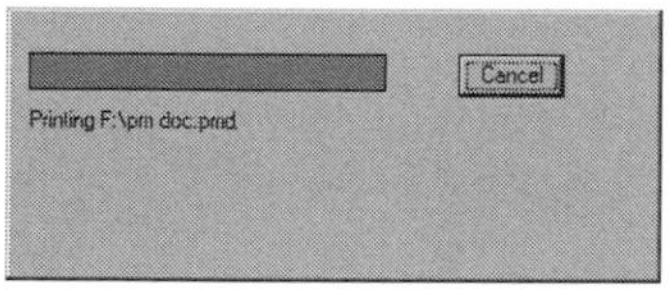

Figure 21.6 The Printing progress bar dialog box.

Printing a Document

PageMaker comes with specific printer drivers for a range of printers. Although PageMaker can print to any printer you might be using, PostScript printers will provide the best print quality. Check your printer's documentation to make sure it is set up correctly, and that you have selected the appropriate printer driver for it.

To print a document:

1. Open the document you want to print.

2. Choose File > Save, or Ctrl+S/ Command+S.

   Since errors and file corruption can happen during printing, it is a good habit to save files just before you print them.

3. Choose File > Print, or Ctrl+P/ Command+P.

   The Print Document dialog box appears (**Figure 21.4**).

4. Make sure the All option is chosen in the Pages section. If it isn't, not all of the pages in your document will print.

5. Click Print.

   The Sending pages dialog box appears. It will count the pages as they are sent to your printer (**Figure 21.5**).

   Soon thereafter (almost instantly for a small publication), the Printing progress bar appears (**Figure 21.6**).

   Printing a larger document can take several minutes. The dialog boxes remain onscreen until each process is completed.

✔ Tip

■ If you have trouble printing, make sure your printer is attached to your system and is turned on. If you're using a network printer, check to make sure the printer is connected to the network.

Printing Specific Page Ranges

PageMaker deals with page ranges a little differently than other software. Instead of From and To text fields that define the starting and ending page to be printed, PageMaker allows you to print noncontiguous page ranges by entering values in one text field (Ranges). The general rule of thumb is to separate contiguous page ranges with hyphens, and noncontiguous page ranges with commas.

To print a specific range of pages:

1. In the Print Document dialog box, click the Ranges radio button (**Figure 21.7**).

2. Enter the page range you want to print.

3. Click the Print button.

   Only the pages you specified are printed.

To print contiguous pages:

◆ Enter a page range with a hyphen between the first and last pages.

   For instance, to print from page 4 to page 8, you would type 4 - 8.

To print noncontiguous pages:

◆ Enter each page or page range, separated by commas.

   For instance, to print pages 6, 8, 11, and 14, type 6 , 8 , 11 , 14.

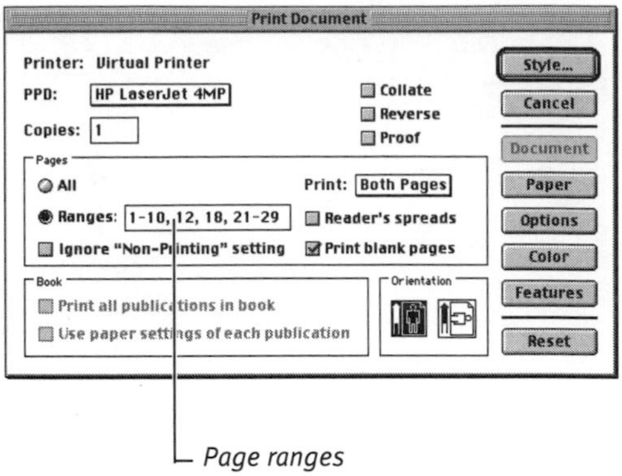

Page ranges

Figure 21.7 The Print Document dialog box, with a mix of noncontiguous and contiguous page ranges specified.

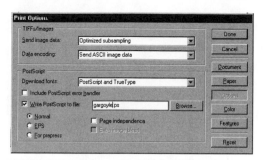

Figure 21.8 The Print Options dialog box. Write PostScript to file is selected.

Printing to Files

In some cases, you'll want to print your document directly to your hard drive in the form of a PostScript file. This file can be sent to any PostScript printer, to a service bureau, or distilled by Acrobat Distiller into a PDF file.

To print to a file:

1. Choose File > Print.

The Print Document dialog box appears.

2. Click the Options button in the Print Document dialog box.

The Print Options dialog box appears (**Figure 21.8**).

3. Select Write PostScript to file.

Checking this box allows you to enter a name for the file.

4. In the text box, type the name of the PostScript file you want to create.

By clicking the Browse button (Windows) or the Save As button (Mac), you can define the location as well as the name of the file. If you don't specify a location, the PostScript file will be saved in the same folder as your PageMaker document.

5. Click the Print button.

The PostScript file is written to your hard drive.

The PostScript file you've created can be downloaded to any printer, using a utility program such as LaserWriter Utility.

✔ Tip

■ PostScript files can be extremely large, so make sure you have several megabytes of free space on the destination disk.

Printing Color Separations

If you have only black in your document, the only output from the printer will be a single, black separation per page. If you have full-color artwork or color photographs, you'll get a separate sheet for cyan, magenta, yellow, and black—four color separations per page. If you've included objects in the document that contain spot colors, a sheet will be printed for each spot color.

To print color separations:

1. Choose File > Print.

   The Print dialog box appears.

2. In the Print Document dialog box, click the Color button.

   The Print Color dialog box appears (**Figure 21.9**).

3. Choose the Separations option.

4. Click the Print button.

   Separations for each color in your document will be printed.

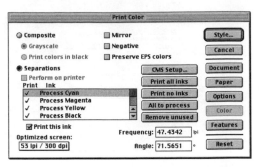

Figure 21.9 The Print Color dialog box. The options are set to print all color separations.

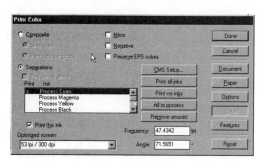

Figure 21.10 The Print Color dialog box. Only the Cyan color separation will print.

Printing a Specific Separation

For a two-color print job (say, black and blue), you won't need all the color plates. When it's time to make color separations, you can save time and printing supplies by printing only the plates you need.

To print a specific color:

1. Choose File > Print.

   The Print dialog box appears.

2. In the Print Document dialog box, click the Color button.

   The Print Color dialog box appears (**Figure 21.10**).

3. Choose the Separations option in the Print Color dialog box.

   By default, all color separations will print.

4. In the list of separations, click the name of the first color you don't want to print.

5. Deselect the Print this ink option.

6. Repeat for all colors you don't want to print.

✔ Tip

- Double-click a color with a checkmark to remove the checkmark and prevent the color from printing.

PRINTING A SPECIFIC SEPARATION

Printing Crop Marks

Printing crop marks can be useful if your printed page will need to be trimmed, that is, when you print on paper that's larger than the final document pages will be. Crop marks, which help the service bureau trim the paper properly, appear on composite and separation printouts.

To print a document with crop marks:

1. Choose File > Print.

   The Print Document dialog box appears.

2. In the Print Document dialog box, click the Paper button.

   The Print Paper dialog box appears (**Figure 21.11**).

3. Click the Printer's marks check box.

   Checking the inset box 'Crops and bleeds only' prevents additional information, such as registration marks and color bars, from appearing on your page. Check this box only if you'll be printing single-color documents.

4. Click the Print button.

   The publication is printed with crop marks.

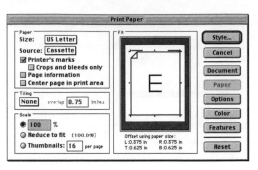

Figure 21.11 The Paper panel of the Print dialog box. Printer's marks and crop marks are set to print.

Figure 21.12 The Define Printer Styles dialog box before a new style has been created.

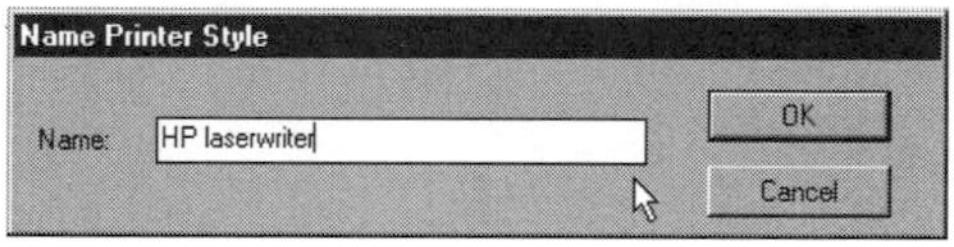

Figure 21.13 The Name Printer Style dialog box.

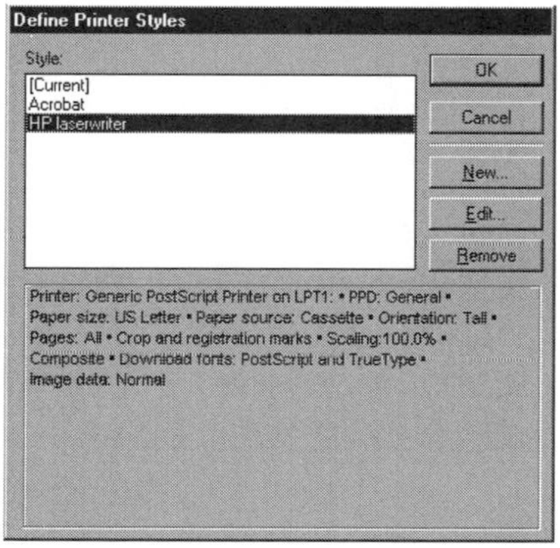

Figure 21.14 The Define Printer Styles dialog box after a new style has been created. Note the style definition in the bottom half of the dialog box.

Defining a Printer Style

If you find yourself constantly switching between two or more different sets of printing options, you'll find PageMaker's 'hidden' feature of Printer Styles a godsend. For instance, I'm constantly printing out documents to my black-and-white laser printer that need crop marks, or to my color printer without bleeds or crop marks but sized smaller to fit on the color sheets, or to PostScript files for which I have other special requirements.

PageMaker lets me set up each of these combinations of printing options as Printer Styles. When I want to print, I can choose the appropriate printer style from the File menu, and then press Enter.

To define a Printer Style:

1. Choose File > Printer Styles > Define.
   The Define Printer Styles dialog box appears (**Figure 21.12**).

2. Click New.
   The Name Printer Style dialog box appears (**Figure 21.13**).

3. Type a name for your new Printer Style.
   Be descriptive, so it will be easy to figure out which Printer Style to use under which circumstances.

4. Click OK.
   The Name Printer Styles dialog box closes, and the Define Printer Styles dialog box remains.

5. Click Edit.
   The Print dialog box appears.

6. Set print options as appropriate for your new Printer Style.

7. Click OK.
   The new Printer Style is created (**Figure 21.14**).

8. Click OK.
   The Define Printer Styles dialog box closes.

Printing Using a Printer Style

Now that you've created all those helpful Printer Styles, it's time to use them to make your work more efficient.

To print using a Printer Style:

1. Choose File > Printer Styles > [Your Style].

   The Printer Styles you've created appear in the submenu (**Figure 21.15**).

   The Print dialog box appears, complete with all the settings you specified for the style when you defined it.

2. Make any needed changes to the Print dialog box panels.

3. Click Print.

   The publication is printed to your specifications.

Figure 21.15 The Printer Styles menu contains a list of all the Printer Styles you've defined.

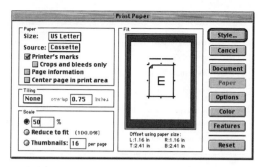

Figure 21.16 The Paper panel of the Print dialog box. These settings will reduce the publication to 50 percent.

Enlarging or Reducing a Printout

It's often useful to be able to reduce or enlarge the dimensions of a printout. Maybe your final printed output will use a paper size that your proof printer doesn't support. In that case, you'd want to reduce your publication's page size to fit on your current printer's paper.

Perhaps you're printing a periodical and have placed all your ads, but none of your feature articles. It's very helpful to have a printout of the available space for content. In that case, you might want to print thumbnails, with two or three pages reduced to fit on a page. If you're repurposing a layout used on a previous project, you might also enlarge a printout to make it fill available space.

To enlarge or reduce your printout:

1. Choose File > Print, Ctrl+P/Command+P.
   The Print Document dialog box appears.

2. Click the Paper button.
   The Print Paper dialog box appears (**Figure 21.16**).

3. In the Scale box, enter a percentage for reduction or enlargement.

4. Click Print.
   The publication is printed to your specifications.

Trapping

When your document uses multiple colors, especially spot colors, gaps can appear where the colors should butt up against each other. This isn't a PageMaker problem. It's due to mechanical variations that occur with most commercial printing presses. A slight slip of alignment of a plate on a printing press, and disaster strikes. The process used to reduce or eliminate these gaps is called 'trapping.'

There are lots of ways to make trapping adjustments from your end. But your best bet is to talk to your commercial printer before you do anything. This will tell you what kind of trapping (if any) you should apply to your document. Many commercial printers prefer to make trapping adjustments themselves.

Sometimes your service bureau or commercial printer will give you specifications for trapping on their presses. Talk to your printer! This can't be emphasized enough. Each printer has different presses with different requirements, so don't accept what one printer says and apply it to a job that's going to be printed by his rival across town. Also, many commercial printers use different presses for different jobs, so the settings for one job may not work for your next job. Remember to ask, and to be specific.

To trap in PageMaker:

1. Choose File > Preferences > Trapping.
   The Trapping Preferences dialog box appears (**Figure 21.17**).

2. Set options according to your service bureau or commercial printer's instructions.

3. Click OK.

4. Save the document.
   Your trapping preferences are saved with the document.

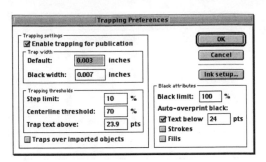

Figure 21.17 The settings in the Trapping Preferences dialog box should be set only after consultation with your printer.

MACINTOSH SHORTCUTS

Text Editing

Task	Action
Select word	Double-click with cursor
Select paragraph	Triple-click with cursor
Up one line	Up Arrow
Down one line	Down Arrow
Up one screen	Page Up
Down one screen	Page Down
Left one character	Left Arrow
Right one character	Right Arrow
Left one word	Shift + Left Arrow
Right one word	Shift + Right Arrow
Up one paragraph	Shift + Up Arrow
Down one paragraph	Shift + Down Arrow
With cursor in text, select words to the left	Command +Shift + Left Arrow
With cursor in text, select words to the right	Command +Shift + Right Arrow
Drag left-indent marker only	Shift + drag indent
Move to beginning of story	Home
Move to end of story	End
Close current story window only	Shift + W
Close all open stories in current pub	Shift + Story > Close Story
Cascade all open stories in all open pubs	Shift + Window > Cascade
Tile all open stories in all open pubs	Shift + Window > Tile

Special Characters

Task	Action
Bullet (·)	Option + 8
Copyright symbol (©)	Option + G
Ellipsis (...)	Option + ;
Degree (°)	Option + Shift + 8
Paragraph (¶)	Option + 7
Open typographer's quotations (")	Option + [
Close typographer's quotations (")	Option + Shift + [
Open single quotations (')	Option +]
Close single quotations (')	Option + Shift +]
Foot mark (')	Command + Option + "
Inch mark (")	Command + Option +Shift + "
Registered trademark (®)	Option + R
Section (§)	Option + 6
Trademark (™)	Option + 2
Page number	Command + Option + P
Em space	Command + Shift + M
En space	Command + Shift + N
Thin space (1/4 em)	Command + Shift + T
Nonbreaking (fixed) space	Option + spacebar
Forced line break or soft return	Shift + Return
Discretionary (soft) hyphen	Command + Shift + -
Nonbreaking hyphen	Command + Option + -
Nonbreaking slash	Command + Option + /
Em dash (—)	Command + Shift + -
En dash (–)	Command + -
English pound (£)	Option + 3
Japanese yen (¥)	Option + Y
Cent (¢)	Option + 4
Pi (π)	Option + P
Ligature (fi)	Option + Shift + 5
Ligature (fl)	Option + Shift + 6

MACINTOSH SHORTCUTS

Typographical Controls

Task	Action
Increase one point size (Layout view only)	Command + Shift + >
Increase to next standard menu size (Layout view only)	Command + Option + >
Decrease one point size (Layout view only)	Command + Shift + <
Decrease to next standard menu size (Layout view only)	Command + Option + <
All caps (toggle on and off)	Command + Shift + K
Small caps (toggle on and off)	Command + Shift + H
Subscript (toggle on and off)	Command + \
Superscript (toggle on and off)	Command + Shift + \
Kern apart .01 em (Layout view only)	Option + Right Arrow
Kern together .01 em (Layout view only)	Option + Left Arrow
Kern apart .04 em (Layout view only)	Command + Option + Right Arrow
Kern together .04 em (Layout view only)	Command + Option + Left Arrow
Clear manual kerning (Layout view only)	Command + Option + K

Viewing a Publication

Task	Action
Set all pages to same view	Option + View > any view
Change page to fit in window	Command + 0 (zero)
100% view	Double-click Zoom tool or Command +1
100%/Fit in Window view (toggle)	Command + Option + click page
100% / 200% view (toggle)	Command + Option + Shift + click page
Send window to back	Option + click title bar
Edit story or text frame	Triple-click text object with Pointer tool
Redraw page in high resolution	Control + View > any view
Cycle through pages	Shift + Layout > Go to Page (click mouse or press any key to stop)
Go to next page	Page Down
Go to previous page	Page Up
Go forward to previous page selected	Command + Page Down
Go back to previous page selected	Command + Page Up
Zoom in / zoom out	Command + plus key (+) / Command + minus key (-)
View hyperlinks	F10

Layout

Task	Action
Open a copy of a publication or the original of a template	Option + File > Recent Publications
Revert to last mini-save	Shift + File > Revert
Save all open pubs (Save All)	Option + File > Save
Close all open pubs (Close All)	Option + File > Close
Insert one page	Command + Option + Shift + G
Auto/manual text flow (toggle)	Command + flow text
Semi-automatic text flow	Shift + flow text
Proportional resize	Shift + drag corner handle
Defer text redraw while adjusting text wrap	Hold spacebar
Select multiple elements	Shift + click each element
Select elements behind others	Command + click
Mask and Group	Option + Element > Mask and Group
Unmask and Ungroup	Option + Element > Unmask and Ungroup
Constrain move vertically or horizontally	Shift + drag element
Paste Multiple without dialog box	Option + Edit > Paste Multiple
Paste items in the same position as the original (Power Paste)	Command + Shift + V
Edit original	Option + double-click object
Nudge selected object	Press arrow keys
Rotate from center of bounding box or text block	Command + Rotating tool
Constrain rotation to 45-degree increments	Shift + Rotating tool

WINDOWS SHORTCUTS

Text Editing

Task	Action
Select word	Double-click with cursor
Select paragraph	Triple-click with cursor
Up one line	Up Arrow
Down one line	Down Arrow
To beginning of line	Home
To end of line	End
Left one character	Left Arrow
Right one character	Right Arrow
Left one word	Ctrl + Left Arrow
Right one word	Ctrl + Right Arrow
Up one paragraph	Ctrl + Up Arrow
Down one paragraph	Ctrl + Down Arrow
Move to beginning of story	Ctrl + Page up
Move to end of story	Ctrl + Page down
Up one screen	Page up
Down one screen	Page down
Close current story window only	Ctrl + W
Close all open stories in current pub	Shift + Story > Close Story
Cascade all open stories in all open pubs	Shift + Window > Cascade
Tile all open stories in all open pubs	Shift + Window > Tile

Special Characters

Task	Action
Bullet (·)	Alt + 8
Copyright symbol (©)	Alt + G
Ellipsis (...)	Alt + 0133 (on numeric keypad)
Degree (°)	Alt + 0176 (on numeric keypad)
Paragraph (¶)	Alt + 7
Open typographer's quotations (")	Alt + Shift + [
Close typographer's quotations (")	Alt + Shift +]
Open single quotations (')	Alt + [
Close single quotations (')	Alt +]
Foot mark (')	Ctrl + Alt + Shift + '
Inch mark (")	Ctrl + Alt + Shift + "
Registered trademark (®)	Alt + R
Section (§)	Alt + 6
Trademark (™)	Alt + 0153 (on numeric keypad)
Page number	Ctrl + Alt + P
Em space	Ctrl + Shift + M
En space	Ctrl + Shift + N
Thin space (1/4 em)	Ctrl + Shift + T
Nonbreaking (fixed) space	Ctrl + Alt + spacebar
Forced line break or soft return	Shift + Enter
Discretionary (soft) hyphen	Ctrl + Shift + -
Nonbreaking hyphen	Ctrl + Alt + -
Nonbreaking slash	Ctrl + Alt + /
Em dash (—)	Alt +Shift + -
En dash (–)	Alt + -
Cent (¢)	Alt + 0162 (on numeric keypad)

Typographical Controls

Task	Action
Increase one point size (Layout view only)	Ctrl + Shift + >
Increase to next standard menu size (Layout view only)	Ctrl + Alt + >
Decrease one point size (Layout view only)	Ctrl + Shift + <
Decrease to next standard menu size (Layout view only)	Ctrl + Alt + <
All caps (toggle on and off)	Ctrl + Shift + K
Subscript (toggle on and off)	Ctrl + \
Superscript (toggle on and off)	Ctrl + Shift + \
Kern apart .01 em (Layout view only)	Alt + Right Arrow
Kern together .01 em (Layout view only)	Alt + Left Arrow
Kern apart .04 em (Layout view only)	Ctrl + Alt + Right Arrow
Kern together .04 em (Layout view only)	Ctrl + Alt + Left Arrow
Clear manual kerning (Layout view only)	Ctrl + Alt + K

Viewing a Publication

Task	Action
Set all pages to same view	Alt + View > any view
Change page to fit in window	Ctrl + 0
100% view	Double-click Zoom tool or Ctrl + 1
100%/Fit in Window view (toggle)	Ctrl + Alt + click page
Edit story or text frame	Triple-click text object with Pointer tool
Redraw current page	Use shortcut for current view
Redraw page in high resolution	Ctrl + Shift + F12
Cycle through pages	Shift + Layout > Go to Page (click mouse or press any key to stop)
Go to next page	Page Down
Go to previous page	Page Up
Go forward to previous page selected	Ctrl + Page Down
Go back to previous page selected	Ctrl + Page Up
Zoom in / zoom out	Ctrl + plus key (+) / Ctrl + minus key (-)
View hyperlinks	F10

Layout

Task	Action
Open a copy of a publication or the original of a template	Shift + File > Recent Publications
Revert to last mini-save	Shift + File > Revert
Save all open pubs (Save All)	Shift + File > Save All
Close all open pubs (Close All)	Shift + File > Close All
Insert one page	Ctrl + Alt + Shift + G
Auto/manual text flow (toggle)	Ctrl + flow text
Semi-automatic text flow	Shift + flow text
Proportional resize	Shift + drag any handle
Defer text redraw while adjusting text wrap	Hold spacebar
Select multiple elements	Shift + click each element
Select multiple elements behind others	Ctrl + click
Mask and Group	Shift + Element > Mask and Group
Unmask and Ungroup	Shift + Element > Unmask and Ungroup
Constrain move vertically or horizontally	Shift + drag element
Paste items in same position as original (Power Paste)	Ctrl + Alt + V
Edit OLE object	Double-click object
Edit original	Alt + double-click object
Nudge selected object	Press arrow keys
Nudge selected object by ten times the amount in Preferences	Shift + press arrow keys
Rotate from center of bounding box or text block	Ctrl + Rotating tool
Constrain rotation to 45-degree increments	Shift + Rotating tool

INDEX

C

INDEX

INDEX

U

underline text, 79
Undo command, 199. *See also* Revert command
Ungroup command, 9, 202
Unlock command, 203
Unmask command, 9, 204
Use Snap To Constraints option, 46
Utilities menu, 10

V

vector-based graphics, 134
vector files, 279
Vertical nudge, 46
View HTML option, 263
View menu, 11

W

Web browsers, 263, 264, 270
Web pages, 259–271
    adding hyperlinks to, 265
    editing hyperlinks in, 266
    exporting to HTML, 5, 262–263
    formatting hyperlinks, 268–269
    HTML export options, 260–261
    preferences, 270
    removing hyperlinks, 267
    styles, 261
    viewing hyperlinks, 271
    viewing in browser, 264
white space, 97
widow control, 100
Width nudge icon, 190
Window menu, 12, 36
windows
    commands for, 12
    fitting document in, 11, 42

Windows-based systems. *See also* cross-platform issues
    conversion logs, 153
    extensions and, 155
    fonts, 156
    keyboard shortcuts, 297–300
    Photoshop filters, 145
    special characters, 298
    typographical controls, 299
windowshades, 49, 52, 53
WMF format, 134
Word Counter dialog box, 67
word processing, 3
words. *See also* text
    adding to spell checker, 69
    changing case, 82
    counting, 67
    deselecting, 6
    dragging to selection, 58
    hyphenating, 8, 66
    replacing misspelled, 68, 69
    selecting, 6, 58
    spacing, 99
wrapping text, 9, 136–137

Z

Zero Lock command, 11
zero point, 11
Zoom controls, 28
Zoom In command, 41
Zoom Out command, 41
Zoom To command, 41
Zoom tool, 41, 43, 44
zooming
    custom, 44
    magnifying view, 41, 43
    reducing view, 43
    in specific area, 44
    step-at-a-time, 43

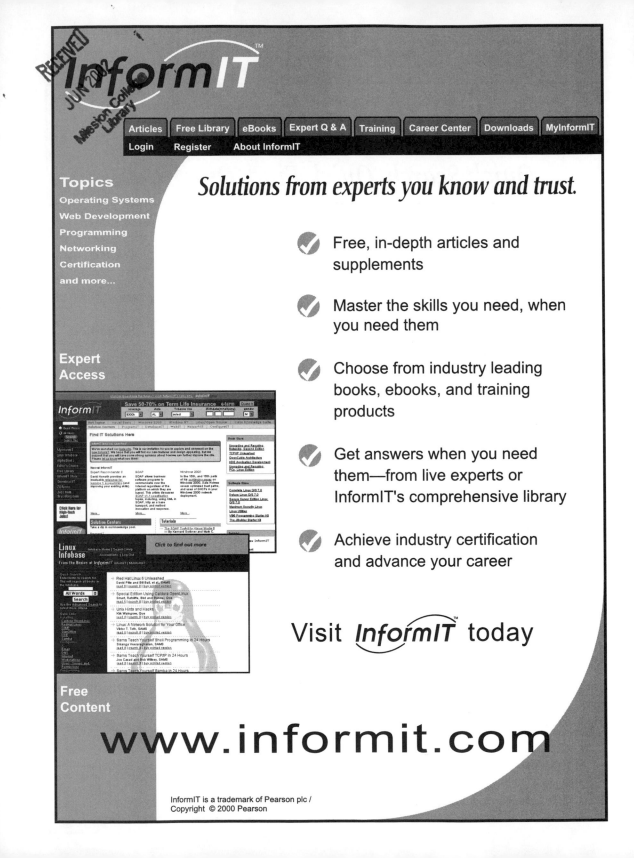